Literature and the Land

Literature and the Land

Reading and Writing for Environmental Literacy, 7–12

Emma Wood Rous

Boynton/Cook Publishers
HEINEMANN
Portsmouth, NH

Boynton/Cook Publishers, Inc.
A subsidiary of Reed Elsevier Inc.
361 Hanover Street
Portsmouth, NH 03801–3912
www.boyntoncook.com

Offices and agents throughout the world

The author and publisher wish to thank those who have generously given permission to reprint borrowed material:

Excerpts from *Ovid's Metamorphoses* translated by Rolfe Humphries. Copyright © 1955. Published by Indiana University Press. Reprinted by permission of Indiana University Press.

Excerpts from "The Lake Isle of Innisfree" reprinted with the permission of Scribner, a Division of Simon & Schuster from *The Collected Poems of W. B. Yeats*, Revised Second Edition edited by Richard J. Finneran. Copyright © 1983, 1989 by Anne Yeats.

Excerpts from "The Lake Isle of Innisfree" by W. B. Yeats reprinted by permission of A. P. Watts Ltd on behalf of Michael B. Yeats.

"How Poetry Comes to Me" from *No Nature: New and Selected Poems* by Gary Snyder. Copyright © 1992 by Gary Snyder. Reprinted by permission of Pantheon Books, a division of Random House, Inc.

Excerpt from "Dreaming America" from *The Fabulous Beasts* by Joyce Carol Oates. Copyright © 1975 by Joyce Carol Oates. Published by Louisiana State University Press. Reprinted by permission of the author.

Library of Congress Cataloging-in-Publication Data
Rous, Emma Wood.
    Literature and the land : reading and writing for environmental literacy, 7–12 / Emma Wood Rous.
      p. cm.
Includes bibliographical references and index.
ISBN 0-86709-568-7
    1. Readers—Nature. 2. Environmental protection—Problems, exercises, etc. 3. English language—Composition and exercises. 4. Readers—Environmental protection.
5. Nature—Problems, exercises, etc. 6. Readers (Secondary) I. Title.

PE1127.S3 R65 2000
363.7'0071'273—dc21
                                        00-039779

Editor: William Varner
Production service: Denise Botelho, Colophon
Production coordinator: Elizabeth Valway
Cover design: Jenny Jensen Greenleaf
Manufacturing: Louise Richardson

Printed in the United States of America on acid-free paper
04 03 02 01 00 RRD 1 2 3 4 5

"In every deliberation, we must consider the impact
on the next seven generations."
Great Law of the Hau de no sau nee
(Six Nations Iroquois Confederacy)

For the Seventh Generation

Contents

Contents

Foreword

The teachers I love most have grace. Their work is not proficiency and outcome, it's poetry and ministry.

Jonathan Kozol
National Education Association
April 2000

Emma Rous has grace. Her teaching and writing are both poetry and ministry, both elegance and precision. As I read this book, I felt as if I had stepped into the pages of Annie Dillard or John McPhee or Mary Oliver or John Muir. But Emma is more than a writer who pulls us into worlds through words. She is a teacher who shows us explicitly how to invite and teach our students how to be the strongest readers, writers, and thinkers they can be, by offering them an intellectually rigorous program, in this case, focused on the literature of the land.

Emma is passionate about teaching, about reading and writing, and about the earth. Through her work, she has found a way to combine these deep interests. And it is a very powerful combination. In these pages, Emma's vivid descriptions, from her backyard overlooking Great Bay to the walking trail of Franconia Notch to the teepee at David Langley's bison farm, let me step into this classroom and experience her deep passions. But Emma does far more than simply bring me into the world of her classroom, she shows me precisely what to do to offer this world to my students. This is a book so rich with the what and how and why. Readers will marvel at the way Emma shares so much practical information. She gives them the freedom to frame a course that could be taught as is, or reshaped to fit the needs and interests of other students and teachers anywhere. What Emma Rous asks students to do in her high school Literature and the Land course is challenging, provocative, and important work. She asks them to pay attention to the world so that they may make a difference personally, locally, and globally. She asks them to be close observers of the land and to think and act deeply and widely on all they notice. In the time it takes us to inhale deeply, Emma's introduction to *Literature and the Land* moves us from the bucolic scene we all imagine when we think "nature," to the reality of the way we too often abuse what the environment offers us. In a compelling, poignant, and evocative style that weaves her own journal entries and experiences with the richly annotated literature of classic and contemporary authors, storytellers, historians, artists, and environmentalists, Emma shows us explicitly how to prepare our students to be "responsible stewards of the earth."

Literature and the Land is at once about literature and writing, but it is also about science and poetry, history and philosophy, humanity and ecology, mythology and culture. It is about observing the world in a serious way through many different perspectives. Emma guides us every step of the way through her own small town and the search for the history of the land she lives on, to an understanding of the history and mythology of the way our land has been treated, to thinking about the issues of land today. She systematically leads students from their own backyards to the Southwest and Alaska through nonfiction, fiction, and poetry. She uses contemporary and classic literature, art, and photography to stimulate conversation and writing.

Each chapter is rich with annotated resources and precise explanations of how Emma uses them with students. There are so many examples from extraordinarily excellent pieces of literature, from William Shakespeare to Henry David Thoreau to Barbara Kingsolver, that it seems the needs of a full range of students could be met by choosing from this collection of offerings. Woven throughout are a range of ways even the most challenging student can find success, from a multitude of examples of kinds of journal writing, to oral presentations, essay writing, field trips to outdoor sites, or weeklong hiking experiences. Emma always sets the standards high, yet offers a myriad of ways for students to access information and to present what they've learned and think.

As a middle school teacher I found myself reading this book with pen in hand, pulling out practical ideas for interdisciplinary teaching and learning with my seventh and eighth graders. *Literature and the Land* offers high school and middle school teachers a way to slow down and concentrate more deeply, while enhancing the challenges of thoughtful observing, reading, and writing.

I want my students to be the most literate, articulate young men and women they can be by the time they leave my classroom. I want them to do important work that matters in the world. I want them to be challenged intellectually. Emma Rous does all of that in this book. This is a book about teaching thoroughly and thoughtfully because it asks students to consider complex issues through compelling literature. Emma offers no easy answers. But she teaches students how to grapple with important questions. If we don't teach our students how to understand each other's perspective, and how to be responsible, respectful, articulate citizens of the world, then what else is worth learning?

Emma quotes Baba Dioum, an African conservationist, as saying, "In the end, we will conserve only what we love and respect. We will love only what we understand. We will understand only what we are taught or allowed to experience." This is what *Literature and the Land* teaches and allows us, and ultimately our students, to experience.

Emma Rous's work is "poetry and ministry." It can be our work too.

Acknowledgments

Many inspiring and supportive people helped make "Literature and the Land," the course and the book, possible. I owe heartfelt thanks to:

All of the teachers, interns, friends, and students who ever recommended a book, shared an idea, or suggested a trail.

My friends and mentors in the Oyster River High School English Department—Liz Whaley, Liz Dodge, Richard Tappan, Paul Gasowski, and Kay Morgan, who inspired and challenged me—and the supportive school district philosophy that made this course possible.

Bob Byrnes, my biology teacher for over fifteen years; Kathleen Kentner, friend and dedicated librarian, who led me to sources and showed me how easy it is to click on loc.gov; and the long list of colleagues, particularly Doug Knight, who patiently undid the disasters I created on the computer.

My good friends in the Great Bay Art Colony—Kay and Vin Morgan, and Bev and Will Conway—who first made me believe I could write this and supported me along the way.

The Farmer's Hill Group—my home away from home; and the Wilderness Writing Workshop hikers who, in one week, revitalize me for a year.

Janet Ward for creating the Scientist as Humanist project and inspiring dozens of New Hampshire teachers.

Tom Newkirk, who also loves nature writing, for his advice and introduction to the intricacies of publishing.

My editor, Bill Varner, who found me just when I was looking for him, and never prescribed but, like a good teacher, encouraged me to open new doors.

Bev Conway for her skillful, loving work with my photographs.

My mother, Fil Wood, who admires natural beauty and is always ready for an adventure.

Ben Rous for our shared days of creative effort—him at the piano, me at the computer.

Kay Morgan, Walter Rous, and Nahanni Rous, who read every word, sometimes several times, and made many of them better.

Linda Rief who inspired Nahanni who in turn inspired me.

And especially Walter, the best reading, hiking, and living partner I could ever have.

It has been my privilege to work with wonderful students over the years; for sharing this journey, in the classroom and on the trail, I thank you. I often wonder who is the teacher and who the student.

Introduction

Why Teach Environmental Literature?

October, 1997

Walking around Adams Point today, I see a white heron peering into the
shallow salt marsh, a hawk keeping watch from high in a pine, Great Bay's
surface wrinkling and heaving under a heavy southerly wind, a flock of geese
heading perversely north, a solitary monarch butterfly clinging to a purple
aster, a clear-cut lot violating shoreline protection rules, and cigarette packages
and cans scattered across the brilliant red and yellow October fields.

    In each case I think of my students and implications for my teaching.
What would they make of these sights? How can I help them be more aware of
their surroundings? How will we consider issues of land use or dwindling
species or disrupted ecological systems?

It is now three weeks since I walked and wrote about Adams Point. Two days ago,
I took my students on the same walk. I asked them to keep their eyes open and tell
me what they noticed. As we walked, I told them about the role of glaciers in the
formation of Great Bay, about estuaries and the importance of salt marshes in the
food chain and as natural filtration devices, about Evelyn Browne who helped
Great Bay become a National Estuarine Research Reserve, about bedrock and
thin soils and coniferous trees and blow downs, about horseshoe crabs. Some used
a trail guide and read to us about the history of the bay—the shallow draft gun-
dalows in the 1800s that carried bricks from these shores to Beacon Hill in Boston,
the Adams family farm and inn, and Pulpit Rock where sermons were given in the
grove. We saw oyster shells in the woods (dropped by seagulls to crack them open)
and fragments of old shells exposed in the eroding bank of the shore (left by sum-
mering Abenakis).

Students pointed out fish jumping, cormorants on buoys drying out their
wings, milkweed plants from which monarchs had recently departed, a swan on
the far shore, stone walls in grown-over, former fields. With binoculars, they
scanned the tops of trees for eagles but saw none. We noted the clear-cut house

lots around the bay and discussed the rights of property owners versus the impact of cutting on soil erosion and wildlife. We considered the aesthetic impact of shoreline cutting. A student hunter questioned the right of large property owners to post their land against hunters and trespassers.

Eventually we spread out along the shore to write and draw in journals. I gave them ideas to think about: Imagine being an Abenaki or an Adams living here. What adaptations are needed to live in the various habitats? What rights should property owners have with their own land? Most chose to simply describe their surroundings: the stillness of the air and calm of the water, the peacefulness they felt, the respite from school. Like most of us who are no longer pioneers struggling to survive, students see nature as a refuge from busy schedules and the stress of school work. Although this wildlife area is only five miles from the center of town, few had ever been here; one who lives in the neighborhood had never walked the trails. All appreciated this "outdoor classroom" opportunity. A diverse group of students, ranging from motivated to alienated, had enjoyed an experience together and established a rapport that would facilitate future learning.

I considered the day a success—proof of the value of field trips and an example of the interdisciplinary integration possible in the study of land. The trip is one of many I have taken while teaching "Literature and the Land," a one-semester environmental studies class designed for a high school language arts curriculum.

When I resumed teaching sixteen years ago, I entered an English department committed to teaching the skills of thinking, reading, writing, speaking, and viewing through a curriculum based on student choice and teacher expertise. From tenth grade on, we offer a nontracked, mixed-grade elective program: teachers teach what they know best; students choose courses based on interest and post-high school goals. The department embraces an interdisciplinary and inclusive philosophy. Everything in my early teaching experiences supported this student-centered approach: I had worked on interdisciplinary teams, organized field experiences, and facilitated group processing and problem solving. During the time off after my children were born, I had also acquired a new expertise and interest—environmental literature.

Looking back, I can trace widening circles in my love for nature, from the lilac bushes and pheasants in my childhood backyard, to the ocean sunsets of my early teens and the first mountain hikes in my twenties. The only high school essay I can still recall was a lament for a sledding hill cut into house lots and a skating pond filled in for a bridge project. As an adult, I have canoed on lakes, oceans, rivers, and marshes; camped in rainforests and desert canyons; biked; ski toured; and backpacked in Yosemite, the Wind River Range and Alaska's Brooks Range. Some of my best walks are in the woods right around my house. As my experiences in the out-of-doors have broadened, so has my commitment to living a sustainable lifestyle: my husband and I built a passive solar house, choose fuel-efficient cars and appliances, take recycling for granted, and try to ignore America's rampant advertising and consumerism. Twenty-five years ago, we joined friends to build a self-sufficient, cooperative house in the Maine woods using only local and recycled materials, wood heat, a composting toilet, and a spring-fed cistern. We are also acutely aware of how much work is still to be done in our own lives and in the world community.

My personal reading history mirrors these ever-growing circles. An early Golden Book about the changing seasons on a farm and *Heidi* formed the archetypal "golden age" I have been trying to regain ever since childhood. In high school, I loved the British romantic poets, and when I first read Thoreau, I imagined living alone in an abandoned house I knew on the beach. Much later, after college, marriage, work, and children, a like-minded friend, Ken Olson from our Maine house group, handed my husband and me a copy of John McPhee's *The Survival of the Bark Canoe*. We were enthralled. We became McPhee converts. We read other titles, including *Coming Into the Country*, and dreamed of Alaska. McPhee led us to Barry Lopez and Annie Dillard, Norman McLean, Gretel Ehrlich, Edward Abbey and Aldo Leopold. When the Oyster River High School English teachers asked me what I could contribute to their elective program, I was ready. With their enthusiasm and support, I launched a Literature and the Land elective which has been taught every semester since 1984 and is now also offered by two of my colleagues. This book is a description of that course.

Teaching "Literature and the Land" has given me the rare opportunity to turn my avocation into my vocation. With this course, everything comes together: my belief in experiential, interdisciplinary, student-centered learning; my love of outdoor activity; a commitment to sustaining the natural environment; the enjoyment of nature literature; and the pleasure of sharing literature and outdoor experiences with students. Whether teachers and outdoor educators use this material for a year, a semester, or only a few weeks, all have the opportunity to combine personal enjoyment and commitment with teaching that inspires and makes a difference—personally, locally, and globally.

I see this difference now in the lives of former students like Todd who once studied a park on the river near his home and now teaches high school social studies. He introduced an interdisciplinary course on landscape in which students study nature poetry, map their school grounds, and look at landscapes in films. Todd turned his early interest in Oyster River Park into a unit on urban land use and the work of Frederick Law Olmsted.

Rick, another former student, hiked the entire Appalachian Trail, wrote to my students en route, and showed slides and read from his journal when he returned. He currently studies hydro-geology in Arizona, and hopes to someday help to restore clean groundwater. Jon, inspired by William Least Heat-Moon's *Blue Highways*, outfitted a van and traveled for a year; he now studies "green design" as an architecture student in Montana. James has combined his interest in outdoor adventure and filmmaking to make videos about backcountry skiing. Bianca spent a semester studying ecological problems in Madagascar. Gabe majored in outdoor education; Chris and Ted work for the Appalachian Mountain Club. In the values and choices of these former students, I see the ripples, starting with my childhood and first nature writers, spreading ever outward.

Young people are concerned about the health of the planet. Returning from a day of advocacy training on behalf of the Arctic National Wildlife Refuge, my husband and I marveled that the participants—and facilitators—were mostly in their twenties! Surveys indicate that the state of the environment is one political issue that motivates a seemingly apolitical generation (*Atlantic Monthly*, 8/99). "Literature and the Land" uses something most students already care about, the out-of-doors and a healthy environment—to engage them in significant reading and writing. A student like Claire can move from her appreciation of the river and falls near her house to a greater awareness of historical environmental attitudes. John's love for his favorite fishing hole becomes a desire to know more about pollution and species depletion. From an urban student's daily exposure to trash and air pollution comes the motivation to solve the problems of solid waste and air quality.

"Literature and the Land" is about appreciating nature and defining attitudes toward it. The course and this book explore many perspectives toward land—scientific, poetic, historical, artistic, religious, economic, and cultural. Understanding these varied perspectives and their effect on the treatment of land, now and in the past, provides the organizing principle of this curriculum. By increasing students' understanding of past attitudes and actions, I hope to influence responsible decision-making in the present and future. The course does not advocate particular solutions, but by presenting issues as complex and many sided, it offers students a process for thoughtful problem solving.

Environmental questions are personal and ethical as well as scientific and economic. Property rights and nature's rights deeply divide public opinion. There are no easy answers, as much as we would sometimes like the world to be black and white ("Wolves are always good; cutting a tree is always wrong."). We must all learn to listen, understand a variety of points of view, and practice consensus building skills (sharing ideas, finding common ground, compromising). It is not a teacher's role to tell students what to believe. Nor should we encourage the belief that any idea is "right" because "it's all relative anyway." We need to help students develop standards for judging and solving ethical dilemmas.

While a growing body of material helps teachers and students study, monitor, and work to improve the natural environment, this material is usually written with a science or elementary classroom in mind. This book suggests some science activities and resources, but its focus is on literature and writing at the secondary level.

Nature writing is a rich and flourishing genre. Some of the best authors publishing today—writers such as Dillard, Ehrlich, Lopez, and McPhee—work in this field. Many respected scientists such as Rachel Carson, Loren Eiseley, and Lewis Thomas are also poetic writers. There is now a *Norton Book of Nature Writing* (Finch and Elder) and a yearly collection of outstanding nature writing, *American Nature Writing*, from Sierra Club Books. The nature sections of every bookstore include best-sellers such as Jon Krakauer's *Into Thin Air* and *Into the Wild*. Classics of the past such as O. E. Rolvaag's *Giants in the Earth* or Willa Cather's *My Antonia*, or less well-known writings such as John Smith and William Percy's colonial exploration journals, can be read from an environmental perspective. In this course, students read fiction, poetry, and nonfiction including journals, diaries, science writing, and stories of adventure, exploration, and survival. There is something for every student—from *The Tempest* to *Alive*. While I believe that students benefit from studying environmental issues in heterogeneous groups, the material can easily be adapted for an Advanced Placement course by putting more emphasis on challenging readings such as Dillard, Thoreau, or McPhee. For lower-level, tracked courses, the most difficult readings can be omitted in favor of more hands-on activities. Each chapter ends with a list of student readings and resources for teachers.

I have attempted to use female and male authors equally in the course and throughout this book, and I make sure that males and females play equal leadership roles in classroom activities, discussion, and outings. I sometimes have to counteract tradition and expectation to be sure that this happens. Women have not always received equal credit as leaders in the conservation movement, although the efforts of scientists and activists like Rachel Carson, Jane Goodall, Marjory Stoneman Douglas (Everglades protector) or Katharine Ordway (prairie conservationist) were crucial in advancing environmental science. We are careful to include their names alongside those of John Muir and Aldo Leopold. Similarly, female adventurers are featured along with males.

Environmental themes suggest a wealth of writing possibilities, including narrative writing, descriptive or persuasive essays, poetry, adventure stories, research papers, comparison-contrast essays, and journal keeping. A variety of writing topics, teaching strategies, and examples of student work are given in Chapter Two. Many topics are interspersed throughout the course, but are also collected in this chapter for ease of access. The writing process includes brainstorming, drafting, conferencing with peers and teacher, and rewriting.

Writing is not the only method of assessment used in "Literature and the Land." There are occasional quizzes and final tests consisting of short answers and essays. Students do individual and group research, action projects, and oral presentations in the form of reports, debates, or discussion leading. They might do creative responses to reading, accompanied by written rationales, as described in Chapter Six.

Variety and student involvement are two keys to successful assessment. If we use only one form of assessment we may only see a student's weakest (or strongest) area. When projects and presentations are part of the assessment program, students show how they gather information, think, and solve problems, as well as what they remember. If students do not assess themselves, they learn to measure themselves only against someone else's judgment. But when self reflection and goal setting are part of the process, then assessment goes beyond being a testing device and becomes a learning tool.

While the primary focus of "Literature and the Land" is literature and writing, the course encourages an interdisciplinary approach to the study of land. Understanding ecology and sustainability requires thinking of the earth as an interconnected system: we cannot understand and sustain soils, vegetation, wildlife, or social relationships without understanding how these elements interact. To be truly interdisciplinary, this course should be team taught with a biology teacher. An alternative is to link two courses, so that the same students are simultaneously scheduled to take biology and environmental literature. Teachers can plan coordinated activities though they do not actually teach together. If the courses occur back to back and each teacher is free when the other is with the class, the option to teach together or to conduct a two-hour activity is available. In my own case, neither team teaching nor linked courses have been an option, but I owe much to ongoing conversations with my colleague, biology teacher Bob Byrnes, and I have taken many opportunities to incorporate readings, speakers, and activities from science, math, history, and the arts. With its holistic approach, the course helps students see connections between their academic subjects, and between school and the larger community.

An environmental literature course is not only interdisciplinary; it is experiential. Since John Dewey and probably before, teachers have believed that students learn best by doing. In addition to field trips, there are countless activities that can be done right on school grounds. Even in urban environments, students can examine people's impacts on the natural environment and nature's adaptations to the built environment. Many exploration, observation, writing, environmental monitoring, and problem-solving activities are described in the following chapters.

Increasingly, teachers are asked to make their course work relevant. Students ask, "Why do we need to know this?" and businesses complain that students are not equipped to function in the work place. Relevancy does not have to mean specific job training. Learning how to think and problem-solve, how to find information and apply it, how to work with others, and how to demand excellence of oneself are equally relevant. A course on the environment offers specific career awareness, as well as thinking and problem-solving skills.

The same leadership skills that help students work together effectively in the classroom or the field also prepare them for future workplaces. Whether they are on a strenuous mountain hike or considering how to implement sound energy practice, students can learn that real leadership is not telling others what to do but helping a group cooperate and use all members' skills and ideas. Chapter Seven describes team-building exercises and lists outdoor education resources.

The skills that constitute good leadership are also integral to good teaching. The "Literature and the Land" course described here is designed for a heterogeneous classroom and is based on a student-centered pedagogy. The challenge is to find readings, activities, and assignments that allow all students to develop their strengths. The reward is seeing that all students can learn from each other. We sit in a circle or in small groups. As a discussion moderator, I look for questions that encourage dialogue among students and I try to stay in the background as much as possible. The worst questions make students try to guess the answer I am looking for. The best questions help students grapple with what they believe and look for the information to support this belief. Students themselves often lead discussion.

Good teaching encourages leadership from each student and facilitates an atmosphere in which the creativity and power of each individual supports the learning of every other member of the class. Like geese flying in V-formation, each benefiting from the energy of the others, we all learn best when everyone contributes to the process.

This book is generally organized in the same sequence as the course, which begins with an exploration of perception and defines a variety of points of view toward the environment (Chapter One). Chapter Two applies the ideas of perception to student writing about nature. The ideas in this chapter can be used at any point in the course. Chapters Three and Four explore the history of human perceptions and treatment of land, from mythological times to the present, particularly in America. Chapter Five applies these perspectives to selected contemporary environmental issues—water use in the Southwest, land use in Alaska, and wolf reintroduction—and introduces options for student involvement in community projects. Chapter Six focuses on fiction and poetry, and Chapter Seven discusses outdoor adventure; either of these chapters can be used at any point in the course. Each unit uses quality literature as its starting point. Environmental philosophy, authors, and books are described for readers who have limited familiarity with this literature. For others, the classroom strategies may be the most useful part of the book. Appendix A gives time estimates for units and suggestions for teachers who will teach a unit rather than a semester of nature literature.

While nothing in education works every time for every student, and I have always resented curriculum advocates who suggest otherwise, some of these strategies, honed over fifteen years, should prove effective in classrooms and provide a framework for teachers' own creativity and expertise.

Although some teenagers may prefer a mall and pavement to the woods, students usually come to this course caring about some aspect of the material. They may like to hunt, fish, and camp. They like to be outside whether at a lake, the beach, or in the mountains. They may be risk-takers, rock climbers, or mountain bikers. They may be nature lovers, hikers, poets. They may be environmentalists, concerned about clean air and water or endangered species. They may even be activists, involved in recycling or monitoring projects. They may be budding scientists, eager to learn how nature works and do their part to improve our relationship with the natural world.

The satisfaction of teaching an environmental studies course is that it integrates the personal with the "objective," and the philosophical with the practical. It starts where students are, explores how their attitudes developed historically, and considers the implications of these attitudes for their own and the earth's future. The 1992 United Nations Earth Summit in Rio de Janeiro set the task of achieving a sustainable relationship with the earth as humanity's top priority. We can start with ourselves and our students.

Works Cited

Elder, J., and R. Finch, eds. 1990. *Norton Book of Nature Writing*. New York: W. W. Norton & Co.

Halstead, T. 1999. "A Politics for Generation X," *The Atlantic Monthly*. August.

Least Heat-Moon, W. 1983. *Blue Highways: A Journey Into America*. Boston: G. K. Hall.

McPhee, J. 1975. *The Survival of the Bark Canoe*. New York: Farrar, Straus and Giroux.

———. 1977. *Coming Into the Country*. New York: Farrar, Straus and Giroux.

Murray, J. A., ed. 1998. *American Nature Writing*. Vol. 4. San Francisco, CA: Sierra Club Books.

1

Perception

To see a world in a grain of sand
And a heaven in a wild flower
Hold infinity in the palm of your hand,
And eternity in an hour.

William Blake, "Songs of Innocence"

"The quality of life is in proportion to the capacity for delight. The capacity for delight is the gift of paying attention. Attention is an act of connection."

J. A., The Artist's Way

June, 1998

I have just returned from a five day backpacking trip with students in the White Mountains and I have been thinking a lot about "perception." It is an act of sheer determination and tremendous effort for me to carry fifty pounds up 3,000 feet in ninety degree weather. Hiking uphill, all I am aware of is the pounding of my pulse, the sweat trickling down my back, the ache in my thighs, and the placement of each boot as it gains another fifteen inches on the mountain. I think of the comforts of home and wonder why I am here; I feel tired and inadequate. But as the grade moderates, my eyes lift from the trail and begin to notice the lady slippers and bunchberry blossoms, the hardwoods giving way to softwoods, the slight breeze cooling my sweaty head, the views opening out across the valley. My stride lengthens; I feel confident and strong. Coming down the same trail will be easy, a question of footing and some strain on the knees, but not the torturous labor of climbing. I will regret ending the trip and leaving the mountains behind. Same trail; totally different perspectives—it's all in your state of mind—and body!

"Attention," a friend tells me; "perception is really about attention." "Pay attention," I say to my students, and what I usually mean is "Listen to me." But my real goal is to help students pay "attention" and listen to the world around them; to see the world unencumbered by personal agendas—or at least to become aware of the effects of those agendas. From such seeing, with attention, comes appreciation and discovery, the keys to understanding and even revelation.

9

Perception could be the theme of an entire interdisciplinary course rather than an introductory unit to a course on the environment. After a particularly intense discussion of perception and the nature of reality, a student once suggested that the course be called "Literature, Land, and Life." The guiding questions for the course and this three-week unit are:

How do we view the world? What influences what we see?
How does our point of view affect the way we treat the world?

The goals are to help students learn to look closely at the world around them and to gain a new appreciation for it, to recognize a range of points of view in the way people see the world, to clarify their own point of view toward the environment, and to consider the effect of their views on their actions.

I often begin the course by asking students to observe carefully an actual tree and describe it in any manner they choose. Although I do not specify a format, students usually describe their tree in writing. A few may draw. Once, a student brought in a branch, saying that reality was better than any description. Some students write nostalgic pieces about tree forts, buried pets, Christmas decorations, or first climbs to the highest branches. Others write careful measurements of height and girth. Some pay close attention to sensory detail—to textures, colors, and smells. Some write poems, or use metaphoric writing, including personification, in their descriptions. Surprisingly few name the species of tree.

The next day, students share their descriptions in groups and develop lists of the types of descriptions they used, for example, historical, scientific, sensory, metaphoric, or personal. We discuss the differences in the kind of information each description provides and why different students notice different details. Would we use different descriptions for different purposes? Which are closest to the "real" tree? Is a drawing more "real" than writing? than a photograph? If we read the descriptions before we saw the trees, would they affect what we saw? how?

To reinforce the idea that purpose and point of view influence what we see and how we describe what we see, I give students a collection of published descriptions of trees, including a dictionary definition, a page on the economics of tree harvesting, an explanation of photosynthesis, a description of white pines for identification purposes, Edward Abbey's description of the "grandmother" juniper tree "hold[ing] skyward a sapless claw" in *Desert Solitaire*, Alice Walker's mystical realization that "if I cut a tree, my arm would bleed" in *The Color Purple*, and the mythological Norse description of the world tree, Yggdrasill. Martin Buber's "I contemplate a tree," in *I and Thou*, also works well for this assignment. Buber sees the tree as "a picture . . . movement . . . a species . . . a number. . . . Throughout all of this the tree remains my object. . . . But it can also happen . . . that . . . I am drawn into a relation, and the tree ceases to be an It." Any range of tree descriptions will do.

Again, students label these "points of view," and discuss what kind of picture each gives and how these descriptions affect how we see and treat trees. Is personification good or bad? Does it distort our view of the actual tree? Does it lead us to respect the tree more? Is science more "real" than poetry? Which descriptions do they prefer and why? Kirk and Linda addressed some of these questions in a final writing on perception:

> The different descriptions of trees . . . showed just how different people can be while writing about simple trees. There was poetry, fiction, fact, and myth—all different points of view while viewing the same object. . . . The way I see it, poetic descriptions are subjective pieces of writing because the authors can use imagination and creativity to expand on ideas and opinions. Scientific descriptions are objective pieces of writing because they tell pure fact and leave no room to expand and be creative.
> —*Kirk R.*

> The [descriptions of trees] are written by people in different fields: scientists, farmers, and poets. Therefore, the format of writing and their descriptions are greatly different. This shows how much a person's point of view can influence his/her "observations." For a scientist, he focuses more on the functions of plants and their effects in the ecosystem. For a poet, none of those things matter; it's the tree itself and the poet's feelings toward the tree. . . . that enable him/her to draw connections between themselves and the plant.
> —*Linda L.*

To keep the discussion of point of view from getting too abstract, I set up a group of objects in the center of our discussion circle and ask students from different sides of the circle to describe what they see. Some objects are obstructed, some are hidden inside others, some have writing which no one is close enough to read, one might be a musical instrument which is better "perceived" by ear, etc. By analogy, we discuss how our view is affected by where we "sit": by our personality, our ability to "see," our past, and our motives. We notice that first impressions can be deceiving (a point made again later with optical illusions), and that other points of view may help us get closer to the "truth."

Exercises using art and photography can enrich a discussion of point of view. Almost invariably, a student will say that drawings and "definitely" photographs are more accurate representations than verbal descriptions of trees. When all students are asked to draw the same tree or houseplant, an activity they find engrossing and relaxing, they immediately see the fallacy of believing that a drawing is more "real" than a written description. Of course, every drawing is different and they discuss why.

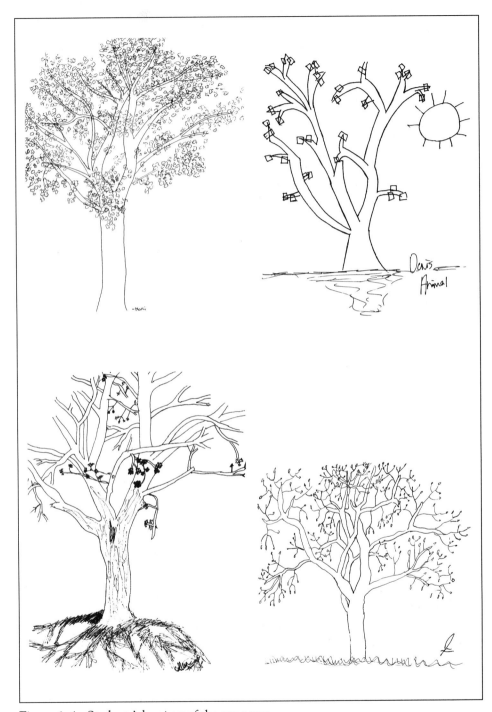

Figure 1–1. Students' drawings of the same tree.

I illustrate the same point with reproductions of tree paintings in a range of styles (see bibliography) and contrasting photographs of trees. Students pass these paintings and photographs from group to group and generate descriptive labels for them, just as they labeled the written tree descriptions. In comparing writing, painting, and photography, they consider what kind of information or feelings each medium is best suited to convey, and which require closer observation of the tree. They generally conclude that subjectivity is inherent in all perception, even photography.

These point of view discussions open the door to several topics and readings, including subjectivity versus objectivity, science versus poetry, and the effect of the medium (writing, painting, photography) on the message. A number of discussion techniques may be used for the readings associated with these topics. Sometimes I ask students to read the assignment at home and come to class with written comments and questions to raise during class. The next day I ask any volunteer to begin the discussion or simply go around the room for a more structured way of sharing. I have experimented with student-led discussions as described by Robert Schaible and Gale Rhodes from the University of Southern Maine in which discussion leaders are randomly selected on the day of class so that everyone must come prepared to lead. (This may not work as well in a widely heterogeneous class where the weakest students often struggle to maintain discussion.) In the case of difficult readings, such as Annie Dillard's, I may assign specific questions for students to answer in writing at home.

Dillard's "Seeing" chapter from *Pilgrim at Tinker Creek* is the first reading we discuss in class. Her descriptions of the natural world are vividly concrete while at the same time creating a mystical sense of unity between the visible and the spiritual. In Dillard's writing, metaphor is the key that unlocks meaning in ordinary experiences. The concrete symbolizes and points to the abstract; she is a modern transcendentalist. For students, her work is challenging, but also highly engaging and inspiring. In the "Seeing" chapter, Dillard explores the limits and wonder of human perception. Below are effective homework questions, followed by discussion topics and exercises, for this reading:

What is the point of Dillard's anecdote about finding pennies?

What do you think Dillard means by the "artificial obvious?"

How does the world look to the newly sighted and why? How does Dillard try to apply this experience to the way she looks at the world?

According to Dillard, what role do words play in the way we see? How do words both help and interfere with the way we see?

Explain the "camera metaphor." What is the difference between seeing with and without a camera, according to Dillard?

What does Dillard say about "the secret of seeing?"

The chapter begins with an anecdote about Dillard's childhood game of hiding pennies for others to find. Writing about this "game," Joel says:

> Annie Dillard . . . looks for the little things in life which mean a lot to her. We should do the same thing. We should take care and notice the details in life, not just see a generalization, but look closer, for if you do you will see a whole other world. Hiding the penny was a symbol of how Annie Dillard looked with more thought and a little bit closer at life than many of us do today.
> —Joel S.

I once heard Annie Dillard answer a university student's question about the "artificial obvious" by saying, "I don't know!" I think she means the heightened awareness that comes with specialized knowledge, for example the herpetologist's ability to find snakes where others see none. I have students apply this to themselves by thinking of their own areas of expertise. While a spectator might just see action on the basketball court, the athlete sees plays and strategy. Musicians hear music differently. Interest as well as knowledge affects vision; for example, someone in the market for shoes or a house suddenly notices others' shoes or realtors' "for sale" signs. To a new car owner, it appears that every other car on the road is their model; pregnant women seem to see nothing but other pregnant women!

But our vision can be hampered if our knowledge is limited by stereotypes or preconceptions, for example Dillard looking for a "green" frog that is really mottled brown. One January, I illustrated this effect by asking students to draw a tree with no other instruction. Eighty percent of them drew a silhouette of a "Christmas" tree with three points on each side! Is that what they always "see" in their minds when they hear the word "tree?" Can they see beyond this image when they look at actual trees? Do they really look? And how is this similar to the effects of having stereotypes of people?

Dillard describes the way the world looks to patients who were born with cataracts and have them removed as adults. That these newly sighted patients at first have no notions of space and distance leads to interesting discussion of how anyone learns depth perception. Without the experience of connecting spatial dimension with visual images, the formerly blind see the world as flat, as "color patches" where shadows are as substantial as objects. They are the "unscrupulous observers" Dillard later tries to emulate; they see without preconceptions, without verbalizing, and without a conscious mental "camera" framing each "shot." Dillard says the newly-sighted are like one-celled organisms that see the world as it is because their brain does not edit their "sense impressions." This observation brings up a subject of keen interest to students—animal perception. How does a cat or an owl's night vision affect its perception of the world, or a bat's use of sonar, a bee's ability to see ultra-violet, a dog's sense of smell or sound, a fly's segmented vision? Are these animals seeing the world as it "is?" Are we?

The discussion of sight provokes interesting responses from students. Erin wrote:

> I thought a lot about that experiment with blind people and what the world would be like to someone who used to be blind. As hard as I tried, I couldn't see the world as flat and one-dimensional. . . . If I saw in color patches with no sense of depth, it would be very distressing. . . . For some reason, the thought of being able to "see" more things when not thinking offends me. Well, maybe not offends, but annoys me a little. As humans, we are thinking all the time and we can't help it! I, for one, don't really see a problem with thinking. You can see a tree without knowing it is a tree, but I think it's more fun to think about it. So, you could look at the tree and you could say, "That's a maple tree. They make maple syrup from its sap. That bird sitting on top is a chickadee, and that bug crawling on it is a cicada." If you just look at something blankly, without thinking, it is just a meaningless thing.
> —*Erin Q.*

To simulate Dillard's attempts to see the world fresh and without bias, I use two exercises. One is simply to put a number of optical illusions on the board and pass around others. The familiar old woman/young woman illusion demonstrates how difficult it can be to see beyond our first interpretation of an image. The same effect is achieved by looking at the outline of a cube and forcing our eyes to play with which cube face appears to be closer to us.

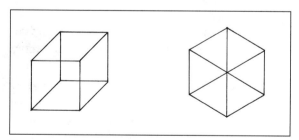

Figure 1–2. Which cube face appears to be closer?

A student once taught the class to focus on the lines converging at the corner of the room and try to make the corner appear to be coming toward us rather than receding. Books of holograms are also excellent tools to illustrate the ability to see the same thing in more than one way

Other illusions show how influenced we are by the context of an image:

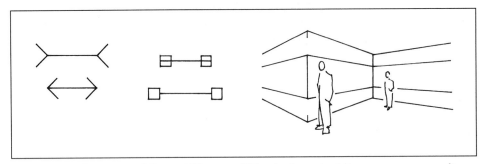

Figure 1–3. Context and Optical Illusions: Why do the paired lines appear unequal?

Children's puzzle pictures with hidden objects can be used to illustrate how easily we overlook things in our surroundings.

Another exercise, a blindfolded walk with a partner, raises issues about trust as well as about perception. Students without blindfolds are told not to give their blindfolded partners instructions about where to step but only to warn them if they are in danger of hurting themselves. Students should use their hands, feet, and ears to guide themselves. After 10–15 minutes, partners switch blindfolds. A variation on this exercise is to have the blindfolded student pick an object such as a tree and try to locate it again when the blindfolds are removed. If an outdoor walk is not feasible, students can work in pairs and pass around objects in bags that the blindfolded partners describe while the other partners take notes. Students can switch roles after four or five objects.

Students' writing and discussion about being blindfolded and being a partner demonstrate that it is a powerful experience. Many say that they become more aware of other senses, even in this brief time. They may feel frightened and insecure. Often they comment that they appreciate their ability to see more after they remove the blindfolds. Unblindfolded partners usually have two feelings: one of power and one of responsibility. When I ask students to apply this observation to their relationships with other people and the environment, they note that a position of strength should carry with it responsibility for others' welfare.

> If I were blind, what would I perceive things as? If I didn't know color, what would a leaf look like? Or if I didn't know shape, . . . what sort of picture would I be creating in my thoughts? Not only that, but what would names of things mean to me, like 'triangle,' or 'tree?' When someone told me their perception of a tree, what would I picture in my head?
> —*Tara B.*

Guiding people, you had to see a different way. You had to think about what they would care about, like a little dip in the ground for example, that you could just subconsciously see and avoid.

—*Erin Q.*

John Searle (*The Artist's Way*) says, "We do not describe the world we see; we see the world we can describe." Dillard's discussion of the role of words in seeing and the symbolism of looking at the world through a camera is another way to approach the idea of the "artificial obvious" or to weigh the virtues of selective vision versus unedited, "unscrupulous" seeing. Students can ponder whether words carry preconceptions and therefore interfere with seeing (as in the tree drawing exercise described above). Do we have a running verbal commentary in our heads about everything we see, and does this improve or interfere with our vision? What are the pros and cons of seeing the world through a camera lens? How much does a word predetermine what we will see?

Students also consider whether the same word has the same meaning for everyone. How does the word "round" differ for a sighted and a blind person? Does everyone picture the same thing when they hear the word "green"? What if you're colorblind?

Dillard has two seemingly different ideas about the "secret of seeing." One, "unless I call my attention to what passes before my eyes, I simply won't see it," and, on the other hand, that "although the pearl (seeing) may be found, it may not be sought." Students can discuss whether these two "secrets" are contradictory or complementary. The chapter ends with a "vision" of vision, a realization that we can make ourselves ready to see but cannot control what we will see: "I cannot cause light; the most I can do is try to put myself in the path of its beam . . ."

Following the Dillard reading, I turn to two previously discussed modes of perception: science and poetry. We usually presume that artists and scientists see the world through vastly different lenses. Objective versus subjective, facts versus fantasies, right brain versus left, experimentation versus expression: these views are often seen not only as different but as conflicting. In an interdisciplinary learning environment, students learn a new appreciation for the wonders science reveals to the artist, and the philosophical and historical context that the arts and humanities provide for science. In learning the value of breaking down walls and seeing from new points of view, students also learn that the distance between science and art need not be unbridgeable, that we are all engaged in the human search for meaning.

When I ask students, they almost invariably say that science and poetry have little to do with each other, and most will also usually (and unfortunately) say that they prefer the world of subjectivity and imagination to the world of objectivity and rigorous measurement. Other students are uncomfortable with what they perceive as the sentimentality of poetry. The goal of this discussion is to reexamine student stereotypes about science and poetry.

Two poems by Edgar Allan Poe and Walt Whitman reinforce the stereotype that poetry deals with beauty and the imagination while science deals with facts and figures. "Science! . . . Who alterest all things with thy peering eyes. / Why preyest thou thus upon the poet's heart, / Vulture, whose wings are dull realities?" (Poe, "Sonnet—To Science"). Whitman ("When I Heard the Learned Astronomer") describes the boredom of listening to an astronomer's lecture with "proofs . . . figures . . . columns . . . charts and diagrams,"

> Till rising and gliding out I wandered off by myself,
> In the mystical moist night air, and from time to time,
> Looked up in perfect silence at the stars.

Having discussed the two poets' views of science and whether students agree, I ask students to write two descriptions, one "poetic" and one "scientific," of the same scene or object, and to comment on their process and results. I take students outside for this exercise, or use pictures or a natural object like a plant or large shell. Here are Tammie's scientific and poetic descriptions and drawing of a potted cactus plant:

Cactus: one main trunk two inches wide, one half inch thick. Three branches off of the main trunk. The largest one goes straight up and is about one and a half inches wide. A second branch goes to the right and starts off about one inch round and gets wider ($1\frac{1}{2}$ inch at the widest) and slowly narrows. Off the main middle branch there are 13 additional branches over three inches tall. And approximately 30 more under three inches. The main branch is about a foot tall and leans (three inches from the top) to the back. The right branch is about $1\frac{1}{2}$ feet tall and has approximately 25 buds. The left branch is about 8 inches tall and has one bud about 2 inches and an additional 10–15 buds.

Green, water-filled branches reach toward the sun's rays. Weaving between each plant, the nuclear family branch entwines its relatives. Proud but lonely, the grandson towers above the rest; he is the first to touch nourishment but has no one to share with. The banished member curves, ashamedly, away from its family, its pain clear in faded yellow streaks. One of its children, a daughter, reaches back to the larger family, aching to be part again—she flourishes. Father and mother of all slowly fade—their children to take their place and grow from them. Even alone in a desolate desert, the cactus breeds and loves each that it breeds—one family.

—Tammie S.

18

Finally, we list the qualities of scientific and poetic description and usually end up with words like "factual, numerical, quantifiable, impersonal, objective" for science and "sensory, metaphoric, imaginative, personal, emotional" for poetry. I push the issue and ask students to look for overlaps in the two lists. "What do scientists and poets have in common?" Don't both scientists and poets begin by observing? And don't both disciplines rely on what their senses tell them? Science and art both deal with patterns in nature. Students note that science looks for patterns in order to explain them and as a clue to an underlying order. They point out that artists see and recreate patterns with line, color, shape, sound, rhythm, and movement. We assume that poetry is subjective while science is objective, but can scientists ever be completely impersonal and objective? What about pre-conceptions, ambition, commercialism, or politics? What about "seeing" what you hoped

Figure 1–4. Tammie's drawing of a potted cactus.

would be "true" (as in the false announcement in 1989 that cold-fusion had been achieved)? Or "seeing" what pre-existing beliefs and models assume will be true (as in the geo-centric model of the universe, "proven" for hundreds of years)?

There is also the question of whether science *should* be solely objective. I ask students to list the pros and cons of scientists having an emotional investment in their subject. I tell students about the work of scientist Evelyn Fox Keller who writes about the inescapability of some subjectivity in scientists' work and of the value of having feelings for a subject as illustrated by Barbara McClintock's study of genetics and corn. In her biography of McClintock, *A Feeling for the Organism*, Keller describes McClintock's ability to pay attention to individual and exceptional kernels of corn and to develop an intimacy with her material, an ability that led her to groundbreaking discoveries about genes. Has the traditional "objectivity" of science led us to *objectify* our world and to manipulate it for our own ends? McClintock's admonitions to have "a feeling for the organism" and to "listen to the material" sound a lot like what an Inuit said he does when he first enters a new territory: "I listen" (Barry Lopez, *Rediscovering North America*). The Inuit question scientific generalizations about wolves because, they say, each wolf must be seen as an individual. How, I ask students, might our treatment of the world change if our relationship with it were more personal?

The use of metaphoric thinking is another link between science and art and gets added to the "in common" list. At first glance, it seems that metaphor belongs solely in the realm of imagination, art, and poetry. We describe an idea or object indirectly, by analogy to something else, and the richness of the associations between the two illuminates the initial object in ways that direct description alone could not. The poetic mind makes the leap of imagination that enables us to see the connection between the object and its analogous symbol. Scientists describe similar leaps of imagination, what Einstein calls an "intuitive leap" and Jacob Bronowski refers to as "speculative induction," in their process of creating axioms to explain natural phenomena. While "discovery" involves finding something already in existence and could be done by anyone, "creation" is personal and individual, whether it occurs in the arts or in science. For the student or spectator, the process of vicariously reliving the creative process through viewing art or learning science can be a source of joy and inspiration. As Brendan writes,

One of the best things we discussed was how interesting things like mythology were replaced by boring science. Personally, I think that science is just as interesting as a dream world with no rules, because the bizarre reality of the universe often stretches the imagination just as much. I don't like how people always seem to associate cold facts and no emotion with science. I think that a lot of it comes from feelings, and that is how creative discoveries are made.

—*Brendan C.*

Beyond the creative process, the *explanations* scientists offer us are often, of necessity, in metaphoric terms. We discuss the idea that, since humans cannot reproduce reality, we are forced to deal with symbols. Using language in itself is metaphoric; we use words to represent reality. We compare the scientific "model" to poetic "metaphor." Scientists use "models" like the structure of an atom or of the solar system to represent their theory of reality. Science is a continuous process of testing the model against reality; scientists get into trouble when they go to great lengths to force aberrations in the evidence to fit the model, as did the mathematicians who invented retrograde motion to explain planetary orbits in a geocentric model of the universe. At this point in the discussion, a thoughtful student will wonder what "models" currently accepted as fact may some day be rejected.

So both scientists and poets observe, find patterns, seek explanations, use individual creativity, and describe their world symbolically. Neither can avoid a degree of subjectivity. If students do not think of all of these points, I bring them up myself. Why explore these parallels with students? Not to negate the differences but to counter the negative assumptions and stereotypes about science or poetry expressed too often by students. Hopefully, they will begin to see science as a creative process of discovery, not just another set of facts to memorize, and poetry as another way to acquire and interpret knowledge of the world, not just a superficial expression of feelings. Science and art are equally involved in our attempt to explain the world around us; they are complementary rather than antithetical to each other.

N. Scott Momaday's "A Vision Beyond Time and Place" and an excerpt on Maya, or illusion, from *The Snow Leopard* by Peter Matthiessen are good follow-up readings to Dillard's ideas on perception and also raise interesting questions about the role of science in shaping our view of the world. Along with the film "Mindwalk" by Bernt Capra, based on the book, *The Turning Point* by Fritjof Capra, these readings raise provocative questions about the nature of reality.

Momaday, a Native American novelist, describes "old man Cheney . . . whose vision extended far beyond the physical boundaries of his time and place," who could "in his mind's eye . . . integrate all the realities and illusions of the earth and sky."

This native vision, this gift of seeing truly, with wonder and delight, into the natural world, is informed by a certain attitude of reverence and self-respect. It is a matter of extra-sensory as well as sensory perception, I believe. In addition to the eye, it

involves the intelligence, the instinct, and the imagination. It is the perception not only of objects and forms but also of essences and ideals.
—*N. Scott Momaday (1971)*

Responding to this piece, Linda writes:

"A Vision Beyond Time and Place" by Momaday was the article I liked the best. It showed us it's possible for humans to see beyond the "obvious." It's just us, our culture that has limited our views. "Our eyes, it may be, have been trained too long upon the superficial, and artificial, aspects of our environment." After all, I believe the first step to truly see is to open up your heart to nature.
—*Linda L.*

Peter Matthiessen (1996) reminds us that both Buddhism and science teach that "we do not see the universe as it is."

Today science is telling us what the Vedas have taught mankind for three thousand years, that we do not see the universe as it is. What we see is Maya, or Illusion, the "magic show" of Nature, a collective hallucination of that part of our consciousness which is shared with all of our own kind, and which gives a common ground, a continuity to the life experience. According to Buddhists, this world perceived by the senses, this relative but not absolute reality, this dream, also exists, also has meaning; but it is only one aspect of the truth. . . . (66, 67)

In the film "Mindwalk," Liv Ullman, playing an astrophysicist, teaches a skeptical politician and an appreciative poet that the old mechanistic, Newtonian view of the universe must be redefined by ecological thinking. Her comparison of an atom's structure to an orange in the center of Mont St. Michel orbited by a tiny electron at the periphery of the island vividly illustrates for students the point that the universe is not the mass of solidity it appears to be. If you have the good fortune to team teach with a science teacher, this material offers an opportunity for philosophical examination of scientific principles—and in my experience, students love philosophy. Engaging in such discussion might dispel the all-too-prevalent idea that science deals only in "dull realities."

At the end of the introductory unit on perception, students write an in-class essay on what they have learned about looking at the world, with reference to all of the readings and exercises done in the unit. A review sheet of topics can help to break this task down for students. Some excerpts from students' final papers have been included in this chapter.

To apply their newly sharpened observational skills, students begin keeping weekly journals about a piece of land for the rest of the semester. The land journals are discussed in detail in the following chapter.

Works Cited

Works Cited for Students

Abbey, E. 1968. *Desert Solitaire*. New York: Ballantine.

Blake, W. 1974. "Songs of Innocence," *The Portable Blake*. New York: Viking Press.

Buber, M. 1970. *I and Thou*. Walter Kaufmann, trans. New York: Charles Scribner's Sons.

Dillard, A. 1975. *Pilgrim at Tinker Creek*. New York: Harper & Row. Chapter two: "Seeing," nonfiction, philosophical discussion of vision and perception.

Eiseley, L. 1957. *The Immense Journey*. NY: Random House. Essays on evolution.

Lawrence, G. 1991. "The Naturalist's Journal," *Habitat,* Journal of the Maine Audubon Society.

Lopez, B. 1991. "The Rediscovery of North America," *The Amicus Journal*, Fall. (From *The Rediscovery of North America*, Kentucky: University Press, 1991.)

Matthiessen, P. 1996. *The Snow Leopard* (1978). New York: Penguin. Nonfiction travel writing about philosophy and searching for illusive snow leopards in the Himalayas.

Momaday, S. 1971. "A Vision Beyond Time and Space," *Life*, 7/2/71. New York: Time, Inc. Nonfiction essay about Native American ways of seeing the world.

N. E. Thing Enterprises. 1994. *Magic Eye Gallery, Magic Eye II*. Kansas City: Andrews and McMeel. Two collections of 3D hologram illusions.

Walker, A. 1982. *The Color Purple*. New York: Harcourt Brace Jovanovich.

Works Cited for Teachers

Cameron, J. 1995. *The Artist's Way: A Spiritual Path to Higher Creativity*. Los Angeles: Jeremy P. Tarcher/Perigee.

Bronowski, J. 1970. "The Creative Process." In *Creativity: A Discussion at the Nobel Conference*, ed. John D. Roslansky. New York: Fleet Academic Editions.

Bronowski, J. 1974. *The Ascent of Man*. Boston: Little Brown.

Capra, F. 1983. *The Turning Point: Science, Society, and the Rising Culture*. New York: Bantam Books. About the interconnectedness of fields of knowledge and the current "crisis of perception."

Horning, B. 1993. "The Controversial Career of Evelyn Fox Keller," *Technology Review*, MIT, Jan. 58–68. Discusses Keller's work on McClintock and subjectivity and objectivity in science.

Keller, E. F. 1983. *A Feeling for the Organism*. San Francisco: W. H. Freeman. A biography of Barbara McClintock and her work with genetics and corn.

Rhodes, G. and R. S. 1990. "User's Manual for Student-Led Discussion." In *The Joy of Learning*, eds. Callender et. al., 89–98. Portland, ME: The University of Southern Maine.

Additional Resources for Teachers

Ferris, T. 1988. *Coming of Age in the Milky Way*. New York: Doubleday. A history of our scientific understanding of the universe.

Gordon, B., ed. 1985. *Songs from Unsung Worlds*. Boston: Birkhauser. Science in poetry and poems by scientists.

Kuhn, T. S. 1962. *The Structure of Scientific Revolutions*. Chicago: University Press. The original description of paradigms, or world views, and paradigm shifts.

Quine, W. V. and J. S. Ullian. 1978. *The Web of Belief*. New York: Random House. An introduction to the study of rational belief.

Videos

The Ascent of Man, PBS, narrated by Jacob Bronowski; particularly episode 11, "Knowledge or Certainty," which explores the paradox that our world cannot be known separate from our perception of it.

Mindwalk, directed by Bernt Capra, Triton Pictures. A physicist (Liv Ullman), a politician (Sam Waterston), and a poet (John Heard), walk around Mont St. Michel and discuss the history of scientific perception and the effects of these perceptions on our treatment of the world. Long and philosophical—select one or two relevant segments for class viewing.

Painting Resources

Tree paintings (reproductions used to discuss varieties of perception in artistic renderings, style labels are mine; any varied collection will work):

A-Hunting He Would Go, Patrick J. Sullivan, 1940 (stylized primitivism)

Cradling Wheat, Thomas Hart Benton, 1938 (stylized realism)

Gnarled Trees, Chaim Soutine, 1921 (expressionism)

Hide-and-Seek, Pavel Tchelitchew, 1942 (surrealism)

Kindred Spirits, Asher Brown Durand, 1849 (Hudson River School, grandiose romanticism)

Siegfried and the Rhine Maidens, Albert Pinkham Ryder, 1891 (stylized romanticism)

The Trout Pool, Worthington Whittredge, 1820–1910 (Hudson River School, realistic romanticism)

2

Nature Writing and Journal Keeping

East Blue Hill, Maine, July 1997

It's a brilliant morning, the kind you dream of when you are stuck in a fluorescent room in February. The air is clear and every green in the landscape is richly, gloriously green. Patches of pink rogosa, yellow and red Indian paintbrush, and blue vetch dot the ground, and orange lilies and white water parsnip wave on tall stalks, saturated points of color in this green sea. Riding my bike along the cove road, I crest a hill and see a postcard Maine scene: a meadow rolls down to the water, the breeze winnows the grass in currents of tan and green, a split rail fence gets lost in the swales and emerges again by an old family graveyard in the shade of two tall firs, all silhouetted against the sapphire of Blue Hill Bay. The rocky shoreline jags to the horizon, tide-lined by bands of dark and light brown topped with a layer of evergreen. White lobster boats and sail boats ride at anchor facing the outgoing tide, and distant islands beckon. A stranger passes, saying, "Beautiful day." "It doesn't get any better than this," I reply, and mean it. Is this the paradise we all seek? If so, it is a transitory and partly man-made paradise. I'm enjoying the white picket fence and meadow as much as the forest and sea. Can scenes like this give me something that lasts beyond the moment? As often happens when I am overwhelmed by beauty, I wonder how to "capture" it, absorb it, get it right into my pores so I can hold on to it. Do I walk into this scene, sit and revel in it, paint or photograph it, write about it? It's so hard for a human to just "be" in the midst of beauty without wanting to "do" something, usually something having to do with ownership.

Nature Writing

"Capture, ownership"—nature writing is, obviously, about nature, but it is also about people's place in their natural world. Given the writer as observer and word-crafter, this interconnectedness seems inescapable. Edward Hoagland (Introduction, *The Penguin Nature Library*) writes that "nature writing, despite its basis in science, usually rings with rhapsody as well—a belief that nature is an expression of God." This connection of observation and reflection, of the objective and the subjective, outer and inner, I believe to be at the heart of nature writing.

In introducing this genre to students, I tell them it is neither all detailed description nor all personal thoughts and feelings, but some combination of the two. A nature writer begins with the particular and moves to the abstract. Nature, important to understand for itself, also becomes a way to understand ourselves, a touchstone or symbol of our experiences and insights.

Louise Westling, professor of English at the University of Oregon, questions this emphasis on human interpretation—"Do we always have to come back to ourselves? Surely nature writers and ecocritics ought to be looking for a less androcentric approach." Westling advocates a perception of nature that values land for its own sake and not for the meaning we derive from it. Nevertheless, nature literature has traditionally included the human inspiration drawn from nature equally with its discussion of nature itself.

In his chapter, "Nature and the Environment" (*Speaking of Journalism*), Roger Cohn, executive editor of *Audubon*, outlines qualities of good nature writing: "clear, vivid description" of nature and its effect on the writer, based on careful observation; a "strong sense of place" derived from personal involvement with the land and its inhabitants; and, for modern nature writers, a third quality—a consideration of the environmental issues associated with a place. Just as ecological systems must be seen as a whole to be understood, Cohn believes that nature writing must take all aspects of an observed environment into account. "The best kind of article . . . is one that is both a good nature piece and a good issue piece."

Ideally, we can tell students to go out with their journals and look at the world and write what they see and think, and they will come back with beautifully detailed, carefully worded descriptions and insights. This can work for some students some of the time, but not usually as a steady diet. I often have students begin to say, "I don't know what you want me to write about." Or as one student kept repeating to me, "Nothing is happening in nature." Several approaches can help them over these humps. One is to share, with permission, successful examples of students' own writing with the class. Another is to read and discuss examples from published nature writers, usually nonfiction, but also fiction and poetry. And finally, structured writing assignments can help students observe and think in new ways about their natural surroundings.

I intersperse the following exercises throughout the "Literature and the Land" course. Some work well with particular readings; some can be done at any time.

Favorite Place Everyone has a "favorite place," a place they escape to in their imagination, or in reality, in times of joy or trouble. I usually introduce this assignment by asking students to close their eyes and imagine they are in the place they most love in the world. It can be anywhere and any kind of place, but it must be a real place, and one that they have actually been in. (Imagined "best" places can be the subject of another assignment.) I ask these questions: Where do you look forward to being when you are in a place you do not like? Where do you like to spend vacation time? Where do you like to be when you have problems to work out? Where might you like to live as an adult? Where would you rather be than here? Once they have a place, I ask students to imagine its sounds, tastes, smells, sights, and textures. What are their own feelings as they imagine being there now? What feelings do they associate with being there in the past? Why is it their favorite place? Students then write a description (at home or in class) of the "favorite place" with such specificity of physical details and feelings that readers can place themselves in the scene and appreciate it along with the writer.

Students like the personal focus of this paper and it often results in some of their best writing. They have written about a grandparents' vacation home in the mountains, a family cabin where a student spent his last summer with a dying brother, the beach, and even their own bedrooms. Claire called her paper about skiing in Colorado, "Pure Escape":

> I remember everything as though it were yesterday, from the smell of the air to the texture of the powder. It had snowed a foot the night before . . . the kind of snow that you can actually fly through, that cushions your turns perfectly, and dances as you slice through it . . . I had just fallen . . . and tumbled until I stopped. It was that moment I fully realized I was in heaven. Tall dark evergreen trees surrounded either side of the trail. These were just the foreground of the beautiful view in front of me, reaching until the earth curved beneath itself. . . . Mountains leaped up, . . . trying to free themselves from the detaining forces of ground. It stole my breath. . . . Somehow, it just all fit, like I belonged. . . .
> —Claire H.

We share these descriptions in class and consider the range of places and what they have in common that makes them "favorites." While I purposely do not tell them that their "favorite place" must be a place in nature, usually at least three quarters of the pieces describe natural places. Discussion reveals many reasons for this: nature represents an escape; it is different from our normal surroundings; it is beautiful. I use "Favorite Place" to introduce the "Golden Age" readings in Chapter Three.

Land Autobiography A "land autobiography" is a personal narrative in which writers look back over their lives at *all* of the natural places that have been special to them and have shaped who they are. The places can be ordinary, everyday places as well as special places associated with a vacation or trip. The writing should include both vivid, specific description of the places and discussion of what these places mean to the student. To avoid superficial treatment, I limit the number of sites described to four or five (or allow time for a longer paper). Again, this is an opportunity to share the students' papers and discuss the importance of nature in students' lives. (Assignment from Stephanie Kaza, *Turning Wheel,* Winter, 1996)

I try to do assignments along with my students, especially those done in class, and this is one of my favorites. Try it! You'll be amazed at the memories that come flooding back.

> I vividly recall my childhood yard and where each flowering plant and shrub stood: swamp pink in the corner, lilac at the back door with "alcoves" for playing house, phlox so thick I made rooms and passage ways in it, bridal wreath dropping dots of white petals in the rain by the kitchen window, spiny branches of pink quince by the garage, peonies hanging heavily out of their rows along the driveway, tiger lilies in the hedge, two trellises of rambler roses—each bloom greeted with excitement. My mother always called me to see the hummingbirds and Baltimore orioles attracted to the quince, or the flock of pheasants which occasionally fed in the back yard in the Fall. Where did my love for nature begin? With my mother and my yard. In the neighborhood, five old horse chestnut trees grew along my route to school. Every autumn I came home with a skirt full of shiny new brown chestnuts, some still in burrs to preserve their freshness a little longer. I filled shoeboxes with my treasures and was downcast when the lustrous brown skins turned dull and shriveled. My uncle's farm in the Berkshires had goats, a spring at the far corner of the pasture where his cows drank, and mysterious woods beyond. My mother and I spent every summer half a mile from Long Island Sound, and now I never feel properly oriented unless I know I can reach the ocean easily.

I could go on—to travels, places associated with friends, the beach where we walked with our newborn daughter, the homesite we found after years of searching. As I said, this assignment is evocative—and fun!

Mandy, who started out saying she could not write a land autobiography because no place had any special meaning for her, eventually wrote a very effective paper about her field hockey field:

> I like nature and being outside, but there really aren't any places where I feel connected to the land. . . . The places I like to spend a lot of time are the fields where I play sports. . . . I still remember exactly what all of the fields I've played on look like, as well as their surroundings.
>
> It's field hockey season right now and I spend three hours a day on the field hockey field. I know every bump and hole in the field. I know from past mistakes where the ball could hit the ground and bounce into the goal past my diving body. I know how hard I can kick the ball and still keep it on the field, or how there's a hole near one of the goals that's easy to trip on if you're not careful. I've played on that field for four years. . . . It will always be part of me, even long after I graduate and move away.

I will still be able to picture that field and feel the ground hit me as I dive for a ball or get knocked down by an opposing player. I will remember all the times when I played on that field in the mud or the August heat, so tired that I just wanted to give up, but I kept going until I got the ball away from the goal. . . . The scars on my elbows from landing on rocks on that field will always be there. . . .

In the off season I often find myself looking out at the field from the library windows, thinking about all that I've been through on that field. How I've grown up without knowing it, but that field was always there, part of me. I have endless memories on that field, good and bad. From freshman year when we didn't win a single game, to the years of making it to the playoffs only to lose after weeks of practice and pain. . . .

The field hockey field at Oyster River is the one I call home. It's where I grew up playing the sport I loved and learning lessons in life all at the same time. I won't miss this school when I leave, but I sure will miss that field.

—*Mandy G.*

The land autobiographies can result in an awareness and appreciation of how much natural places mean to us and how much they have influenced who we are. It is a good assignment to give early in the course, allowing two to three weeks for drafting, conferencing, and rewriting. The paper serves as a good transition to introducing the land journal project (see end of this chapter) because it demonstrates the importance of developing a personal relationship with a particular area. More than statistics and doomsday predictions, this personal connection and appreciation can give students a sense of place and help them become stewards of land.

Sensory Writing English teachers all have tricks for helping students to become more aware of what their senses perceive and to find a vocabulary to describe these sensations. James Moffett calls these descriptions "sensory monologues." Some ideas include sitting quietly and describing (not naming) every sound that occurs (e.g., "the increasing then fading hum of the truck tires passing on the highway"; not "a truck goes by"); passing around bags of different materials and describing the textures (not just guessing what the object is); having blindfolded students pass around containers with a variety of aromas or a variety of foods to taste (again the object is to describe the sensation, not name the source). I have students bring in oranges and describe every stage of peeling and eating them. One teacher asks students to imagine being inside an orange and working their way out of it.

Students include metaphors and similes in their descriptive writing by finding analogies or comparisons for the sensations they are describing. The brainstorming exercises become drafts for polished poems or prose pieces. Once students have practiced sensory writing in class, I take them outside and have them apply the same awareness to describing their natural surroundings.

As the following journal entry demonstrates, these exercises help students become keen, articulate observers of their surroundings:

> The rains have come and gone, leaving small, nearly dried muddy rivulets on the entrance to the path. The air has a thick, nutty smell to it, . . . the smell of rotting wood. The rain has honed the scent of nearly everything in the field. Today, I stand by an old overgrown asparagus plant. It's a monstrous creature, a thick, matted bramble taller than I am. It looks a bit like a giant, woody hairball. Prickles stick out from every shoot. A bruised light is creeping through the trees to swallow up the last golden rays.
>
> —Mary J.

Extended Metaphor Perhaps the best way to introduce extended metaphor, a comparison of two different elements that extends throughout a piece of writing, is to look at writing that uses nature symbolically. Norman MacLean's *A River Runs Through It* compares the characters of a father and two sons to their individual fly fishing styles. Examples abound in Melville's *Moby Dick*; for example, in "The Fountain," he compares a rainbow in a whale's spout to the divine inspiration that illuminates the "fog" of our doubts. Thoreau's writing is also a rich source of extended metaphors, such as "Time is but the stream I go a-fishing in. . . ." at the end of "Where I Lived and What I Lived For" in *Walden*.

I ask students to find a process in nature (the passing of seasons, the growth of a seed) that could have symbolic significance in their own lives and to describe this process in a way that suggests the parallel, symbolic meaning.

Personification Personification is one form of extended metaphor. In *Desert Solitaire*, Edward Abbey says he does not want to personify nature but rather to see it as it is without the imposition of human constructs and motives. He is seeing with the scientist's eye. Students are of two minds about this. They see the logic of his point, but they also feel that people might care more about something that they can identify with themselves. If a natural object is personified with a divine spirit, that caring expands to reverence and awe which we discuss when we read about early cosmologies (Chapter Three).

While reading myths, I often suggest that students personify something on their land sites as a journal writing option. They imagine that some object in their environment has the ability to think and feel. Emily imagined two stars, "like two bright shining eyes, watching over me, as I watched them." Students write from the point of view of something very small or something very large. How does the world look? How does it feel to be this object? How do you experience the passing of a day or the seasons? How are you treated by people? On hikes, I have asked students to write from the point of view of their boot, a rock or tree along the trail, or the mountain itself.

Lenses—Close-up and Wide-angle Some of us habitually look for broad vistas in the natural landscape; some pay regular attention to the fine details that others ignore. Outside, I ask students to imagine they are looking through two camera lenses. First they focus on something small—an area of bark on a tree, a blade of grass, a leaf, an insect—and describe it in detail. Then they pull back to see the "big picture," including the small object in the scene, and describe this "wide-angle" view in detail. Finally, they discuss any connections (similarities, differences, relationships) found between the close-up and distant view.

> Each blade of grass is different and unique, yet when we look at the whole field we assume every blade is the same. We make the same assumptions about people and expect everyone to be alike. We need to respect differences. Each unique individual is a necessary part of the whole.
> —*Tara B.*

This assignment and the following one are good complements to the discussions of point of view in the introductory unit on perception.

Thirteen Ways of Looking At . . . My colleague Kay Morgan has her class read and briefly discuss Wallace Stevens' poem, "Thirteen Ways of Looking at a Blackbird." Students note that the stanzas are not just random impressions, but reveal a structure and a sequence, from sensory to personal to philosophical and back to a concrete image that can now encompass the other levels of meaning.

Outside, students choose something to observe, then find thirteen ways to describe it. Each description should involve a few lines of writing, not just one word descriptions. This assignment forces the writer to get beyond first impressions and to dig deeper for ideas. Students consider the order of their images and what this order might convey.

A Journey I take several field trips as a part of this course and have students write about their experiences. (See Chapter Seven.) In addition, many students travel in the course of a year, offering excellent opportunities to keep trip journals. These journal entries can be thought of in three stages:

- *Anticipations*: What do you expect from this trip? What do you hope for? What concerns do you have? What are your goals? What might you learn?
- *Observations and reactions*: How does the new environment differ from your home environment? What might you notice as a newcomer that natives may take for granted? What environmental problems are observed? Traveling students should avoid the "bed-to-bed" kind of writing that includes

every daily event and meal and instead concentrate on describing events that are significant to them and why.

- *Reflections*: How did the trip match your expectations? Were your goals met? What surprised you? pleased you? disappointed you? What were the highlights and low points? What did you learn? What effects might your presence have had on this place? How did seeing a new place affect your view of home?

In addition to these selected writing assignments, my students keep weekly land journals.

Land Journals

This spot of land is more than just a place to me; it is a piece of me.
—*Jon M.*

When Thoreau spent two years living by Walden Pond and keeping a journal about his thoughts and surroundings, he set a standard emulated by modern writers like Annie Dillard, Sue Hubbell, Aldo Leopold, Gretel Ehrlich, Edward Abbey, Edward Beston, Terry Tempest Williams, and Bernd Heinrich. A list of nature journals students have enjoyed reading is included at the end of this chapter, and the entire course could be organized around reading these journals and having students keep their own. *Ceremonial Time* by John Mitchell is an excellent example of a modern *Walden*. Mitchell spent a year observing a square mile area around his eastern Massachusetts home, walking the land at all times of day and night and in all seasons. By the end of his journeys in space and time, he senses a spiritual link between himself, the land, and the Native Americans who inhabited the land before him. His book and many others like it have inspired the "land journal" project.

In *To Compose*, Thomas Newkirk says that, within the context of a course, a journal is neither a diary nor a class notebook but borrows features from both. Like diaries, journals are written in the first person about issues the writer cares about; like class notebooks, journals are about the content of a particular course. The "land journal" is about a chosen piece of land and all of the observations and reflections the land inspires in the writer.

Students in "Literature and the Land" each keep a journal about a piece of land that is special to them. The land journal is used weekly throughout the semester and is usually introduced after the perception unit. When I first introduced these journals, I had a somewhat formal land-study approach in mind (see Appendix B). The following motivator still appears at the beginning of my land journal assignment sheet, but over the years the goals for keeping a land journal have evolved to be much broader and more personal than what I first envisioned:

Many people have made important discoveries by looking closely at their immediate environment. Loren Eiseley's favorite 'laboratory' was the vacant lot next door. The man who invented Velcro did it by studying burrs. Closely studying a piece of local land this semester may or may not bring new knowledge to the world at large, but it should bring *you* a new awareness of the interaction of human and natural history.

Students themselves have helped me to understand what is important to them about keeping land journals. The goals we have developed together are:

- to increase awareness and powers of observation about the natural world, including seeing changes over time
- to apply a variety of points of view in looking at land, including poetic, historic, scientific, personal, artistic, and political
- to see land as an integrated, ecological whole
- to learn a variety of journal keeping styles and to discover and develop a personal voice
- to develop a personal relationship with and a sense of caring for a piece of land
- to have a weekly "time out" from routine activity.

In *Earth in Mind*, David Orr says, "I do not know whether it is possible to love the planet or not, but I do know that it is possible to love the places we can see, touch, smell, and experience. And I believe that rootedness in a place is the most important and least recognized need of the human soul." Barry Lopez talks about land we know well as a "querencia," the place a bull goes to gather strength in a fight, or "a place on the ground where one feels secure, a place from which one's strength of character is drawn" (*The Rediscovery of North America*). Students often say their land sites are just such a source of strength to them.

> "The best part of keeping this journal is that it gave me time to get off by myself and just think and relax. If I didn't have to do this for an assignment, I probably never would."
> —Jenny M.

The intimate knowledge of our natural surroundings advocated by Lopez is for the good of our environment as well as our own good. As a student once said, "Imagine if every place on earth had a person who knew it well and cared for it passionately!"

> Keeping this journal has taught me about preserving land. I have gotten attached to my land after having to write about it. I've always gone down there on my own time to think or fish or whatever. But writing about the land has gotten me attached to it in different ways. When I write about the land and use words to describe it, I'm seeing

the land differently and really observing it. So, because I'm so attached to this land now, I want it to be preserved the way it is forever. I'm sure that's how most environmentalists feel about the wilderness.

—*Peter J.*

Logistics

Choice of Site Students choose a piece of land they already know and like, or would like to know better. It must be a place they can get to weekly. The size is up to them: there are virtues both in a small plot, which forces the observer to look hard at detail, and in a larger area (up to a half-mile square) which provides more variety. Students have chosen their own yards, a family homestead, a favorite park or pond, a beach, a cross-country running trail, a mountain bike trail, a fishing hole, a water fall, even the local laundromat. In the process of reading their journals, I have learned a lot about my area! Urban students do not have to restrict themselves to parks or vacant lots; any exterior space—street markets, intersections, alleys, plazas—can provoke interesting reflections about the way people use outdoor spaces and the impact of human use on the environment.

Our bulletin board has a large topographic map of our area covered in contact paper. Every semester, students locate and label their journal site on the map with erasable marker. Students enjoy comparing notes about their sites and helping each other find their sites on the map—a task some find surprisingly difficult. (See mapping activities in Chapter Seven and Appendix B.) At the end of the semester, I wash off the lines and start over.

Two variations: Students can write about contrasting sites, for example a wild versus a developed site; two contrasting ecological systems, or a site that has undergone some significant change in recent years. I offer an optional site switch mid-semester to students who are feeling bogged down in their journals. Another option is to divide the local area on a map, and "auction off" sites to the class; at the end of the semester a display of final projects surveys the entire environs.

Problems with journals: This assignment is not for everyone. For some, the very word "journal" sets off alarm bells. Some start hopefully, and quickly run out of things to say. Some are too action-oriented to be comfortable with observation and self-reflection. If suggested topics or changes of site do not help, I would rather design an alternative assignment, such as collecting and writing about media articles on the environment, than have these students struggle and bluff their way through the semester.

The Journal Students get their own journals, which must be separate notebooks especially for this purpose. My instructions are: "Get yourself a beautiful journal, a book you will look forward to writing and drawing in. The size is up to you. If you choose one without lines, you will be able to draw as well as write in it." Students can slip lined paper behind unlined journal pages for writing. Some students buy attractive commercial journals. Others make their own, or decorate regular notebooks with collages, quotations, and drawings. I show a variety of former journals as examples.

Due Dates Students go to their site at least once a week. Shannon and Amanda describe the benefits of writing on the site or at home:

> While I was at my site, I would try to write there if possible. I think when I was able to do this my writing was more creative and I saw more. When I couldn't write there—because of snow, rain, cold—then I would take many mental notes. Sometimes I would write short phrases in my head.
> —*Shannon B.*

> I learned more when I wrote later. I think it gave me more time to absorb.
> —*Amanda L.*

I usually know when students are not going to their site but are writing their entries in the cafeteria five minutes before class; they say things like, "The leaves are turning color and starting to fall off" and run out of things to write after half a page. I expect students to go out in all weather; contrasts make for good observations and writing. Some will complain about this and actually need to learn to dress appropriately in order to be comfortable! Night time visits are also a good source of material. (*Moon Journals* by Chancer and Rester-Zodrow has excellent ideas for observing nature at night.)

I collect journals every Tuesday and try to return them by Thursday. This allows students to have them for two weekdays and the weekend, but does not force them to write on the weekend. I accept late entries until Thursday because I can still return the journal by Friday, but I do not allow make-up entries after that because one point of the assignment is to observe the site and write regularly and frequently.

Length I ask students to write about 700 words or make the equivalent effort in drawing or collecting. They may write one long entry, or several shorter ones. I encourage them to try a variety of approaches—drawing, mapping, collecting samples, pressing flowers, or photographing. Students have also included news articles and historical documents related to their land.

Feedback I read and comment on the entries every week. I write my responses on post-it notes or just insert scrap paper. I try to respect the personal nature of these journals by not writing in them myself, although not every student minds and I often find my note permanently taped into the journal as another "artifact." I use my comments as a way to open a dialogue with the student about their land. I ask questions (and expect answers!); I share related anecdotes of my own; and I tell them which part of their writing I enjoyed, found interesting, surprising, or effectively written. I do not make editing marks in the journals, but I do include a list of spelling words on the post-it. To give myself a break as the sole source of feedback, I occasionally have students read and comment on each other's entries, but the class has to agree to this beforehand; not all students want others reading their entries. Sharing journals in class also provides students with a wide range of journal writing ideas and styles to consider as models.

What to Write About and How

The content of journal entries can be assigned and structured, completely open-ended, or a combination of the two. While some students prefer the structure of specific questions, others like to follow their own muse. Offering students optional topics or alternating "free writes" with assigned topics are effective compromises.

When we begin the land journals, students read an excellent article called "The Naturalist's Journal" by Dale Laurence (author of *The Beginning Naturalist*),

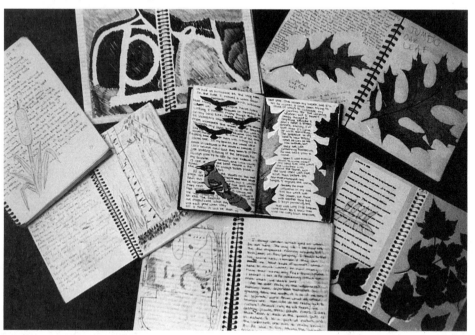

Figure 2–1. Journals. (Photo by Bev Conway)

36

which appeared in the Maine Audubon magazine, *Habitat,* and which delineates six types or styles of journal keeping for naturalists. Illustrations in the article feature pages from the journals described. I ask different students to be responsible for summarizing one of the six journal styles. Students find their earlier discussions of perception and subjectivity versus objectivity reinforced by these six styles. The models provide a range of options for students to try in their own journals, and we discuss the merits of each approach, which students prefer, and why. While I do not expect them to choose and stick to one model, certain styles will naturally suit certain students. I encourage them to experiment, to see what they can learn from different approaches, and to find a style they like.

The "Day Book" The first model Laurence describes is the methodical "day book" kept for forty years in the 1700s by a British curate named Gilbert White. White observed daily and noted seasonal occurrences for all of the plants and creatures in his garden, including a long-lived tortoise he called Timothy. This style of journal keeping does not include personal reflection or poetic description, but over time can reveal patterns in natural phenomena. An example of the usefulness of such amateur data collection is the lake water monitoring done by Albert and Alfred Smiley, who in 1869 established the Mohonk Mountain House and preserve in the New York Shawangunks. Their long-term records of the increasing acidity levels in Mohonk's lakes provided scientists with key evidence about the history of acid rain.

I encourage students to notice small things like the order in which trees turn color in the fall, when various flowers bloom, what birds come to their feeders and how they behave, or which varieties of seeds form when. With access to simple monitoring equipment and a little training, they can check water quality or take stock of tree health. Science teachers can support these efforts, and many communities have volunteer monitoring projects students can participate in. (See Appendix C.) Over time, students may be able to notice recurring patterns or correlations, for example, between temperature and insect activity. For the scientifically inclined student, the "day book" is an effective journal keeping style.

The "Exploratory Journal" The next journal type, what Laurence calls an "exploratory journal," is exemplified by Charles Darwin. For five years, Darwin kept field notes which he expanded into diaries while traveling around the world on the Beagle and making the observations that resulted in *The Origin of the Species.* Laurence describes *The Voyage of the Beagle* as "part autobiography, part travelogue, part science, part speculation, and part youthful enthusiasm." Darwin's diary offers a model of how to combine scientific observation with personal feeling and discovery. It also demonstrates that scientific writing need not be dull and boring.

The "Literary Journal" Next Laurence turns to Henry David Thoreau and the "literary journal." Laurence says, "Thoreau's journal offers a model for naturalists willing to engage in an intense literary, intellectual, and spiritual dialogue with nature. In a journal emerging from this relationship, the observer is as important as the observed, the response is as important as that responded to, the metaphor is as important as the fact. . . ." Ideas for reading selections from *Walden* with students are described in Chapter Four.

The "Field Journal" John Muir provides the example of the "field journal" kept "with minimal separation between the experience and the writing about it" and "filled with ecstasies, enthusiasms, and verbal celebrations." Muir carried his journal with him as he walked from Indiana to Florida at age 29, on glaciers in the Pacific Northwest, and when he first explored Yosemite Valley. This style of journal keeping encourages students to make entries right on their sites. (Muir's My *First Summer in the Sierra* is discussed in Chapter Four.)

Figure 2–2. Illuminated Journal

The "Naturalist's Sketchbook" Clare Walker Leslie, a New England artist, provides a model of "the naturalist's sketchbook," which combines verbal observations and illustrations. Drawing forces us to look more closely and results in attractive pages, though there is no pressure to make the drawings polished, finished products. Many students enjoy drawing from nature in their journals and also include maps, designs, fantasies, story illustrations, and cartoons.

The juxtaposition and interaction of the visual and the verbal can spark creativity and lead to new insight and understanding. Hannah Hinchman, an artist, writer, and naturalist, has created what she calls an "illuminated" nature journal every year since her youth. Her book, *A Trail Through Leaves, The Journal as a Path to Place,* includes descriptions of techniques and materials along with many pages from her own journals. Her excerpts include illustrated maps of places and nature walks along with geology, botany, and astronomy drawings and text. The book is so inspiring that I immediately started my own "illuminated" journal! The page below is an entry made in the Wind River Range in Wyoming.

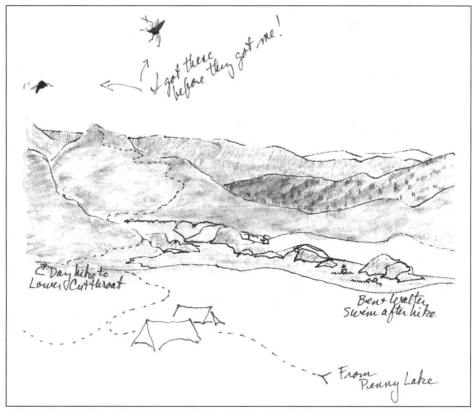

Figure 2–2. *(continued)*

The "Renaissance Journal" Laurence's final example is the "renaissance journal," as illustrated by Bernd Heinrich, zoologist and author of *One Man's Owl, Ravens in Winter, A Year in the Maine Woods,* and *The Trees in My Forest.* Heinrich combines scientific field observation, personal experience, illustration, and photography. This eclectic approach offers the most options for students and is probably the most popular.

Having read and discussed Laurence's article on nature journal styles, students are ready to begin their own entries. I ask them to somehow introduce their site in the first entry, but how to do this is their own choice.

> To begin this journal, I've decided to follow Barry Lopez's advice, and meet the land as our ancestors should have. I want to begin this "observation experience" the "right" way. I hope to fit my place.
>
> My place is a spot of woods, close to my home. It is a kind of mound; at the foot there is a small shed that resembles an old fashioned school house. I often sit on a special rock and look at my semi-distorted reflection in the windows.
>
> I'm quite excited about this journal/activity/class. I feel that it will be an excellent learning experience. I wish to learn more about the land, and my place in it. This is important for everyone; we must identify our place and responsibility. In a sense, the world and life are a game. The land is our board; we must learn the lay of "our" land, how we can be a part of it and how we can "use" it (unfortunately). We need an ultimate strategy—goals, aspirations, dreams. We need the board to carry out our strategy. In today's society, the land isn't more than an assumed possession, which is wrong. The land is in no way "ours." I think the Indians are correct in saying that deeds, boundaries and property are meaningless. The land is there for our enjoyment, and in some circumstances our asset. But until we know and respect the land, we have no right to all that it offers. When/if we stop destroying the land, we can enjoy/have it.
>
> Unfortunately, I don't see the human race rearranging their priorities to benefit the earth. Even if we did, I feel it's too late. "What's done is done;" we can't take it back. That is, collectively rather than individually. I think that if we individually try to "rediscover" the land, then we can partially redress our past actions.
>
> The only panacea for our earth is caring.
> —*Amanda L.*

As the semester progresses, I offer students a few additional approaches to journal writing suggested by Solly and Lloyd in *Journey Notes* (1989). I introduce these techniques one at a time, when the mood seems right, the style fits a topic we are discussing in class, or students are running out of ideas for their weekly entries.

Stream of Consciousness One day, when discussion lagged and students seemed stressed and out of sorts, I turned the lights out and asked students to take out paper and pen and just start "speed writing" or putting down whatever went through their minds. One thought should lead to another without regard for logic or grammar. This process can take some getting used to; students will say, "You mean we can put down *anything?*" but once they catch on, they find it relaxing and liberating. Students were surprised and pleased when I encouraged them to try this on their land sites.

Listing Listing is just a form of brainstorming. Students list sense impressions, wildlife sightings, plants, or memories, then choose three items from their list and describe them in detail. The lists and descriptions can be further developed as prose or poems, or left as they are.

Shifting Point of View Writing from another point of view (also discussed under "personification") can be applied to writing from the view of another person. For example, when we read Native American myths (Chapter Three), I suggest students imagine being a pre-contact native living on what is now the student's land site; when we read European accounts of early America (Chapter Four), I suggest pretending to be an explorer seeing the student's land site for the first time. When conflicting philosophies of land use are the subject of discussion, students can write a dialogue in their journal between a developer, a conservationist, an ecologist, and a preservationist (see Chapter Four) about how their own sites should be treated now and in the future.

Letter Writing Students can use their journals to write "letters" and pose questions to previous owners of their land. They also write to someone living a hundred years in the future about their feelings and hopes for their site. If they are reading about the travels of John Muir or the sojourns of Gretel Ehrlich, they "write" to these authors about explorations of their own land.

Storytelling Students do a lot of storytelling in their journals: They write about childhood experiences and recent events with family or friends. They make up a "story" about how their place came to be. They imagine a story about what happens on their site when no one is there. A squirrel reminded Diane of the day she learned that her dear cat, Snowflake, had been hit by a car while chasing a squirrel.

> When I saw "little gray" twitch his bent tail, I wondered if he was related to Snowflake's prize. I make noises to him and he sees me. He sits up almost like he's saluting me! With a squirrelly, cocky look, he bounces happily away. Well, he shook his sorrow. I will do the same by remembering my darling Snowflake!
> —Diane J.

41

Poetry Land journals also create opportunities for student poets. More examples of poetry are in Chapter Seven.

Environmental Unconsciousness

Shoveling plastered
flakes off the milky cliffs
of the basin, you rhythmically
clank your spoon on the glass.
The morning paper blankets
the table in front of your
careless mind.
Scanning the dull pages
on your way to another essential episode
of Peanuts, bits of
oil spills and dead elephants
paste themselves to your always preoccupied
brain, like the fragments of flooded
fields on the side of your bowl.

Amanda L.

Data Collection and Research Entries The land journal project offers many possibilities for research in the social and natural sciences. Students can gather information in geology, botany, zoology, human history, current use, and options for the future. By applying all of these categories to the study of one land site, students gain a deeper understanding of the concept of an "ecosystem" and of the interconnectedness of knowledge in general. Students can map their sites, research historical documents, collect oral histories, do archeological digs, or learn zoning and land protection ordinances; they can dig soil test pits, survey plants and animals, monitor water quality or tree health, and observe the relationships between soils, plants, and animals. Suggested activities for such research are described in Appendices B and C.

Evaluation and Final Presentations

Since self-evaluation is so important, I ask students halfway through the semester to write (in the journals) what they have learned so far about themselves, their land, and journal keeping, and to set goals for the remainder of the semester. What approaches have worked and what new approaches would they like to try? What else do they want to know? At the end of the course, students write an extensive final entry, using the stated goals, to evaluate what they have learned from the process of keeping a land journal.

I grade journals twice a quarter: mid-quarter to give students a "progress" report and at the end of the quarter. Grades are based on consistency and quality of effort. Have they turned in a full entry every week? Do the entries show observations and reflection that go beyond a cursory, superficial description? Has the writer tried a variety of journal keeping approaches? If all expectations are thoroughly met, I am generous with my grade.

In addition to the self-evaluation entry, I ask students to prepare an oral presentation on their land sites for the end of the course. Their presentations include 1) thoughts from the self-evaluation and personal reflections on the journal keeping process, 2) selected excerpts from their journals, 3) information they have researched or gathered about soils, plants, animals, and history (including any documents and interviews), 4) possible future uses, 5) environmental problems associated with their site and possible solutions, and 6) some visual representation of their land. Some students mount photos on poster board; some enlarge their maps; some make videotapes, drawings or murals. One student made periodic videos to accompany her weekly written entries; she used the camera to introduce the site to me, then continued to film seasonal changes throughout the semester. To share students' work beyond the classroom, I occasionally arrange their journals, drawings, maps, and collections in a hallway display case.

Samples of Student Journals

An exerpt from an opening journal entry:

> Once I start to feel comfortable with this place, I will begin to live when I am there, not just remember and record. I will discuss the people I take there, the thoughts I'm thinking or the feelings I'm experiencing when I go there, the songs I sing, and the poems I write, and the reasons I laugh and cry. I think that then I can begin to understand the importance of the bull's corner of the ring [Lopez's "querencia"], the importance of the environment to me, the impact of my surroundings on my life and my interaction with my human and non-human environment. And then, I hope, I can begin to find the ways in which I can give something back.
> —*Kasey E.*

This excerpt from Aaron's journal shows how his affection for a piece of land starts and grows. Aaron's "field of dreams:"

> It was 1990 and I was as scared as could be. We had to move out of our house that we were renting. It was my idea to build on a plot of land, and after a long search, we finally decided that that is what we were going to do. As soon as we saw this land, I loved it. I could envision my baseball field; I could see my house. My parents immediately saw something that they liked as well, because, soon after, we were the proud

owners of a new lot. . . . My favorite thing was the prospect of a baseball field. The yard dimensions were ideal, and I quickly went to work on a pitcher's mound, a backstop and bases. Soon after I finished with that, I added the needed touch—a wall extending from left field all the way to right field. Everyone old enough to throw a ball was there seeing if they could hit a home run on the Ward's "field of dreams." It was truly a childhood dream come true. Although the field is far less used now than it once was, I still occasionally play a game, and it is one of the main reasons I like the land.
—*Aaron W.*

Entries on extraordinary events—a snowstorm:

I can't imagine not being able to take showers, use the microwave, the oven, the heater, and the TV for two days. Nature is really powerful. Every time we think we have reached another level of intelligence or have invented another powerful machine, nature wipes everything out in two seconds.
—*Linda L.*

We are still without power. At first I don't think it is too bad and it is kind of nice not having the TV on; it forces my family and me to talk. It was kind of fun doing my homework by candle light. I got an idea of what it was like for Abe Lincoln when he was a kid. After a while this whole power thing started to get to me and I wasn't enjoying it anymore. I wanted to watch the Patriots game. But how could I do this without any power? I even went to bed early because I had nothing better to do with my time.
—*Eric J.*

—a lunar eclipse:

We looked at the eclipse through [a friend's telescope] . . . It was strange thinking that the darkness on the moon was the earth's shadow! I wondered if there was something really large on the side of the earth, could it make a lump in the shadow going across the moon? It would have to be a really large thing, though. The moon turned orange as the shadow went over it. Someone explained to me why, and it has to do with the light rays that make it over the earth and the light rays that don't, but that's all I remember.
—*Erin Q.*

Animal sightings:

I searched around, looking at tracks and seeing how old they were by seeing if the edges had melted and refrozen, and matching the surrounding snow with the snow in the track—if they match, the track could be fairly recent. . . . The habitat was perfect for rabbits; there were a few downed trees to provide cover and patches of thick vegetation that the rabbits eat and hide in. I was standing looking at where a grouse had slept two nights ago when I heard a sound on my right. I looked up and saw a flash of pure white. The rabbit took a few leaps and then paused behind a tree for a second. It then bounded another ten yards and paused again. This time I was able to get a good look at it. It was snow white with a black nose and dark eyes; it blended in with the snow almost perfectly. . . . After a few seconds, the rabbit continued its flight, taking huge eight to ten foot leaps that carried it away at an amazing speed. It ran along a ridge . . . I waited for a couple minutes and then started after the rabbit. The fresh tracks went over logs and through small groups of young pine trees. After about fifty yards of going through pretty thick cover, the rabbit started to circle back to where I had scared it up. The tracks became a little closer together indicating that the rabbit was slowing down. I expected the rabbit to go back to where it had started, but it must have known that I was following it so it kept circling until it was on the track it had just made. It did this to confuse any pursuers because the two sets of tracks and scent trails and my tracks would all help to confuse me or any animal like a dog or bobcat.

—*Jeff F.*

Final entries:

Keeping a journal takes discipline, which is one thing that this assignment taught me. Another thing that I noticed was my increased concern for the environment: it made me think about the condition of my land in twenty or thirty years. By discipline, I mean that I had to make time to write in the journal and think about what I was writing. In a way, this got me away from other things and gave me time to think.

—*Krissy D.*

The journal also got me thinking of the fishing areas and how many of the visitors couldn't give a darn how they left the area with fishing twine, beer bottles, and other garbage . . . it got me thinking of environmental impact on a grand scale and where we are all headed. I guess what I learned most was to not take for granted the land which I lived on for most of my life.

—*Diego S.*

I guess the major thing keeping this journal taught me about my land, and land in general, is that it is always changing. . . . Every time I went out to "my" land, I noticed something different. To think of all the changes that happen in just the small portion of land I observed for such a short time, makes me think of all of the changes that must take place all over the world. Keeping a journal about a piece of land makes me realize how insignificant I am in nature. The role of any one person is very small, but put together is very important. . . . The actions that I take promote some of the changes that occur on my land.

—*Greg S.*

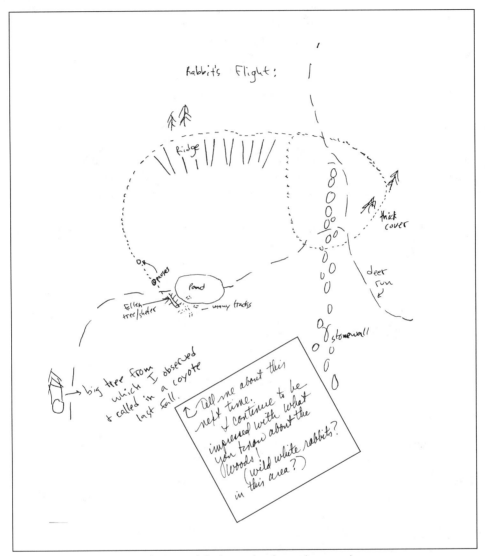

Figure 2–3. Jeff's Journal–Animal Sighting (with teacher note).

In the beginning of the year, I knew my journal wouldn't just be about my land. It would be about me as well. . . . I looked and observed my land and connected that to my personal experience. When I was depressed, the wind blowing through my hair seemed to understand exactly what I was going through. When I was happy, the cos-

mos seemed to be sharing my joy. . . . I never thought I could see my feelings through the land. I never thought it could comfort me like a friend.
—*Linda L.*

Keeping this journal has opened my eyes to my surroundings. . . . I consciously hear the chirping crickets and see the forest in a new way. . . . While my land changes through the seasons, I have been changing through my life. With every experience, I have been able to get a glimpse of the real me. Of who I really am.
—*Karen Z.*

I haven't noticed anything concretely different about my land, but it seems like a completely different place. I'm not sure if that is because I've explored it more, or if it changed so drastically that I just can't pinpoint the change. In fact, when I showed the pictures to my mother, she said, "Where's that?" "It's our back yard," I said. "Nah, really? It didn't look like that when I've been out there." I've noticed a lot of things I never did before. I saw many bones and skulls, rabbit and snake holes, and a beauty I never noticed.
—*Amanda L.*

Works Cited

Works Cited for Students

Abbey, E. 1968. *Desert Solitaire*. New York: Ballantine.

Buber, M. 1970. *I and Thou*. Walter Kaufmann, trans. New York: Scribners.

Elder, J., and R. Finch, eds. 1990. *Norton Book of Nature Writing*. New York: W. W. Norton & Co.

Heinrich, B. 1994. *A Year in the Maine Woods*. Reading, MA: Addison Wesley.

Hinchman, H. 1997. *A Trail Through Leaves, The Journal as a Path to Place*. New York: W. W. Norton & Co.

Hoagland, E, ed. 1988. *The Penguin Nature Library: Thoreau's Maine Woods*. New York: Penguin.

Kaza, S. 1996. *Turning Wheel: Journal of the Buddhist Peace Fellowship*. Winter.

Laurence, G. 1991. "The Naturalist's Journal," *Habitat*. Journal of Maine Audubon Society.

Lopez, B. 1991. "The Rediscovery of North America," *The Amicus Journal*, Fall; also, 1992. *The Rediscovery of North America*. New York: Vintage.

Maclean, N. 1983. *A River Runs Through It*. Chicago: University of Chicago Press.

Melville, H. 1988. *Moby Dick*. Evanston, Ill: Northwestern University Press.

Mitchell, J. 1984. *Ceremonial Time: Fifteen Thousand Years on One Square Mile*. Garden City, NY: Anchor Press/Doubleday.

Muir, J. 1911. *My First Summer in the Sierra*. New York: Penguin.

Stevens, W. 1954. *Collected Poems*. New York: Alfred A. Knopf, Inc.

Thoreau, H. D. 1965. *Walden*. New York: Airmont Publishing Co.

Further Readings and Nature Journals for Students

Austin, M. 1903. *The Land of Little Rain*. Boston: Houghton Mifflin.

Beston, H. 1976. *The Outermost House*. (1928). New York: Penguin.

Dillard, A. 1988. *Pilgrim at Tinker Creek*. New York: Harper.

Douglas, W. O. 1961. *My Wilderness*. New York: Doubleday.

Ehrlich, G. 1985. *The Solace of Open Spaces*. New York: Penguin Books. Sheep herding in Wyoming.

Ferra, L., 1994. *A Crow Doesn't Need a Shadow: A Guide to Writing Poetry from Nature*. Layton, VT: Gibbs Smith. Geared for ages nine to twelve.

Hay, J. 1961. *Nature's Year: The Seasons of Cape Cod*. New York: Doubleday.

Hubbell, S. 1987. *A Country Year: Living the Questions*. New York: Perennial Library. Each chapter can be read alone; about bee keeping and much more.

Hoagland, E. 1982. *Notes from the Century Before: A Journal from British Columbia*. San Francisco: North Point Press.

Leopold, A. 1966. *A Sand County Almanac* (1949). New York: Ballantine.

Lindbergh, A. M. 1978. *Gift from the Sea*. New York: Vintage. Each item found along the beach teaches Lindbergh a life lesson.

Sarton, M. 1964. *The House by the Sea*. New York: W. W. Norton & Co.

Teale, E. W. 1978. *A Walk Through the Year*. New York: Dodd, Mead.

Williams, T. T. 1992. *Refuge, An Unnatural History of Family and Place*. New York: Pantheon Books. Parallels her mother's terminal illness with an unusual rise in the level of Great Salt Lake.

Works Cited for Teachers

Ackerman, D. 1990. *A Natural History of the Senses*. New York: Random House.

Chancer, J., and G. Rester-Zodrow. 1997. *Moon Journals*. Portsmouth, NH: Heinemann.

Cohn, R. 1994. "Nature and the Environment." In *Speaking of Journalism: Twelve Writers and Editors Talk About Their Work*. William Zinsser et. al., eds. New York: Harper Collins.

Solly, R. and R. Lloyd. 1989. *Journeynotes: Writing for Recovery and Spiritual Growth*. San Francisco: Harper & Row.

Moffett, J. 1968. *Teaching the Universe of Discourse*. Boston: Houghton Mifflin.

Murray, J. A. 1995. *The Sierra Club Nature Writing Handbook: A Creative Guide*. San Francisco: Sierra Club Books.

Newkirk, T, ed. 1990. *To Compose: Teaching Writing in High School and College.* Portsmouth, NH: Heinemann.

Orr, D. 1994. *Earth in Mind.* Washington, DC: Island Press.

Westling, L. 8/9/96. *The Chronicle of Higher Education.* vol. XLII, no. 48, A8.

Further Resources for Teachers

Cameron, J. 1995. *The Artist's Way: A Spiritual Path to High Creativity.* Los Angeles: J. P. Tarcher/Perigee.

Heard, G. 1995. *Writing Toward Home: Tales and Lessons to Find Your Way Home.* Portsmouth, NH: Heinemann. Writing, autobiography, and travelogue. Each short chapter ends with writing "assignments."

Johnson, C. 1997. *The Sierra Club Guide to Sketching in Nature.* San Francisco: Sierra Club Books.

3

Myths, The Golden Age, and "The Tempest"

So dawn goes down to day.
Nothing gold can stay.
                              Robert Frost

October, 1997

It's a brisk but bright October morning; the sugar maples are golden yellow, the oak leaves just beginning to rust. A small herd of buffalo grazes against the backdrop of a glittering bay as we stand at the edge of David Langley's pasture. He is telling us that these animals are not actually "buffalo" but bison and that a grown male can weigh 2,000 pounds and outrun a human. Twenty million animals were reduced to only 550 by 1889 when William Hornaday helped pass protective measures enabling them to recover. Now 15,000 bison live in fenced game reserves in the United States, and private farmers like David raise several thousand more. Raising meat is one of his goals; another is keeping his third generation water-front farm undeveloped but sustainably used.

As my students and I walk down the hill toward the water, we see signs of the rich history of this farm. An old foundation marks the spot where a lone settler held off a band of raiding Indians from up the coast. The tip of the peninsula was the landing for the ferry from Portsmouth and the start of the main roadway into Durham. Darby Field, the first European to climb Mt. Washington, once maintained a tavern at this point.

We are heading for the Blackfoot Indian teepee David erected by the edge of the water. As we lift the flap and step through the opening, we enter silence and shadow and the feeling of being in another time and place. Coals smolder in the center firepit and David adds a few logs as the students crowd around the fire. We are here to tell, from memory, Native American stories learned back in the classroom. Some students shift uncomfortably as we wait for someone to volunteer to begin. Gradually the ice breaks, and we hear, "Long ago, Gluscabi lived with his grandmother, Woodchuck, in a small lodge beside the big water." In this Abenaki tale about Gluscabi and the Wind Eagle, Gluscabi learns that his efforts to control and stop the wind only create more trouble and that all of the forces of nature have a purpose.

Mythology

Native American Literature

Sharing Native American stories is a motivating introduction to a historical study of human perceptions of the natural world. While students would groan at a phrase like "historical overview," they are happy to learn more about Native Americans. Rather than teach a comprehensive history of land use, I do a selective study that begins with early human attitudes toward nature as reflected in world mythology, then focuses on land use in North America (Chapter Four). My goal is to help students understand how present attitudes toward nature have developed and the impacts of these attitudes on ourselves and our world.

Native American storytelling immerses students, if only briefly, in the experience of oral tradition and helps them discover the storytellers' values regarding the environment. Students work with a partner to learn stories taken from Joseph Bruchac's collections, *Keepers of the Earth* and *Keepers of the Animals*. I remind students that these stories were told by people who had no written language. To simulate oral tradition, each student hears their story read aloud by a partner before reading it from the page. One student, Mike, described how unusual it was as an adult to hear rather than read a story. He began to imagine that, in a nonliterate culture, words might carry a different kind of force, calling to mind feelings and visual images rather than letters.

Students read and practice telling their stories. They do not need to learn them word for word, but retell them in as much detail as possible, using animated voices and body language. This activity appeals to the outgoing student with a flair for drama, but can intimidate a shy student who never speaks in class. For both, it offers an opportunity to experience the concept of "story" in a new context. It is often especially engaging for students who do not usually like reading.

I encourage students to incorporate a visual "prop" with the storytelling: a drum, a flute, or an object such as a rock, branch or ear of corn that might appear in the story. Tom donned his Boy Scout troop's bear skin to tell "Awi Usdi, the Little Deer," a Cherokee story about hunting wisely and respectfully. Christine, a theater student, used a scarf and movement to act out the Nisqually story of conflict and resolution, "Loo-Wit, the Fire Keeper." Students say that these objects help them to focus and absorb the details of the stories.

We have just one class period and one night to rehearse our stories; I tell a story as well. The next day we share stories, often outside—and sometimes in a teepee!

Follow-up discussion focuses on the question: What do these stories tell us about Native Americans' view of the natural world? Students point out the powerful role played by animals as characters and as creators in the stories, and about the absence of anthropomorphic divinities. For example, the Onondaga believe that the earth was created on a turtle's back. In the Lakota story of "The First Flute," a young man makes a flute and wins a woman with the help of a woodpecker and the beautiful sounds in nature. The prominence of animals shows a profound respect for the natural world and its creatures. Stories, such as "Gluscabi and the Wind Eagle" and "Awi Usdi," also teach explicit lessons about respecting nature. In my favorite story, the White Buffalo Calf Woman brings buffalo to the Lakota Sioux people, presents them with a Sacred Pipe, and teaches them to give thanks for their blessings.

> "The bowl of the Pipe," she said, "is made of the red stone. It represents the flesh and blood of the Buffalo People and all other Peoples. The wooden stem of the Pipe represents all the trees and plants, all the things green and growing on this Earth. The smoke that passes through the Pipe represents the sacred wind, the breath that carries prayers up to Wakan Tanka, the Creator." (Bruchac 1991, 129)

She taught the Sioux to offer the pipe to the Earth and Sky and to each of the four directions, and to remember that "all things were as connected as parts of the Pipe" (Bruchac, 131).

Writing I ask students to write a response in which they discuss the values and views of nature revealed by the stories, using at least five or six of the stories as examples.

By the time students are in high school, they already have certain assumptions about Native American lifestyles. They say things like, "They didn't do anything to hurt the land," or "They didn't waste anything; they used everything they killed." To challenge oversimplifications and consider the inevitability of some human impact on land, I share with them information from William Cronon's *Changes in the Land.* For example, New England natives cut thousand of acres around Boston and Narragansett Bay for firewood and regularly burned over fields to maintain the right habitat for game animals such as deer, rabbit, turkey, and quail. Natives in the west drove herds of bison over cliffs, and some anthropologists believe that the die-off of mammoth species during the Pleistocene era may have been due to a combination of climate change and overhunting by pre-historic humans. We discuss these questions: Is it possible to live on the earth without affecting it? If change is natural, how much change and what kinds of changes are reasonable?

Contemporary works on Native American beliefs discussed elsewhere in this book include Scott Momaday's "A Vision Beyond Time and Place" (in Chapter One) and *Animal Dreams* by Barbara Kingsolver (in Chapter Six).

Journal Writing While students are in the midst of reading and discussing Native American traditions and beliefs regarding the land, they use their weekly land journal entry to try an imaginary exercise. I ask them to pretend they are living on their land before European settlers arrived. They consider what the land might have looked like, how the plant and animal life would differ, and what it would be like to live a subsistence existence using the resources in the vicinity of their land. Eric wrote this imaginary story about a New England Abenaki family:

> It is the time of shortening days. Soon the land will be covered in white snows. We have come to the river to gather foods to keep us during the cold days to come. Our wigwam of bent saplings and sheets of bark sits in a grove of old, spreading oak trees. There is little underbrush and it is easy to move about in the forest. My oldest son and I awake at dawn to throw my wife's finely woven nets over the ducks that landed on the river to rest for their long flight south. Today my wife works alongside the squirrels to gather acorns. She must begin the long process of soaking and boiling these nuts to remove their acids, then pounding them into meal. Tomorrow morning, my son and I will go to the spot where the deer beds for the night. If the deer's spirit looks favorably on us and lets our arrows find it, we will give thanks, smoke the meat, and stretch and dry the skin for warm, dry clothing. We carve the deer's antlers into tools for punching and sewing skins. For everything, we find a use. We fish in the river with nets and spears, and where the river meets the salt water, we dig clams and oysters and cook them over hot coals. We add their shells to our parents' shell mound from years past. The spirits of the animals are generous with us as they have been with our ancestors, and when we gather with other relatives for the winter we will celebrate together.
>
> —*Eric M.*

These three or four days of storytelling, discussion, and writing highlight important aspects of Native American beliefs regarding nature. By seeing themselves as part of a web of natural relationships, Native Americans neither romanticized nor exploited their world. They teach us that "all things are as connected as parts of the Pipe."

World Myths

Having used Native American tales to introduce storytelling and early people's perception and treatment of the earth, I turn to myths from other parts of the world. Donna Rosenberg's *World Mythology* covers creation, fertility, hero, and death mythology from every continent. This text along with Joseph Campbell's writings and public television series with Bill Moyers, *The Power of Myth*, are invaluable for understanding the universality of mythological themes. I select a few myths to read and discuss with students, and use Campbell for my own under-standing and occasional in-class viewing.

I look for myths that reveal a culture's attitude toward the natural world. In many creation myths, the earth is created from the parts of a divine figure's de-feated or dying body. The Chinese story of Pan Ku, the Norse story of Ymir, the Babylonian story of Tiamat, and the Aztec creation story all follow this pattern. The personification of elements of nature is the essence of polytheistic, animistic religion. In Greek myth, earth and sky are personified as the first divine beings, Gaea and Uranus. Having discussed these common elements, I ask students, "How might people regard the earth if they believe it is, or was made from, a god?" "With respect," they answer. "Perhaps also fear, awe, or love, but definitely respect."

In many myths, the world begins in chaos out of which the gods create order. A Ugandan creation myth (in Jewkes, *Man the Mythmaker*, [1973, 12] describes how Kabezya-Mpungu, the creator, restrains the desires of Sun to shine continu-ously, Rain to "pour down without cease," and Darkness "to rule forever." He per-suades Sun to take turns with Rain, and Darkness to alternate with Moon, thus allowing creatures to live comfortably on earth. Students discuss what these in-structions to Sun and Rain, Moon and Darkness, tell us about the Ugandan view of the world. Like many myths, including the Abenaki story of Gluscabi and the Wind Eagle, this story demonstrates the belief that there is an order and balance in the world, a balance that should not be disturbed by selfish desires for control.

Genesis

In contrast to these animistic stories, the Biblical story of creation depicts a world created by God and separate from God, a world that is not divine but is beautiful and good. I read Genesis 1 and 2 with my classes, using Ackerman and Warshaw's *The Bible as Literature* (revised standard version). I explain to those who either never read the Bible or who read it only in a religious context, that I am teaching *about* beliefs, not teaching what to believe, and I have never had an objection to this study. Modern environmentalists (whose critics sometimes equate the love of nature with paganism) are often hard on Genesis. They point to the admonitions by God "to be fruitful and multiply, and fill the earth and subdue it; and have do-minion over . . . every living thing that moves upon the earth" as the source of western civilization's feeling of entitlement and justification for exploiting the earth. But the creation story continues in Genesis 2 and shows Adam being put in the Garden of Eden "to till it and keep it," to use the earth but also to care for it. In Genesis, we care for the earth not because it *is* a god but because it is God's *gift*. Some commentaries interpret these two stories as representing two sides of human nature: the side that seeks to control and dominate versus the side that seeks to nurture and sustain. Questions I use to help students consider these ideas, either in discussion or on paper, are:

> What is the relationship between people and the earth as described in each Biblical story? And what implications do these stories have for how people should treat the earth?
>
> How do the Genesis stories compare with other creation stories we have studied in how people view the earth and how they treat it?

In one class discussion of these questions, Tracy begins, "If the Chinese thought the earth was made from Pan Ku's body, they would respect it because they respect the gods and they respect their ancestors." Mike adds, "The Greeks thought Poseidon lived in the sea, so they prayed to the god of the sea for protection. They feared the sea and respected it."

Reflecting on a difference between early polytheism and western monotheism, Rick observes, "But the Bible seems to encourage us to see ourselves as superior to the rest of nature. Words like 'subdue' and 'have dominion over' sound like permission from God to use our power to our own advantage." "True," responds Celeste, "but God does not want us to abuse that power. He also tells us to 'keep' the earth, to care for it. We may be superior to the rest of nature, but we have a responsibility to take care of nature." "I don't think we are superior; we just like to think we are because it suits us," says Sarah. "Maybe we think God gave us permission to 'subdue' the earth because it's what we want to do anyway."

I point to Adam's first job in Eden, naming the animals, and ask, "For Adam to carry out this assignment, what ability must he have which the animals do not have?" "Language," they answer. "We're not the only ones who can communicate," someone will counter. "Look at dolphins' clicking, whale songs, chimpanzee sign language, bird songs, and bee dances." "My dog understands when I say 'Bad dog!' or 'Do you want to go out?'"

Students love to debate this point but eventually they concede that humans use language to symbolize and conceptualize at a level animals do not reach—at least as far as we know! People are verbal "tool users."

I continue. "What does the capacity for language imply about our relationship with animals?" "It gives us an advantage." "We can store knowledge and pass it on instead of having to rediscover things over and over." "We can not only communicate our feelings but explain them as well." "Poets create metaphors with language. By 'naming' our insights and feelings, they preserve and interpret our experiences." "We name things we own or discover. Language is power!"

Language might also be seen as symbolic of our separation and alienation from the natural world. I tell students the Babylonian story of Gilgamesh in which the wild man, Enkidu, loses his innocence and closeness to nature when he learns language and falls in love with a woman. In "She Unnames Them," a story I sometimes have students read, Ursula Le Guin imagines that Eve overrides Adam and offers "namelessness" to the animal world. "They [the animals] seemed far closer than when their names had stood between myself and them like a clear barrier: so close that my fear of them and their fear of me became one same fear." In the act of returning her own name to Adam, Eve liberates herself and re-enters the world without self-consciousness. Both of these stories enrich a discussion of humans' relationship to the natural world, particularly the symbolic role of language in this relationship.

When I ask students to think of an everyday relationship in which one creature names another, they mention naming their pets and the parent-child relationship, connections that contain both authority and loving care. While language might be associated with the human ability to manipulate and exploit nature, it can also be part of our capacity to redefine and recreate a sustainable relationship with nature.

By studying myths and religious texts, students discover a wide variety of ways humans have conceived of their own identity in relationship to nature. For Native Americans, people are part of the web of nature and respect it as one would a parent. In other creation myths, nature is revealed as inhabited by divine beings and is regarded with a mixture of fear, awe, and piety. Genesis conceives of God and people as separate from nature, superior and with the power to dominate but the responsibility to care for the earth. Each of these views has implications for how the earth is treated and for present attitudes toward the natural environment.

The Golden Age

The mythical archetype of a "golden age," a time when people lived without work or hate, in perfect harmony with nature as in the Garden of Eden, has special significance for a study of the environment. The so-called "pastoral vision" was strong in Virgil's day, it was strong for Rousseau and Emerson and John Muir, and it is strong now. Its impulse helped establish national parks and is exploited today to sell sport utility vehicles (SUVs).

Writing, My Favorite Place Before starting this three- or four-day unit, I ask students to describe their favorite place, without telling them why. I carefully do not specify that it be a natural place. We do this in writing, using vivid sensory detail, and sometimes we also paint our favorite place. (See Chapter Two.)

Some students describe the coziness and privacy of their bedrooms, one painted a stage set up with instruments for a rock concert, and one girl described the Boston Garden before a Celtics' game so vividly that I could smell the hotdogs and hear the crowd roar. But at least seventy-five percent of the descriptions and paintings are of natural places. Students paint or describe mountain scenes, tropical islands, waterfalls, or the beach.

"Why is this so?," I ask. "What is it about being in nature that attracts us?"

"Because nature is beautiful," Tracy responds.

"Because it is different from our normal surroundings. We live surrounded by walls, in school and at home, in cars and stores. Nature is an escape from ourselves and what we create," says Rick.

"It's also an escape from our responsibilities and worries. We associate nature with vacation. We go to nature to play—to ski, to go to the beach," says Celeste. "In nature we can relax, do whatever we want."

"In nature, your own cares feel small and insignificant. You get a sense of where you really belong in the world."

Eventually I ask, "Would we feel the same way if we lived close to nature every day and our lives depended on what we could catch and grow?"

Rick answers, "Maybe not, because then nature wouldn't be an escape. We would be worried about survival."

Mike adds, "We might be afraid of nature then."

But Sarah says, "But maybe, because we needed to understand nature so well in order to survive, we would appreciate it even more."

Nature in Advertising After a wrap-up discussion acknowledging how strong our yearning for nature can be, I sometimes ask students to bring in advertisements that exploit this yearning in order to sell products. They have no trouble finding such ads. We use nature and wilderness to sell beer, cigarettes, clothes, insurance, travel, outdoor gear, and cars. As with so many things we have learned to value in a positive way—wilderness preservation, diversity, strong women, and caring fathers—advertising has co-opted our love for nature and seduced us into buying products that actually destroy the wilderness we desire. An electric indoor waterfall may soothe us, but will it also lull us into oblivion about the environment's limited ability to sustain useless consumption? The consumer economy exploits nature almost as much as it exploits sex, an important lesson in media awareness for students. As students share their ads, they comment on the way nature has been used to make products appealing and how the products could actually have a detrimental effect on the environment.

One ad pictures an SUV parked deep in a mossy-floored forest, no road in sight. Touting its product as a vehicle for "self-discovery," the ad quotes Thoreau, "I never found the companion that was so companionable as solitude." Imagine Thoreau's reaction to seeing this ad! I have students try this in writing.

Having described our own favorite places and why we seek them, we are ready to consider some mythical and literary expressions of the longing for nature.

W. T. Jewkes' *Man the Mythmaker* has a short unit of readings on the Golden Age, including the Greek myth of "The Four Ages," a reading by Loren Eiseley, and poems by William Wordsworth, William Butler Yeats, and Joni Mitchell. In addition, we read more in Genesis, and use Robert Frost's poem, "Nothing Gold Can Stay."

Building on our reading of the Greek creation story, we first read Ovid's "The Four Ages" starting with the Golden Age which is characterized by eternal spring, the ready availability in nature of everything needed to survive, and the lack of work, laws, towns, evil, or suffering.

> Earth, untroubled,
> Unharried by hoe or plowshare, brought forth all
> That men had need for, and those men were happy,
> Gathering berries from the mountainsides,
> Cherries, or blackcaps, and the edible acorns.
> Spring was forever, with a west wind blowing
> Softly across the flowers no man had planted,
> And Earth, unplowed, brought forth rich grain; the field,
> Unfallowed, whitened with wheat, and there were rivers
> Of milk, and rivers of honey, and golden nectar
> Dripped from the dark-green oak trees.
> —*Ovid, Rolfe Humphries, translator* (14)

In the Silver Age, the seasons change. Some versions blame this change on violence among the gods: Cronos murders his father, Uranus, and is then killed by his own son, Zeus. Work becomes necessary to provide food and shelter, and commerce begins. Greed enters the world because people now have possessions. In the Bronze Age people acquire weapons and use violence to defend what they have and to acquire more. The myth ends in the Iron Age, full of evil, deceit, and so much violence that hosts kill guests and family members kill each other.

> . . . . the ground,
> Free, once, to everyone, like air and sunshine,
> Was stepped off by surveyors. The rich Earth,
> Good giver of all the bounty of the harvest,
> Was asked for more; they dug into her vitals,
> Pried out the wealth a kinder lord had hidden
> In Stygian shadow, all that precious metal,
> The root of evil.
> —*Ovid, Rolfe Humphries, translator* (15)

Other myths with recurring cycles of good and evil include the Hindu story of Dharma and the Maha Yugas, and the Norse story of Ragnarok and the New Day.

We read chapter three of Genesis and compare the story of Adam and Eve's expulsion from Eden to the Four Ages myth. One important difference is that in Genesis evil is equated with knowledge and self-consciousness or self-awareness, as symbolized by nakedness and shame.

> In Genesis, Adam and Eve eat the forbidden fruit and attain knowledge. They can no longer see the world as innocently, so they are banished from Eden—their perfect world.
> —Meg F.

We list the characteristics of each age and discuss these questions:

Why would living close to nature be part of a Golden Age?
Why does evil come along with knowledge?
Would you want to live in such a time? What would you gain?
What would you lose? Would you give up knowledge to live without work or suffering?
What age do you think we are living in now?
Do you think a golden age ever existed? Do you think life was easier in the past? (If not, why do you think this story is so universally appealing?)

As in most discussions, I do not try to lead students to particular answers. I listen carefully, probe for elaboration, occasionally play devil's advocate, let students question and answer each other, but do not push for resolution. The questions can generate quite different responses: Some students will insist they would love a world with no work; others say it would be boring. Some will point out how much evil has resulted from human knowledge, including the destruction of natural habitat; others will argue that our knowledge also alleviates suffering and the search for knowledge makes life worthwhile. Some will think hunter-gatherers lived in a golden age and cite how much leisure time they had; others will say they suffered from disease, fear, and hunger. Often someone points out that without suffering and evil, we cannot appreciate beauty and good, that innocence also means unconsciousness, no awareness. "Does that mean," I ask, "that the world is about right as it is?" None of these questions can be easily resolved, and that should not be the goal of the exploration.

Usually some student will conclude that we believe in a golden age because the possibility gives us hope for the future. I allude to the romanticism of the 1800s, the back-to-the-land movement of the 1960s, and utopian literature such as Ernest Callenbach's *Ecotopia* as examples of modern attempts to achieve a golden age. On the other hand, William Golding's *Lord of the Flies* and Alex Garland's *The Beach* explore the violence inherent in human nature and question the possibility of utopia. If we have already read Jon Krakauer's *Into the Wild* (Chapter

Seven), we recall Chris McCandless and his quest for a better, purer life away from society. Chris' story raises many questions about the causes and risks of utopian thinking. These titles all offer opportunities for further reading and study.

After discussing the mythical "golden age," I divide the class into three groups to discuss three poems incorporating golden age thinking: "The World Is Too Much with Us" by Wordsworth, "The Lake Isle of Innisfree" by Yeats, and "Woodstock" by Joni Mitchell. With a mixed group, I make sure a few stronger students are in the Wordsworth group. Their instructions are to use the six points generic to any discussion of poetry (see Chapter Six) and to ask themselves: How does the poem convey a longing for a golden age?

Students select a note taker and reporter, often electing to do both as a group. As they discuss the questions, I circulate from group to group, helping with confusing lines and asking questions that extend the discussion and their understanding.

In "The World Is Too Much with Us," Wordsworth uses the Italian sonnet form to lament our preoccupation with "getting and spending" and our neglect of nature: "we are out of tune; / It moves us not." Wordsworth says he would rather follow a pagan religion if it would help him restore the magic of nature.

> Great God! I'd rather be
> A pagan suckled in a creed outworn;
> So might I, standing on this pleasant lea,
> Have glimpses that would make me less forlorn;
> Have sight of Proteus rising from the sea;
> Or hear old Triton blow his wreathed horn. (ll. 9–14)

Students need to look up words like "sordid," "boon," "pagan, "creed," and "lea"; they need help with the mythological allusions to Proteus and Triton. But once students paraphrase these lines, they notice the shift in tone from the prosaic wording of the first four lines about the daily grind in which "we lay waste our powers," to the poetic alliteration and metaphors in the descriptions of nature: "This sea that bares her bosom to the moon; / The winds that will be howling at all hours, / And up-gathered now like sleeping flowers" (ll. 5–7). They see that in Wordsworth's mind there is a clear separation between the world we work in and the world of nature. They also see once again that the romantics believe that polytheists feel greater regard for nature because they worship it as the abode of the gods.

Yeats' poem, "The Lake Isle of Innisfree" expresses a similar desire to leave "the roadway" and "the pavements gray" (l. 11) and go to Innisfree where "peace comes dropping slow" (l. 5). Yeats' poem was inspired by Thoreau's sojourn at Walden Pond, hence the allusions to the "small cabin" and the "nine bean-rows." Students discuss the richness of sounds in the poem: "the bee-loud glade," (l. 4);

"peace . . . dropping slow, / Dropping from the veils of the morning to where the cricket sings" (l. 5, 6); an "evening full of the linnet's wings" (l. 8); and "lake water lapping with low sounds by the shore" (l. 10). Not only are peaceful sounds described, but the lines themselves sound soothing. The visual imagery is equally lush: "midnight's all a glimmer, and noon a purple glow" (l. 7). Students note both the longing and the contentment expressed in these lines. They brainstorm about the name "Innisfree:" Is it real or imaginary? What does the poem have to do with freedom? And they discuss the position of the narrator and the meaning of the last line:

I will arise and go now, for always night and day
I hear lake water lapping with low sounds by the shore,
While I stand on the roadway, or on the pavements gray,
I hear it in the deep heart's core.

This final phrase could refer either to Yeats' heart, which aches for the truly sensual, refreshing experience of Innisfree, or to the core/heart of the earth itself, where all beauty like that of Innisfree has been covered with the dull gray of the roadways.
—*Kasey E.*

I think he is thinking more of a place in the mind. . . . He doesn't hear the sounds of his lake with his ears, but with his mind and in his heart.
—*Meg F.*

The song "Woodstock," by Joni Mitchell, is still familiar to many students, and I play it for the class before discussing the lyrics. Most students will know about the 1969 concert held at Yasgur's Farm in Woodstock, NY. When students discuss the differences between the original concert and Woodstock '99, they consider whether these differences indicate a generational change in attitudes and behavior. In her song, Mitchell imagines a young man going to the concert to free his soul and find himself. Most of the song is expressed as a hope for the future, and even the concert itself is depicted in the third verse through an idealized dream of bombers turned into butterflies. The traveler senses a connection with God and the ancient life of the stars but feels trapped in a world of pollution and evil.

We discuss the repeated reference to getting back to the garden in the chorus.

I think she's talking about the Garden of Eden because then man was open and feared nothing but God. Things were simple then, and everyone loved everything.
—*Meg F.*

A description by Loren Eiseley from *The Unexpected Universe* about his encounter with a fox pup is an excellent short reading on the golden age theme. In this excerpt, Eiseley laments that "one can never, try as he will, get around to the front of the universe. Man is destined to see only its far side, to realize nature only in retreat." But Eiseley, on his hands and knees and smelling of fox, encounters a lone pup that picks up a chicken bone and shakes it playfully at him. "The universe was swinging in some fantastic fashion around to present its face, and the face was so small that the universe itself was laughing." Eiseley also picks up a bone in his mouth.

> Round and round we tumbled for one ecstatic moment. We were the innocent thing in the midst of the bones, born in the egg, born in the den, born in the dark cave with the stone ax close to hand, born at last in human guise to grow coldly remote in the room with the rifle rack upon the wall. But I had seen my miracle. I had seen the universe as it begins for all things. It was, in reality, a child's universe, a tiny and laughing universe. (210)

Students will recognize the golden age archetype in Eiseley's longing to return to nature and a state of innocence. In response to his story, they describe (in class and in their journals) their own encounters with wildlife.

> Last fall I went into the woods to a tree I had been to before that I knew had a good view of the forest all around. I have cleared out enough branches about 40 feet up to provide a good view, but I left enough so that animals will have a hard time seeing me.
>
> This day, I went out to try and see some deer. I brought a pair of shed antlers that I have to rattle for deer. This means to rattle the antlers together to make a noise like two deer fighting. This noise is supposed to attract the dominant buck in the area because he wants to scare away the bucks that are on his territory. This has never worked the few times I have tried it.
>
> I was rattling the antlers on and off for about 45 minutes in the tree when I saw a flash of brown over on my right. I looked over and whatever had moved was now behind a tree. I kept my eyes on the spot about 40 yards away. After a couple seconds I saw a coyote emerge from behind the tree. This surprised me because I had never seen a coyote in these woods before. I had heard that there were coyotes in the area, but now I was seeing one right in front of me.
>
> I was wearing all camouflage clothing and a face mask/hat that was also camo. Without these I think the coyote would have noticed me. The coyote was walk-trotting at an angle slightly away from me. I didn't want the coyote to go away so I made a noise that sounded a little like a retarded crow. At the sound, the coyote stopped moving and looked in my direction. I made the sound again, and it started coming towards me. The wind was going across us and was neither towards me or towards the coyote, so he couldn't smell me. I kept making the noise at short intervals and the coyote kept getting nearer. It was going in kind of a semi-circle so it would get down wind of me and smell to find out what was making the noise. It kept lifting its head up and sticking its nose in the air to try and smell better.

By now the coyote was about 20 yards away and I was getting a great view of it. It looked very healthy and seemed to be in great shape. It was about the size of my dog so it probably weighed about 50–60 pounds. It was just about to get downwind of me when the wind shifted slightly towards him. Now the coyote could smell me and it turned around and ran full speed back the way it had come and was soon out of sight.

I sat for a while in the tree thinking about how neat the animal was.

—*Jeff F.*

Writing To conclude our discussion, I ask students to write a paper responding to the Golden Age myth, its application to the poems, and their own response to the idea of a golden age. While the "favorite place" assignment is a very personal response, this paper is a traditional, literary analysis paper. To help my mixed group of students structure their papers, I outline the written assignment. I give this assignment a few days before it is due, and allot in-class writing and conferencing time.

Introduction: Explain and discuss the "Golden Age" archetype as it applies to Genesis and the Greek myth of "The Four Ages," and as it applies to two of the three poems discussed in class.

Development of paper: Refer to specific lines and images in your discussion of the poems; use specific examples to support your points. Choose two:

"The World Is Too Much with Us," Wordsworth

"The Lake Isle of Innisfree," Yeats

"Woodstock," Joni Mitchell

Conclusion: Some questions to consider:

How do you explain the universality of the idea of the golden age? (i.e., Why do so many cultures have this idea?)

Where do you see signs of this yearning today? (give examples.)

Do you think a "golden age" is desirable? or possible? Why?

Do you think it is an answer to our personal or global problems?

Length: 3–4 pages, about 700–800 words

Ted wrote that a new "golden age" would not be possible because we are too dependent on materialistic comforts:

If we got rid of TV shows such as "Lifestyles of the Rich and Famous," all TV shows for that matter because we see only good lives, and all magazines because we see desirable things and the people don't talk about how good or bad their lives are, then maybe we would be getting on track. However, I can't see it happening. It would be too much of a shock and not everyone would agree to it. It has to be totality.

—*Ted O.*

Meg believes we are too egotistical to achieve a "golden age":

> I think that people are too superficial now for us to be able to go back to the physical golden age. We have many words for hate—racism, sexism, ageism—yet we have only one word for love. I don't think that people are open enough to go back to this simple life. Actually, although I would love to live in a world where there is unconditional love, I don't think everyone would. Some people just enjoy feeling better than others too much.
> —Meg. F.

But Meg does believe a "golden age" can exist as a personal, mental state:

> If each of us has our own place, a state of mind, then we can be happy. Because, without any other people, there is no one to compare yourself to, and then you can't feel jealous or cocky. That is, I think that utopia or a Golden Age can only be found in your own mind and that there is nowhere we can all go that is absolutely perfect; human nature doesn't work that way. We were born to notice faults. . . .
>
> While I don't think a physical Golden Age, such as the one in the Greek myth or Mitchell's song is ever possible, it's a nice thought, especially if it keeps people going. However, I think that if people are happy with themselves, are giving, sharing, and are self-conscious in the true sense of the word, then they can achieve a mental utopia. This state of mind may not be as nice or as permanent as a physical place, but it's definitely better than nothing.
> —Meg F.

Paper Conclusions:

> This ideal is everywhere in human society: the only way to be truly good and free is to go back to the way we were before, whether it be Eden or the Golden Age. But is that what we really want? I, for one, don't think I would want to live in a world where nobody ever has anything to do and everything is "perfect." It would be boring, not even farming the land. . . . The minds of the people who lived in this place would have to be different. . . . Normal people from today would get so bored they might do something bad or make up their own things to do. . . . Although we continue to strive for perfection and harmony in our environment, we probably could not live in an actual Golden Age.
> —Erin Q.

> My final conception of a Golden Age, then, is one in which we are free to exist with one another without competition, without hostility, without evaluation. We are just as free to seek "truths" in such a world as we are in modern scientific pursuits, but truths in such a Golden Age would reflect an acknowledgement of our limited scope of understanding. For as long as we consider our toys—scientific models, currency, Donna Reed's new dishwasher—to be achievements superior to the accomplishments of nature (which include, you know—trivial things . . . like the miracle of

life), we will remain unaware of the silent truths and satisfaction in the serenity of
the Isle of Innisfree and the simple harmony and community of Woodstock.
—*Kasey E.*

While most of us can identify with the poets' desire to escape from our cares
through nature, the question is whether the separation of nature and daily life is
realistic or healthy. I remind students of the overarching questions: How do we
view nature? How does our view affect the way we treat it? We discuss whether trying to achieve or restore a golden age can solve modern environmental problems.
If we continue to view nature quite unrealistically as something untouched, perfect, and static, our treatment may involve appreciation and a desire to preserve
things just as they are (or were), without addressing responsible, sustainable living.
Many environmental theorists such as William Cronon (1995) now reject the romantic separation of nature and civilization that focuses our energies on the
preservation of wilderness areas while ignoring the need to find sustainable, fulfilling daily lifestyles. Tom Kelly, a university sustainability coordinator, shows a
slide of a protected beach, fenced to preserve dunes, while just behind the dunes
are solid rows of cars. His point is that we cannot create "golden" islands of utopia
and ignore the sustainability of the whole system. We should all know by now that
"Nothing gold can stay"; hopefully the search for a sustainable earth is not just another "golden age" impossibility. The sustainability issue is discussed again when
the focus turns to Thoreau or current issues (see Chapters Four and Five).

At this point, I turn to European views of America as a "new" world. I acknowledge regretfully that I am ignoring vast time periods and parts of the world,
and there have been times when I have done more historic or non-western reading but in too cursory a fashion.

For example, we have read passages from Virgil describing his idyllic "pastoral
vision" of nature, and passages from Aristotle demonstrating the new "scientific"
view of a depersonalized nature. *A Green History of the World: The Environment and
the Collapse of Great Civilizations* by Clive Ponting (1993) describes deforestation
and soil erosion throughout the Roman empire and the slaughter of hundreds of
thousands of wild animals in amphitheaters. In the Middle East, the city of Ur
over-irrigated, salts rose in the soils, crops failed, and the city was conquered. The
city of Copan in Central America deforested its surroundings and the population
was forced to move. An excellent Stella modeling program (Appendix D) helps
students graph the correlation between population growth, deforestation, and
flooding in Mahenjo Daro, a Sumerian city in the Indus River Valley. If you
have the time and the resources, particularly if you teach with social studies or science teachers, these are avenues to follow. With limited time, I have focused on
America.

Since many Europeans saw America as a new Garden of Eden, "the new heaven upon the new earth" to quote Samuel Sewall, the transition is thematically smooth. A study of Shakespeare's "The Tempest" can form a good bridge between discussions of the "golden age" and the new world.

"The Tempest"

"The Tempest" was performed for King James in 1611 and was partly based on an accident in 1609 involving nine ships bound from England to the new colony of Jamestown. One of the ships carrying the new governor of Virginia was beached in a storm on the Bermuda islands. The crew survived and a year later arrived in Virginia, where they found hopes for a utopian self-governing colony unraveling because of conflicts among the settlers. Shakespeare based his last play on the sea-storm setting and the settlers' strife, as well as contemporary philosophies about the nobility of nature and human freedom.

When my colleague Richard Tappan and I co-directed a student production of "The Tempest," Abby, a former Literature and Land student, hugged me, saying, "I'm so glad you had us read that play!" But a few days later, Dan, a cast member currently in my class, was saying, "I still don't see what that play has to do with the environment." While reading this play and understanding its relevance to environmental questions can be a stretch, for the right class it is a rewarding experience.

Shakespeare uses the events of "The Tempest" to challenge the idea that civilization is all bad and nature is all good. In the play, civilization and the desire for power and wealth corrupt Alonso and Antonio, but civilization also produces Prospero's books, the source of his wisdom and magical powers. Nature, represented by the play's island setting, produces Caliban, a beastly creature ruled by his appetites, but is also the abode of the airy spirit, Ariel, who teaches Prospero to pity and forgive his suffering former enemies. Shakespeare refuses to accept simple stereotypes about nature or society.

He also questions Rousseau's "noble savage" idea that people, left without laws or government in a golden age utopia, would treat freedom responsibly. In Act II, in an effort to distract King Alonso from the fear that his son has drowned, the aged advisor Gonzalo gives a speech straight out of golden age mythology about how he would rule the island:

> no kind of traffic
> Would I admit; no name of magistrate;
> Letters should not be known; riches, poverty,
> And use of service, none; contract, succession,
> Bourne, bound of land, tilth, vineyard, none;

No use of metal, corn or wine, or oil;
No occupation; all men idle, all;
And women too, but innocent and pure;
No sovereignty . . .
All things in common nature should produce
Without sweat or endeavour. Treason, felony,
Sword, pike, knife, gun, or need of any engine,
Would I not have; but nature should bring forth,
Of its own kind all foison, all abundance,
To feed my innocent people.

. . . .

I would with such perfection govern, sir,
T'excel the golden age. (Iii, 142–162)

Is this golden age possible? No sooner has Gonzalo described his utopia than Antonio persuades Alonso's brother, Sebastian, to join him in a plot to kill Alonso and take over Alonso's kingdom. In a parallel subplot, the comic characters, Trinculo and Stephano, plot with Caliban to kill Prospero and take over the island. So much for having "no magistrate," "no sovereign," and no "letters!" The good forces of nature, combined with the knowledge and magic of Prospero, foil both plots and bring about a "sea-change" (Iii, 400) and the reconciliation of former enemies.

Teenagers are particularly sensitive to abuses of power and authority, and some students criticize Prospero for overly controlling events and people:

"He's like a dictator. He enslaves Ariel, is cruel to Caliban, forces Ferdinand to work, arranges Miranda's marriage, and makes Alonso suffer."

If a student doesn't counter this, I might ask: "What would happen if he didn't exercise this control?"

"Antonio and Sebastian would have killed Alonso, Caliban would have raped Miranda, and Stephano and Trinculo would have killed Prospero."

"So what does this say about human nature? Do we need limits or can we be left to our own devices?"

The ensuing discussion brings out a range of opinions about whether people are good or evil by nature, whether they are corrupted by society, how much control we need, and who should decide. I turn the discussion back to the insights offered by the play.

For Shakespeare, "getting back to nature" is not all it's cracked up to be, whether it be the natural setting of a deserted island or a wild, unfettered human "nature" or "noble savage." Instead, he acknowledges all aspects of human nature—our capacity for treachery and violence as well as for compassion. He understands the role of both reason and emotion, civilization and nature, in our humanity. "The Tempest" rejects extreme positions, and instead teaches the need for balance and the rule of law and knowledge tempered by love and forgiveness. Its ecological message is that retreating to nature and trying to ignore the problems of human civilization is neither possible nor desirable.

Teaching this play involves a combination of reading aloud, assigning some scenes as homework, paraphrasing, acting out selected scenes, and watching scenes on videotape as we read them. We create a timeline to help sort out the events told in flashbacks. We sort characters by place of origin, list their personality traits, and discuss their symbolism. We note that the play follows the classical unities of time and place. We look closely at the imagery in the text and relate it to overall themes of death (sleep) and rebirth; sin, atonement, forgiveness, and reconciliation; purification through suffering; innocence and knowledge; good and evil; nature and civilization.

Students keep a readers' response log in which they write brief scene summaries along with their questions about the text and their reactions to the characters, events, and language. There might be quizzes along the way and a test at the end on lines (passages to identify and discuss), events (e.g., What evil is done, or planned, by Caliban, Antonio, Stephano, and Alonso?) and themes (e.g., What do you think this play teaches about revenge versus forgiveness, and how?).

Writing For a final 800–1,000-word paper, students develop their own theme or use one of the following questions. The questions allow a range of students access to the play. For example, questions one and two are essentially the same, with question one being a simpler version of two. The same is true of questions three and four. Students write drafts of their papers, conference with me and their peers, and/or turn them in for written feedback. I have students read their papers to each other in early and final draft stages. Student readers give valuable feedback about clarity, focus, development, support, and editing; they also learn from the example of their peers' writing. I prefer not to be the only audience for student work.

Writing Ideas for "The Tempest"

1. What does the character of Caliban show about Shakespeare's attitude toward Nature (both human nature and the natural world)?
2. What does "The Tempest" say about the value of the civilized world versus the natural world? Consider:
   - the good and bad aspects of Caliban
   - the good and bad aspects of the civilized characters as represented by Prospero, Ferdinand, Gonzalo, Antonio, Alonso, Sebastian, and Stephano and Trinculo
   - the good and bad aspects of the island and the sea
   - Ariel

3. How do one or more of the following characters change in the course of the play (as a result of experiences on the island), and what brings about these changes: Prospero, Alonso, and Caliban?

4. Ariel says that Alonso has undergone a "sea-change . . . into something rich and strange" (Iii, 400–401), and Gonzalo says, "in one voyage . . . all of us [found] ourselves / When no man was his own" (Vi, 245–250). *Who* "found" themselves? *What* changes does the island make possible, and *how?* Apply to Alonso, Ferdinand, Prospero, Sebastian and Antonio, and Caliban (choose three).

5. Show how Prospero's rule of the island differs from Gonzalo's vision of utopia (IIi, 160–169, 173–178, 181–182); discuss whether this rule is necessary or not and why, given the events in the play.

6. Look closely at images about sleep and death, clothing, and the sea, and consider how these images reinforce the theme of rebirth and renewal in the play. Quote and explain lines containing images you discuss, and discuss specific changes in specific characters.

The class has now studied myths and stories in which people revere, respect or fear nature, stories in which people see themselves as only part of a natural cycle or see themselves as superior and dominant in nature. We have seen the universal association of living in nature with peace and goodness, and the universal longing to regain this state of grace. Each view has its own implications for how we use, abuse, or preserve the environment. They are views that affected the way newcomers to America saw and treated the land, and they are still part of environmental policy making today.

Works Cited for Students and Teachers

Ackerman, J., and T. Warshaw. 1976. *The Bible as/in Literature.* Oakland, NJ: Scott, Foresman and Co. Includes Biblical text from the Revised Standard Version Bible and literature based on the Bible.

Campbell, J. 1991. *The Power of Myth.* With Bill Moyers. New York: Anchor Books. This text accompanies a public television series by the same name.

Cronon, W. 1983. *Changes in the Land: Indians, Colonists, and the Ecology of New England.* New York: Hill and Wang.

———. 1995. "The Trouble with Wilderness," *New York Times Magazine.* Sunday, Aug. 13. Essay adapted from 1995. *Uncommon Ground: Toward Reinventing Nature.* New York: W. W. Norton.

Eiseley, L. 1985. *The Unexpected Universe* (1964). San Diego: Harcourt Brace Jovanovich.

Jewkes, W. T. 1973. *Man the Mythmaker.* New York: Harcourt Brace Jovanovich, Inc.

LeGuin, U. 1985. "She Unnames Them," *The New Yorker* 60 (Jan. 21), p. 27.

Ponting, C. 1993. *A Green History of the World: The Environment and the Collapse of Great Civilizations.* New York: Penguin.

Rosenberg, D. 1992. *World Mythology,* Lincolnwood, IL: National Textbook Co.,

Native Americans

Bruchac, J. 1991. *Native American Stories* from *Keepers of the Earth.* Golden, CO: Fulcrum Publishers.

———. 1992. *Native American Animal Stories* from *Keepers of the Animals.* Golden, CO: Fulcrum Publishers

McLuhan, T. C. 1991. *Touch the Earth.* New York: Promontory Press. "A self-portrait of Indian existence," photos, speeches, prayers, chants.

The Golden Age

Callenbach, E. 1990. *Ecotopia* (1975). New York: Bantam.

Garland, A. 1997. *The Beach.* New York: Riverhead Books.

Golding, W. 1962. *Lord of the Flies.* New York: Coward-McCann.

Shakespeare, William. 1961. *The Tempest.* The Folger Library. New York: Simon & Schuster.

Video

Tempest, Bard Productions, 1983, 127 minutes. Video of staged production of "The Tempest" with Efrem Zimbalist, Jr. as Prospero.

Audio Tapes

Armstrong, Randy, and Genevieve Aichele, *World Tales: A Mosaic of Stories and Music from Around the World,* 1996, Cromson Ark Music, BMI; Uno Mondo Productions, PO Box 128, Dover NH

"The Song of Creation," *Wampanoag Legends, The People of the Morning Light,* told by Manitonquat (Medicine Story), Story Stone, Another Place, Rte. 123, Greenville, NH 03048. Stories include "Sky Woman and the Twins," "How Death Came," "Maushop Builds Turtle Island."

"The Singing Stone, A Play for Children," written and performed by Ellika Linden and Medicine Story. 1989. Story Stone. An adventure about Native American culture and relationship to the natural world.

Additional Resources

Hughes, J. D. 1975. *Ecology in Ancient Civilizations,* Albuquerque, NM: University of New Mexico Press.

Snow, J. T. *Modeling the Earth System or How I Came to Know and Love Stella.* Earth System Models, The University of Oklahoma, Norman, OK.

4

The New World

At first sight, the registry of deeds is an imposing maze of shelved deed books and large maps in flat files. My students and I are here to research the deeds to our local land-journal sites. Armed with only the name of the land's owner and the date of purchase, we can locate a current deed which will in turn lead us to previous deeds and previous owners. The students and I fan out, and I begin to uncover my own land's story.

My family lives on Adams Point, a narrow neck of land separating Little Bay from Great Bay in Durham, NH. Starting with our 1982 deed of purchase, I work backward. I learn that we are only the third family to own our land since 1810, when Richard Kent bought the land from Eunice Crommett. In 1818 Ebenezer Kent paid Richard Kent $2,000 for one hundred acres that included "all the homestead farm where I now reside together with all my salt marsh and thatch bed adjoining." Our thirteen acre parcel was split from the original homestead in 1926 when Ebenezer's grandson, Ralph, sold it to Sherwood Rollins who in turn sold it to us.

In *The History of the Town of Durham to 1913* I learn that Kents have been in Durham at least since 1648 (when they were first taxed), and were officially granted 70 acres in 1656. A Kent fought in the Revolution and three were listed as "able bodied males" during the Civil War. Until the 1990s, after 300 years and ten generations, the Kent land was still in the family. The Kents buried their dead on their own land; I can read the names of Ebenezer and Richard, and their wives, Polly and Dorothy, on their headstones a short walk from my house. Such personal connection to one piece of land is hard to imagine in our transient society.

The Adams' homestead on the land east of ours has been a farm, a brickyard, a religious revival center, a boat-building site, a resort hotel, and, currently, a marine research laboratory. In 1973 Aristotle Onassis proposed building the world's largest oil refinery on the shores of Great Bay, but was stopped by local resistance. Instead, landowners granted conservation easements on their land, and in 1989, Great Bay became part of the National Estuarine Research Reserve system.

In addition to the documentary record, signs of my land's history are waiting to be read on the landscape. The remains of Native American oyster and clam shell middens are gradually revealed in the eroding banks of Adams Point. The rusting barbed wire along the road, the stone wall on our eastern boundary and the thick, spreading branches of the hundred-year-old "field pines" in our woods all indicate that at one time this land was used as pasture. The salt marsh grass along our waterfront was prized by early settlers for the nutritional value of its hay.

The history of where I live, like the history of any piece of land, is a microcosm of changing land use throughout the country. Seasonal use by native hunter-gatherers; farming and fishing by settlers; small scale family industries like gristmills, sawmills, and brick-making; the incursions of political and religious movements; farming abandoned and pastures grown back to trees; the era of grand hotels and rustic get-aways; the threat of large-scale industrial development; suburban sprawl; and conservation efforts—all are represented in the square mile around my house.

My own land research models what students can learn about natural and human history by studying one piece of land. By guiding them through a similar process of discovery, I hope that they will not only perceive history in a new way but also develop a closer, personal relationship with their land. Their discovery process, like mine, involves researching historical documents and books, examining evidence on their land, and gathering oral histories. I intersperse journal assignments related to the history of their land journal sites throughout the history unit. (See Land Journal Project, Chapter 2 and Appendix B.)

Settlement

Journal Writing Students do a journal entry in which they pretend to be a colonial European seeing their land site for the first time, before it has been affected by settlement. Comparing this description with the imaginary Native American entry in the mythology unit (Chapter Three) is another opportunity to consider the conflicting views of land in these two cultures. Here is Rachel's journal entry about a European's arrival in Durham, NH:

11/11/1699

Dear Journal:

We have finally arrived in the New World! No more kings saying what religion we must follow. We have arrived in a town known as Portsmouth. It is no more than a few docks and a few more shops. I hear that in the spring, the banks are covered with strawberries . . . I'm sure Mama will make excellent jam out of any we collect. . . . Papa wants to find a spot that is a good distance away from any other houses. . . . All I know is that I don't want it to be more than a few day's journey from Portsmouth. That is the only town around. Once all of our possessions are unloaded from the ship, we will leave town and set off into the woods.

Dear Journal:

I've never seen so many trees in my life! There are so many different kinds. . . . The good news is Papa has finally found a suitable spot to build a house in front of a rocky outcropping. . . . It is surrounded by many stick trees that have hair instead of leaves. The wildlife here is very strange too. There are many little creatures scurrying about among the branches of the trees. They chirp and chitter and some have very bushy tails. . . . There is also a small animal . . . with black and white stripes on its face . . . that poked its head out from a crevice in one of the rocks. . . . It was the cutest thing I've ever seen. That sighting has made the rocks my special place.

Dear Journal:

Winter has really set in now. We were lucky to finish the house before the first snow. . . . Although most of the trees have lost their leaves, the furry trees are still green. . . . Mama and Papa have decided we shall return to England in the spring. Papa says that the soil is too rocky to grow anything and that these long, dark winter nights are too much to bear. If the family that buys our house has a girl, I will show her my special place among the rocks.

Rachel T.

P.S. Rachel was my great-great-great-great-great-great grandfather's mom. She never actually set eyes on my special place.

Rachel C.

This journal assignment is a good way to introduce historical readings that represent a range of ways Europeans first saw America. The writings of early explorer-settlers reveal responses to the new world ranging from religious awe to materialistic greed. I use excerpts from:

Captain John Smith's *A Description of New England*
Samuel Sewall's "The New Heaven Upon the New Earth"
Robert Beverly's *The History and Present State of Virginia*
George Percy's "A Discourse of the Plantation of the Southern Colony in Virginia"
Michael Wigglesworth's *God's Controversy with New England*
Cotton Mather's *Magnalia*

Some readers can do all of these New World excerpts in one night. With a heterogeneous group, I read the shorter pieces (Smith, Sewall, the Puritan quotes) aloud in class to help them with the seventeenth century language. I ask students to describe each writer's attitude toward the land, and to consider the treatment of land that might result from such a perspective. After discussing the readings, we summarize their notes in chart form.

George Percy arrived in Virginia in 1606 and kept a diary of his five years there. His journal conveys the delight he experienced at the richness of America:

oysters . . . very large and delicate in taste, . . . mussels and oysters, which lay on the ground as thick as stones . . . a little plat of ground full of fine and beautiful strawberries, four times bigger and better than ours in England . . . the soil . . . good and fruitful, with excellent good timber . . . as for sturgeon all the world cannot be compared to it . . . many great and large meadows having excellent good pasture for any cattle.

The natural abundance Percy describes must have seemed even more plentiful when compared with the depleted resources of Europe. My students point out that he may exaggerate the bounties of America in order to encourage others to follow.

This "salesmanship" seems even more pronounced in Captain John Smith's description of the Isles of Shoals off Portsmouth, New Hampshire, formerly called Smith's Isles:

. . . here every man may be master and owner of his own labor and land, or the greatest part, in a small time. If he has nothing but his hands, he may . . . by industry quickly grow rich. . . . The waters are most pure . . . a little boy might take of cunners and pollocks and such delicate fish, at the ship's stern, more than six or ten can eat in a day. . . . And is it not pretty sport to pull two pence, sixpence, and twelve pence as fast as you can haul and veer a line?

We note that clearly some early explorers were looking at natural bounty and seeing dollar (or "pence") signs. Samuel Sewall, on the other hand, looks at nature and sees God. After cataloguing all of the natural riches of Plum Island in Massachusetts, Sewall writes in "The New Heaven Upon the New Earth":

as long as Nature shall not grow old and dote but shall constantly remember to give the rows of Indian corn their education, by pairs: so long shall Christians be born there, and being first made meet, shall from thence be translated, to be made partakers of the inheritance of the saints in light.

Students observe that, for Sewall, America offers a new Garden of Eden, an abundant, generous nature that offers its human (Christian) inhabitants access to heaven. A similar garden image, minus the religious overtones, is conveyed in "Have you pleasure in a Garden?," Robert Beverly's sensuous description of nature's curative powers in 1705 Virginia (see Leo Marx, *The Machine in the Garden*, (1964, 82, 83).

For the Puritans, however, we learn that nature represented something entirely different. Michael Wigglesworth called the New World "a waste and howling wilderness / Where none inhabited / But hellish fiends, and brutish men / That Devils worshipped." North America was a land of "eternal night" and "grim death" without the "Sun of righteousness." "The dark and dismal Western woods" were "the Devil's den." According to Roderick Nash (*Wilderness and the American Mind*), the Puritans equated conquering the wilderness with overcoming the "desolate and outgrowne wildernesse of humaine nature."

The students' notes on these readings can be organized on a continuum going from the least to the most severe impact implied for the land. Ironically, no matter what points of view the writers started from, all of their views except Beverly's probably resulted in abusing the land, and even Beverly may prefer a cultivated garden to a wild one. Here is one class's chart:

Writers	View of Land	Possible Treatment of Land
Robert Beverly	A refuge, a beautiful source of pleasure	Appreciation, care; keep it as it is
Samuel Sewall	Sacred, holy a gift from God	Awe and respect; a sense of entitlement
George Percy	Bountiful, rich resources	Awe and appreciation; use of land for food, fuel, shelter, and pasture
John Smith	Resources for use	Focused on economic profits; exploitation
Puritans	Source of evil	Something to be controlled, tamed, and civilized

I have had students make collages or drawings representing each of these viewpoints. I have also had good results putting students in groups of five, each student adopting one of the above perspectives. The groups get photographs of natural scenes and, through writing or discussion, each student describes the scene the way the character they are role playing would see and use it. Once again, we learn that the same piece of land can be seen in many different ways, depending on who we are and our purpose.

The public television *Land of the Eagle* segment, "The Great Encounter," combines excerpts from first settlers' diaries and natural history segments on the ecology of Chesapeake Bay, and supplements these readings well. It is the first episode from an excellent, region by region series on the history of settlement and environmental issues in the United States.

Students can also sample diaries and journals of American exploration in the 1700s, such as Sarah Kemble Knight's journal of her business trip on horseback from Boston to New York in 1704, William Byrd's *History of the Dividing Line* about surveying the boundary of Virginia and North Carolina in 1728; the journal of William Bartram, a botanist who traveled 5,000 miles in the southeast in 1773; and poet Philip Freneau's descriptions of his travels in 1781–1782.

I refer to the points of view represented in the explorers' and settlers' diaries repeatedly throughout the course, and students see that they are still apparent in our treatment of environmental resources today.

Early Results of Exploration

"I knew the Spaniards exploited the native people in the Caribbean islands," students will often exclaim when they start reading Barry Lopez' *The Rediscovery of North America,* "but I never knew it was this bad!"

I use Lopez' essay to begin discussion of Europeans' treatment of the New World. He opens with a graphic description of the Spaniards' brutal treatment of the Arawak people in Hispaniola, as quoted from first-hand accounts by Bartolome de las Casas in 1502. Students readily understand Lopez' analogy between this cruelty and the explorers' violent exploitation of natural resources. "This incursion . . . quickly became a ruthless, angry search for wealth. It set a tone in the Americas."

Lopez suggests that to reverse this pattern we must "enter the landscape to learn something . . . to pay attention rather than constantly to pose questions. To approach the land as we would a person, by opening an intelligent conversation. . . . In these ways we begin, . . . to find a home, to sense how to fit a place." Like Martin Buber's concept of "I and Thou," Lopez' idea is to stop treating both people and land as objects. To know a place intimately, he says:

> we would have to memorize and remember the land, walk it, eat from its soils and from the animals that ate its plants. We would have to know its winds, inhale its airs, observe the sequence of its flowers in the spring and the range of its birds. . . . To be intimate with the land like this is to enclose it in the same moral universe we occupy, to include it in the meaning of the word community. (33, 34)

In discussing this reading, I remind students that part of the reason for keeping a journal record about one piece of land is to acquire just the sense of awareness and closeness that Lopez is advocating. As Georgia O'Keefe puts it, "Nobody sees a flower—really—it is so small it takes time—we haven't time—and to see takes time, like to have a friend takes time" (from *The Artist's Way*).

Many pieces of literature can be studied to show the results of Europeans' first impressions, explorations, and settlement of the Americas. Thomas Bangs Thorpe's "The Big Bear of Arkansas" and William Faulkner's more difficult "The Bear" (the short story version), are both about hunting legendary bears that represent the grandeur of America as it was first seen by Europeans. Thorpe's protagonist kills his bear; Faulkner's does not.

In "The Passenger Pigeon," John James Audubon (1785–1851) describes countless flocks of now-extinct passenger pigeons, and the reckless slaughter of these birds for food, export and pig fodder, then concludes ironically that "nothing but the gradual diminution of the forest can accomplish their decrease, as they not infrequently quadruple their numbers yearly." But over-hunting as well as habitat loss contributed to the extinction of these once plentiful birds, and students see the fallacy and danger of Audubon's assumption. In James Fenimore Cooper's *The Pioneers*, Natty Bumpo witnesses a pigeon hunt, laments that "the Lord won't see the waste of his creatures for nothing," and admonishes his countrymen to "use, but don't waste." Both pieces help students consider how the belief that a resource is limitless leads inevitably to its destruction.

We look at other works to explore the conflict between loving and using nature. Sarah Orne Jewett's short story, "The White Heron," depicts a country girl's struggle between her desire to please a bird-collecting ornithologist and her appreciation for the wild beauty of the heron he seeks. Walt Whitman's poem, "The Song of the Redwood," shows little regret that the ancient trees must make way for the manifest destiny of the waves of settlers entering the west. In *Roughing It*, Mark Twain describes both the awesome beauty of Lake Tahoe and, without a word of remorse, how he accidentally set fire to several thousand acres of its shoreline.

I generally choose only a few of these selections—Audubon, Twain, and Jewett are three writers students particularly like. After reading them, we either discuss or write about the paradox of destroying the nature we purport to love. "Why do you think this happened?," I ask students. "Greed," some answer. "Because we thought it was limitless; it would never run out," says another. "Can we apply this to any modern situations?" "Yes, some people think the ocean is limitless, but it's not." "Alaska." "The rainforest."

The Romantic Reaction

Thoreau

As some of the readings (Jewett, Faulkner, Cooper) listed above indicate, nostalgia for a lost wilderness has always existed in America alongside reckless development. In the mid-nineteenth century, this enthusiasm for nature was expressed in the writings of America's "romantics," the Transcendentalists.

Ever since I first read Thoreau's *Walden*, I have fantasized about living alone in the woods. My college honors thesis was on Keats. Apply any litmus test that defines the Romantics, and I pass: love nature, see nature as a source of knowledge and inspiration, believe people are good by nature, believe in learning from experience, interested in mysticism and mythology, believe the emotions are as valid as reason, interested in non-technological cultures—all ring true. I'm not an anti-intellectual; I love books. I'm sure Thoreau did too, or he wouldn't have written so many! Whatever their excesses or inconsistencies, I've known since high school that I was a Romantic at heart.

Teaching Thoreau is a must for me, no matter who is in my class. Given the increasing diversity of my class rosters, I have had to work to find ways to engage all students in his writings and ideas.

I start with a very brief introduction to English romanticism, using three poems by William Wordsworth. "Lines Written in Early Spring" (1798) contains several lines that embody the romantic belief in the sacredness of nature, including these closing verses:

> One impulse from a vernal wood
> May teach you more of man,
> Of moral evil and of good,
> Than all the sages can.
>
> Sweet is the lore which Nature brings;
> Our meddling intellect
> Mis-shapes the beauteous forms of things:—
> We murder to dissect.
>
> Enough of Science and of Art;
> Close up those barren leaves;
> Come forth, and bring with you a heart
> That watches and receives.

At a very literal level, this poem leads students straight into a discussion of the ethics of animal dissection in biology classes, and animal rights and experimentation in general. At a more abstract level, we discuss the effects of 'watching and receiving' versus analyzing and categorizing. (See the science and poetry section of Chapter One.)

Two other Wordsworth poems, "Expostulation and Reply" and "The Tables Turned," show the poet, William, absorbed in appreciating nature while his friend, Matthew, tries to draw him away to study books. I stage a reading of these poems with two readers: "Matthew" holds a book; William sits on a "rock" and has the most lines. After enumerating the many beauties of nature—the sun's "sweet evening yellow," "the woodland linnet," the "blithe . . . throstle,"—William urges Matthew: "Come forth into the light of things, / Let Nature be your Teacher," and ends:

> If this belief from heaven be sent,
> If such be Nature's holy plan,

Have I not reason to lament
What man has made of man?

Following these readings, we discuss the historical context of the Romantics' reaction to the industrial revolution, and make a list of the characteristics of Romantic beliefs. To introduce the American version of romanticism, we turn to Thoreau's mentor, Ralph Waldo Emerson, who believed that "The noblest ministry of nature is to stand as the apparition of God." I give students an excerpt from Emerson's essay, "Nature," in which he describes crossing a town common and feeling "a perfect exhilaration . . . uplifted into infinite space—all mean egotism vanishes. I become a transparent eyeball; I am nothing; I see all; the currents of the Universal Being circulate through me; I am part or parcel of God." This is the best definition I know for Transcendentalism, and students seem to either get it or think he's crazy.

I used to assign all of *Walden*, with students taking turns leading discussion of each chapter. Now I am more selective, choosing to assign most of the first three chapters—"Introduction," "Economy," "Where I Lived and What I Lived For"— and the "Conclusion." For each reading assignment, students come to class with three passages to discuss. These might be passages they agree with, disagree with, or do not understand. We go around the room and discuss at least one of every student's selected passages. Using this method, students make the main points, I no longer have to dominate discussion, and I make sure that everyone speaks.

In the course of discussing Thoreau's beliefs about simplifying our lives ("A man is rich in proportion to the number of things which he can afford to let alone . . ."), I ask students to make two lists: one of things they consider necessities, one of luxuries. Is a car a necessity or a luxury? Food is a necessity . . . but caviar? Some students argue that they consider the items on the luxury list to be necessities: "My CD player is part of me." I sometimes come into this discussion wearing a T-shirt that says, "Whoever has the most things when he dies wins."

Simplicity can be a hard sell in our consumer-oriented society. "But Mrs. Rous, what's wrong with materialism?" one student blurted out this fall, prompting the liveliest discussion of the semester. Others quickly jumped on the bandwagon. "Right, I like shopping." "I couldn't live without my car." "If I can afford it and it makes my life easier, why shouldn't I have it?" Other students were ready with responses. "When we get preoccupied with having things, we neglect what is more important, like family and friends." ("Not necessarily. The things I like to do with family and friends, like going to the movies or skiing, cost money!") Finally someone added, "It's not just how materialism affects us personally. It's how it affects the earth." I pointed out that the United States uses twenty to thirty percent more of the earth's resources than any other country. Is this fair? What will happen as other countries try to attain our standard of living? Should we adopt simplicity? . . . cut waste? . . . control population growth? These questions have no easy answers and come up often throughout the semester. (See Chapter Five, "Issues and Actions.")

I use this opportunity to show students a video about Helen and Scott Nearing (*Living the Good Life*) or the "Less is More" segment from public television's *Green Means* about Vicki Robbin and Joe Dominguez. Many students are inspired by these couples' commitment to a lifestyle that fosters both a simpler and better quality of life for people and sustainability for the planet. For every student who says, "I couldn't do that. They work too hard," or "They give up too much," another will say, "I'd like to be able to live my life like that old guy and his wife." We recall Chris McCandless' frequent invocation of Thoreau in *Into the Wild*, and compare his own retreat from the world to Thoreau's. Sections of Mitch Albom's *Tuesdays with Morrie* on family, money, and the perfect day can also prompt students to reconsider materialistic values. I read parts of these chapters aloud to students this year.

In the late 1980s, high-rise office buildings and condominiums were planned on land adjoining the Walden Pond State Reservation, prompting a "Save Walden Woods" action that included a fund-raising concert and an anthology of essays by popular entertainers such as Jack Nicholson and Paula Abdul. The collection, called *Heaven Is Under Our Feet* and edited by Don Henley, is available from the Walden Woods Project of the Thoreau Institute (see bibliography).

After the first three chapters of *Walden*, I talk about the structure of the book which follows the seasonal cycle of a year, with the ponds described in the middle of the book just as Walden Pond was central to Thoreau's experience. I read a few of my favorite descriptions of the ponds (from "The Ponds" and "The Ponds in Winter") such as, "A lake is the landscape's most beautiful and expressive feature. It is the earth's eye, looking into which the beholder measures the depth of his own nature." We note the appropriateness of metaphoric descriptions to the Transcendental belief that the concrete beauty of nature is a doorway to abstract and divine truths.

Writing I give two writing assignments in conjunction with reading Thoreau— one personal and one analytical. The first is entitled: "Where I Want to Live and What I Want to Live For." Students describe family, education, career goals, and living in the country versus the city. They write about making money, being respected, and accomplishing something useful in the world. Some take their cue from Thoreau and vow to make the quality of their lives more important than material wealth, while others reject his philosophy. A few students have protested that they have no idea and are too young to think about the future. But most students are grateful for the opportunity to think through their goals on paper. Because these papers help me know more about my students, I look forward to reading them.

The analytical paper asks students to 1) choose one important passage, 2) explain the meaning of the passage, 3) discuss how the passage relates to other parts of the book and Thoreau's beliefs in general, and 4) discuss whether or not they agree with these beliefs. By providing a format, this assignment helps students learn to organize an analytical paper and can be applied to any reading. For those students who have struggled with the reading, I have a handout of possible quotations to write about.

Once again, before leaving Thoreau, the ultimate question must be asked: Is his philosophy the answer to our environmental problems? Can we all go back to living in the woods? Few of us are ready to give up our modern conveniences, and even if we did, there would soon be no woods left. Nevertheless, Thoreau's advice "to live deliberately," to seek "simplicity" in our use of time and material goods, and to appreciate each moment and each detail in the world around us—all adds up to a better quality of life for each individual and for the earth as a whole. Students who started out skeptical of a man who lived on beans and rice or who touted self-sufficiency while walking into town to do laundry, usually end up inspired by his call to "follow a different drummer" and re-examine what really matters in life.

Hudson River School

Just as 19th century writers turned to nature as their source of truth and inspiration, American painters also found their subject matter in the vast, seemingly unspoiled, American landscape. Studying the works of the "Hudson River" artists as part of a unit on romanticism offers an excellent opportunity to integrate art history with a literature curriculum.

Our former art teacher, Bill Childs, who made presentations to my students on the Hudson River School, began by telling them that for 200 years, America had folk arts but no time for fine arts. Most painting before 1820 was portraiture or narrative painting depicting historical events. "No one thought of going out-of-doors," says Childs.

Working from the 1820s to the 1870s, the Hudson River School created what is considered the first American painting style. Their paintings embody the myth of America as a new Eden and present landscapes that are naturalistic but highly romanticized. While the "school" began with Thomas Cole and Asher Durand in the Catskill Mountains and along the Hudson River, Albert Bierstadt painted in the Rockies and Frederic Church, inspired by German explorer Alexander Von Humboldt, painted in South America. Hudson River School works are characterized by grand panoramas, contrasting elements, dramatic lighting, and careful observation and details which are accurate but heightened in scale and emotional impact. Any human presence is kept small to emphasize the immensity of the landscape. Slides and catalogues of Hudson River School exhibits are available from the Metropolitan Museum of Art in New York City and the National Museum of American Art in Washington, DC (see bibliography).

If I don't have a guest art historian, I have students research and present this information themselves. I develop a list of painters, including local 19th century artists from the "White Mountain School" and the Isles of Shoals (see Chapter Seven), and assign students to present them. They take slides of paintings in art books and give presentations on the artists' lives and styles. CD ROMS and Internet sites are also excellent sources of images. My first intern, Tim Myers, had students sketch copies of paintings from books. This enjoyable activity forced us to pay close attention to composition and detail, and, in spite of the initial groans of "I can't draw," all were surprisingly pleased with the results.

Writing To assess student understanding of the Hudson River School, I give each student a copy of a painting (or project one for the whole class), preferably one they have not already discussed, and ask them to write a short essay describing how the painting is characteristic of the philosophy and style of this movement.

The Frontier: Literature of Exploration and the West

The same views that defined European visions of the Eastern seaboard continued to define American views of the western frontier. Whether the land was viewed positively or negatively, as paradise or a place of hardship, the belief that the West offered limitless opportunities and resources ultimately led to abuse.

Frederick Jackson Turner, writing *The Frontier in American History* in 1920, describes "the frontier" as the defining element of the American character. For Turner, the frontier created a continual rebirth because it necessitated a reversal to the primitive. Westerners "broke with the past and thought to create something finer, more fitting for humanity, more beneficial for the average man than the world had ever seen" (Turner 1962, 355). Because people associated nature with goodness, America's natural abundance was equated with moral superiority. Thomas Jefferson sought to insure this superiority by keeping America agrarian and leaving industry to Europe (see *Notes on the State of Virginia*).

Roderick Nash's *Wilderness and the American Mind*, (1967), distinguishes between the agrarian, "pastoral" vision, and the love of wilderness. Pioneers, according to Nash, seek the pastoral, a tamed landscape, and therefore must destroy wilderness. Only an urban population can afford to indulge in the cult of the wild. Turner and Nash, along with Leo Marx (*The Machine in the Garden*), are excellent resources for understanding the impact of wilderness on American national and literary identity. I read these authors for my own background and occasionally share excerpts with students.

I could easily spend an entire semester on fiction and nonfiction of the West; instead I usually discuss a few representative short works in class, then give students reading lists and an independent reading assignment. I might begin with excerpts from exploration diaries and journals such as Lewis and Clark's journals of their 1804–1806 journey through the Louisiana Territory; an account of Isabella Bird's expedition with mountain man, Jim Bridger; an 1818 journal of Estwick Evans, a New Hampshire lawyer who walked 4,000 miles to the West; or a diary by Virginia Reed Murphy, a Donner Party survivor, coupled with Ruth Whitman's poetic simulation (1977) of Tamsen Donner's lost diary (1846–1847).

Other first person accounts I have excerpted include Anna Howard Shaw's *The Story of A Pioneer*, Mollie Dorsey Sanford's story of her family's life on the Little Nemaha, and Elinore Pruitt Stewart *Letters of A Woman Homesteader*, a story of housekeeper turned homesteader (film version: "Heartland"). In the short story "Neighbor Rosicky" by Willa Cather, farmer Rosicky persuades his sons to resist the lure of the city and live the "good" life of working the land. In many of these works, protagonists struggle between seeing the western lands as a mythical paradise and the reality of having to survive in harsh conditions.

Following class discussion of short works about the West, I have students choose a novel for independent reading (see bibliography). Authors include James Fenimore Cooper, Willa Cather, Ole Rolvaag, John Steinbeck, Wallace Stegner, Ivan Doig, Mary Austin, and Owen Wister. Early American fictional heroes are often characters who measure their worth by their ability to survive in the wilderness. Cooper's Natty Bumpo (*The Deerslayer*) resists the march of civilization into his frontier and glorifies the life of the "savage"; he lives off the land in harmony with nature.

Other frontier characters participate inadvertently and paradoxically in the destruction of the wilderness they extol. A. B. Guthrie's Boone Caudill (*The Big Sky*) is a fearless mountain man who is only happy in the freedom of open spaces but whose own violence destroys his wife, his best friend, and every animal that crosses his path.

Wallace Stegner's *The Big Rock Candy Mountain* depicts the search for paradise in one family's journey from village, to gold rush, to railroad camp, and finally to their own farm, always chasing the father's dream of a better life on the next frontier. That women often suffered from male dreams of greener pastures is revealed in Lillian Schlissel's *Women's Diaries of the Westward Journey*.

Owen Wister's *The Virginian* is about the archetypal western cowboy who is skillful with horses, rope, guns, and cards but never flaunts his talents; his strength is in understatement; he's large, handsome, and rugged; he has no education but is cleverer than those who do; he defends women and animals but is not vengeful; and when the chips are down, he chooses honor over everything else, including friends and his fiancée. The book's plot parallels the progress of development in the west: the Virginian comes from Appalachia, falls in love with a "school marm," and watches the land transformed from open range into settlements. When my students read this, we note how sexist it is; it seems cowboys were in the business of subduing women along with the land. "She knew her cowboy lover, with all that he lacked, to be more than ever she could be, with all that she had. He was her worshipper still, but her master, too." Following the climactic gun duel, Molly Wood and the Virginian spend their honeymoon in a remote mountain valley that is described in purely golden age terms. The place heals his wounds and returns him to a state of innocence. His physical union with his wife is associated with his immersion in the beauty of the place: "Often when I have camped here it has made me want to become the ground, become the water, become the trees, mix with the whole thing. Not know myself from it. Never unmix again."

In "The Frontiersman" chapter of *A Choice of Heroes*, Michael Gerzon re-examines the western hero's treatment of Native Americans, women, and the land and urges us to "redefine masculinity. We must replace our desire to dominate with a willingness to learn humility, respect, nurturance." This chapter can provoke good discussion in class during a unit on the West.

Writing When students do individual reading, I sometimes develop a list of general topics that could apply to any of their choices. I also encourage them to generate their own writing ideas and discuss them with me. Some generic topics for literature of the West include:

1. Why did people go west? What did they hope to find, and what did they actually find?
2. What is the perspective of the protagonist (farmer, trader, explorer, rancher, etc.), and how does that perspective affect the way the land of the West is viewed? Is it seen as rich or poor? Comforting or intimidating? Harsh or generous? Idyllic or menacing? etc. How is the land in turn treated by its new inhabitants?
3. Discuss the character of the western "hero" and the parallels (or differences) between the westward journey and a mythical hero quest (in which a hero separates him- or herself from the ordinary world, seeks a source of power, faces a great challenge and accomplishes a worthy goal, then returns renewed). What role does the land play in the hero's quest?

4.   Describe the roles of women in these stories. Compare their view of the land to that of men.

5.   Describe the roles of Native Americans. Compare their view of the land to that of the new settlers.

6.   How does the book characterize the drawbacks and benefits of settled life versus life on the frontier?

7.   What role does the frontier play in shaping the characters in your book?

8.   What changes are observed in the land over the course of the novel?

Alternatives to writing on a specific topic are the readers' response log or creative projects as described in Chapter Six.

Early Conservationists and Preservationists

While the "golden age" mentality and the Garden of Eden view of America may have its drawbacks, romanticism coupled with the end of the Western frontier did pave the way for 20th century environmental awareness. To understand the beginnings of the conservation movement, I focus on four people: John Muir (1838–1914), Gifford Pinchot (1865–1946), Aldo Leopold (1886–1948), and Rachel Carson (1907–1964).

The materials I use include two outstanding documentary videos by Lawrence Hott and Diane Garey: "The Wilderness Idea," about Muir and Pinchot, and "Wild by Law," about Leopold, Bob Marshall, and Howard Zahniser. For texts, we read excerpts from John Muir's My *First Summer in the Sierra*, Aldo Leopold's *Sand County Almanac*, and Rachel Carson's *Silent Spring*.

Are you a preservationist, an ecologist, a conservationist, an environmental activist, or a developer? After discussing the films and readings, students should understand these labels and be able to compare their own beliefs with those of environmentalists. I tell students this will be the subject of their final writing assignment before we start reading. Each person studied represents a different perspective on land and a different philosophy of land use, perspectives that can be traced right back to the views encountered in early myths and in first European accounts of America.

I begin with a brief introduction to the lives and philosophies of John Muir, and Gifford Pinchot, both covered in detail in "The Wilderness Idea" video (1989). Students watch the film and take notes on each man's biography and beliefs. A *National Geographic* (1973) article calls Muir the "father of Yosemite National Park, savior of the sequoias, guiding light of the national park movement, explorer and mountaineer, naturalist and mystic, adviser to Presidents and gadfly of the establishment." He was also a prolific writer and left over sixty travel journals, 425 published articles, nine full-length books, and thousands of letters.

Muir grew up in a Midwestern Scottish pioneer family. He was hardworking, religious, and inventive. An accident almost cost him his sight and made him resolve to give up human invention and devote himself to nature—God's invention. To give students a taste of Muir's writing, I excerpt passages from *My First Summer in the Sierra* describing Yosemite meadows, mountain ranges, storms, waterfalls, twisted junipers, grouse, and deer, and match these with slides from a family backpacking trip in Yosemite National Park. We read Muir's lyrical descriptions aloud as we view the slides. (See bibliography to order slides and text.) Describing a sunrise, Muir writes, "The whole landscape glows like a human face in a glory of enthusiasm, and the blue sky, pale around the horizon, bends peacefully down over all like one vast flower." Muir called the Sierras "the Range of Light," and two books of Yosemite photographs—by Ansel Adams and Philip Hyde—use this phrase in their titles. Both are good supplements to a study of Muir.

For Muir, wilderness represented an escape from society and a demanding father, but Gifford Pinchot achieved social preeminence through a career chosen by his father—forestry. Pinchot was raised by a prosperous, upper class Eastern family. He studied forestry practices in Europe and went on to become the first chief of the U.S. Forest Service. He was appalled at the waste of natural resources he witnessed in America which had lost ninety percent of its virgin forests by 1900. He advocated a controlled use that could both perpetuate resources and be profitable.

Using *The Wilderness Idea* video, students compiled this chart comparing the lives and beliefs of Muir and Pinchot:

Muir (1828–1914)	Pinchot (1865–1946)
immigrant, lived on frontier	lived in wealthy, established family
worked from 4 A.M. to 9 P.M.	lived a privileged life, used to power
father demanding and restrictive, no books allowed but the Bible	received an expensive education, lived abroad
inventive, clever with technology	enterprising, put new forestry beliefs into practice
rejected technology and "progress"	believed in using technology
left the system, became a tramp and a hermit	held important government posts
wilderness is sacred abode of God	wilderness is a resource to be used
advocated leaving wilderness as is	nature is meant to serve people, advocated multiple-use and scientific forestry: controlled planting and cutting

founder/leader of Sierra Club	first chief of the US Forest Service
influenced Teddy Roosevelt to add to National Park System	influenced Teddy Roosevelt's multiple-use policies
opposed creation of the Hetch Hetchy reservoir in Yosemite National Park	supported Hetch Hetchy reservoir

The debate over flooding the Hetch Hetchy valley to create a water supply for San Francisco was a nationwide controversy from 1903 to 1913. The "wilderness craze" at the turn of the century and the scope of the Hetch Hetchy debate mark the beginning of the modern conservation movement and indicate how much the American view of wilderness had changed. Although Muir lost the Hetch Hetchy battle (and died shortly afterward), Congress subsequently banned such land uses in national parks.

Having established the preservationist (Muir) and conservationist (Pinchot) views, we turn to ecologist Aldo Leopold. In the first half of *A Sand County Almanac*, Leopold keeps a month by-month-journal, his "shack sketches," of the wildlife and seasonal changes around his family's retreat in Wisconsin. He describes the habits of deer, grouse, and rabbit; the migrations of sandhill cranes, plover, and geese; and reveals his love for pines. He and his family planted thousands of pine seedlings to restore the "sand county" habitat. Leopold was a real-life version of the character in Jean Giono's *The Man Who Planted Trees*, a children's book students enjoy.

Journal Writing Leopold's monthly descriptions provide an excellent model for students' land journals. For example, students can imitate Leopold's description of the fantasy odyssey of "X," the atom that begins its journey in a rock then becomes part of an oak, the oak's flower, an acorn, an Indian, the soil, a prairie bluestem leaf, and finally the sea. The same journey can be imagined for a water molecule. Leopold's methods of seeing are also instructive and inspiring to student journal writers. He buries himself in marshmuck to observe the parenting behavior of grebes; he bands chickadees and notes their survival rates; he tracks deer, rabbit, and grouse in fresh snow and estimates the size of their winter ranges. His prose approaches poetry: "a tattered banner of birds, dipping and rising, blown up and blown down, blown together and blown apart, but advancing, the wind wrestling lovingly with each winnowing wing" (1987, 71); and his writing is infused with ecological teachings: "all conservation of wildness is self-defeating, for to cherish we must see and fondle, and when enough have seen and fondled, there is no wilderness left to cherish" (108).

The video "Wild by Law" (1991) is a documentary history of the Wilderness Act. It features Aldo Leopold and Bob Marshall who founded the Wilderness Society, and Howard Zahniser who shepherded the Wilderness Act for eight years through 66 rewrites in Congress until it was finally signed into law by President Johnson in 1964 (four months after Zahniser's death). I focus on the Leopold portions of the video which show pictures of his Wisconsin "shack" and describe his life and the evolution of his environmental philosophy.

In Part IV of A *Sand County Almanac*, Leopold lays out his "land ethic," and it is this reading that I use with students. Both Leopold and Muir understood that each aspect of a biological system affects every other aspect, but it was Leopold who saw the need to protect ecological systems with a new system of ethics. Leopold's breakthrough was in extending the human moral code to all life. I ask students to read "The Land Ethic" and to define terms such as the "community concept" (the "community" we cooperate with expands to include all life), "land health" ("the capacity of the land for self-renewal") and the "A-B Cleavage" ("man the conqueror versus man the biotic citizen; science the sharpener of his sword versus science the searchlight on his universe; land the slave and servant versus land the collective organism").

Leopold begins "The Land Ethic" with a description of Odysseus hanging his unfaithful slave girls upon his return home. While we now understand slavery to be wrong, "there is as yet no ethic dealing with man's relation to land. . . . Land, like Odysseus' slave-girls, is still property. The land relation is still strictly economic, entailing privileges but not obligations." A typical class discussion of Leopold's land ethic begins thus:

"What would happen," I ask, "if we were to liberate land in the same way that we liberated slaves?"
"Everything would change."
"People would lose all of their wealth."
"We would return to a system like the Native Americans' in which no one owned land."
"It would mean that all living things have as much right to exist as we do, no matter how much or how little they benefit us."
"Yes, but we have to use the environment in order to exist. How can we exist if we extend the right to exist to everything else?"

This vital point that no life can exist on earth without having some impact on its surroundings, leads to discussion of which impacts are permissible and which are too much.

I might ask, "How can we extend rights to land without taking the radical step of giving up private ownership? How would Leopold determine what is ethical behavior in relation to land?"

"We need to respect all living things, just as we try to respect each other."

"We have to take into account what the land needs in order to survive and not change it to the point that it cannot restore itself."

"How can we know when we have reached this point?"

"By studying and learning. We need to understand how ecological systems work."

"Too often we destroy habitats before we even know what's in them."

"Is there any way to insure that a land ethic is followed?"

"No, people are too selfish."

"We can have government rules, but people don't like to be told what to do."

"We have punishments for murder; we can have similar punishments for destroying the environment."

"People will never put the environment before their pocketbooks."

"They will if they see that it helps them economically in the long run."

"But Leopold says we should respect the environment even when it doesn't help us economically."

"Some people care enough about the environment to make personal sacrifices."

The question of whether people will act only in self-interest or will choose to act for the good of others and the earth brings out students' basic beliefs about human nature and our capacity to evolve ethically. No one can engage in this discussion without weighing their own moral choices.

When I ask students to arrange Muir, Pinchot, and Leopold on a continuum according to the degree to which each man believes in land rights and land preservation, they quickly come to this arrangement:

Muir	Leopold	Pinchot
Preservationist: the land is sacred as is; leave it alone	*Ecologist:* the land has rights; only use it to the extent that it can renew itself	*Conservationist:* the land is there to be used but not wasted; it should be conserved for future generations

While there are overlaps in the three points of view, there are also clear differences in emphasis.

The final point on the continuum is that of the no-holds-barred land developer. It is not easy to find writers who openly advocate land abuse, but many will criticize limits on development. In the Reagan era, I could call on former Secretary of the Interior, James Watt. In recent years, I have used the views expressed by the so-called "wise use" movement, a label chosen to mislead, often succeeding. The *Time* cover story on October 23, 1995, "Don't Tread On Me: An inside look at the West's growing rebellion," sets out the positions of members of Congress such as Representative James Hansen of Utah who wanted to open mining near Bryce Canyon and close many national parks, or Alaska's Representative Dan Young and Senators Ted Stevens and Frank Murkowski who advocate increased logging in the Tongass National Forest and opening the Arctic National Wildlife Refuge to oil drilling. For each of these men, human and property rights take precedence over environmental rights. Says Young, "Eventually the working class, the poorer people, will realize that [the Endangered Species Act] is saving crickets over saving babies," and Murkowski, "The agenda in our state has been to provide for the economy." We have labeled this fourth position the "developer," defined by a belief in the right of humans to develop land for their own use and profit, and added it to the right end of the continuum:

Muir —————— Leopold ————— Pinchot ————— Developer

Writing Now comes the essential question: Which of these viewpoints most closely represents your own and why? The assignment is in three parts, and students have the questions from the beginning of the unit:

1. Discuss the land use philosophies of Muir, Pinchot, Leopold, and the developers. Give specific examples and quotations from their lives and writings to illustrate their philosophies.
2. Show how each philosophy is paralleled by readings studied earlier in the course.
3. Which philosophy most closely resembles your own beliefs? Explain and justify your personal position.

Students must show, in writing, that they understand the four points of view with explanations and examples from the readings and with comparisons to other course readings (e.g., Native Americans, Genesis, Percy, Smith, Sewall, Beverly, Thoreau, Jewett, Audubon). The paper ends with a discussion of the student's own view.

Most often students reject the outer ends of the spectrum, Muir and the "developers," as too extreme: "You can't live in the world without affecting it, so how can you follow Muir's philosophy, except in a few isolated areas? This is not a solution to everyday life." "The developers can't be allowed to develop without restriction or soon there will be no natural systems left." An occasional romantic will identify with Muir; a few will advocate the right of property owners to do what they want to do with their land; but most students gravitate toward the positions of Leopold and Pinchot. Often, they choose the reasonable, balanced multiple-use approach of Pinchot, with an emphasis on preserving resources for the future along with using them now. Others see Leopold's vision of rights for land as a solution for our own day and line up behind him.

I find this question to be an effective culminating assignment and assessment tool. It is so central to the themes of the course that I often use it as a prepared final exam question. The question forces students to understand a wide range of perspectives on land use, to see how the history of these perspectives affects our current beliefs and actions, and to develop a personal land use philosophy.

Students should be aware that Muir, Pinchot, and Leopold laid the groundwork for the modern environmental movement, our next subject.

Modern Environmentalists

"The lasting pleasures of contact with the natural world are not reserved for scientists but are available to anyone who will place himself under the influence of earth, sea and sky and their amazing life."
—*Rachel Carson*, A Sense of Wonder (1951)

When I was about nine years old, I ordered Rachel Carson's *The Sea Around Us* from a school book club. Sitting in Miss Galligan's winter-gray classroom, I must have been drawn to the title by summer memories of swimming in Long Island Sound and combing the shores for slipper shells and periwinkles. When the book arrived, I entered a water world where hundred-foot waves carry away two thousand-ton piers and seventy-ton sperm whales battle fifty-foot giant squid, where mountain ranges and mile-deep canyons line the ocean bottoms and animals live in tiers between the sea surface and bottom. Two months after *The Sea Around Us* was published in 1951, it was number one on the New York *Times* best-seller list and stayed there for eighty-six weeks. It won the National Book Award and the John Burroughs Medal for natural history writing.

Rachel Carson's life story is as inspiring as her writing. She went to college to be a writer but came out a biologist. Combining these two talents, she worked as a science writer for the U.S. Fish and Wildlife Service for fifteen years, only the second woman they had hired as more than a secretary. She supported her parents, then her widowed mother and two nieces. The success of *The Sea Around Us* enabled her to leave government work and write *The Edge of the Sea*. In 1958, she was working on *A Sense of Wonder* when she received an alarming letter from a friend, Olga Huckins, who wondered if the deaths of birds and bees in her Massachusetts neighborhood were related to the state's new use of DDT on mosquitoes. Carson researched the effects of pesticides and set off a chain of events with *Silent Spring* (1962) that led eventually (after Carson's death) to the banning of DDT and controls for all pesticides. In *Silent Spring*, Carson warned that pesticides sprayed in gardens get into streams and rivers where they pass through plants and fish to end up in human tissues causing, she suspected, cancer and genetic mutations. Instead of creating generations of chemical-resistant insects, she advocated natural controls such as predators and trapping. Her warnings were criticized by some as unsubstantiated and alarmist. Now we recognize them as prophetic and acknowledge our debt to one of the most significant contributors to the modern environmental movement.

Muir, Pinchot, Leopold, and Rachel Carson are only four of the many important environmentalists I would like students to know. To introduce a broader range of people and achievements, I provide a list from which students choose a person to research and present to the class. They read biographies and use sources such as the excellent *Earthkeepers* by Ann T. Keene. Their presentations include oral, visual, and written components. Students also interview local environmental activists and invite some to speak at school. People students present include:

David Brower (1912–), founder, Friends of the Earth and Earth Island Institute; former president of the Sierra Club which went from 7,000 to 70,000 members under his leadership; opposed Glen Canyon dam. John McPhee writes about Brower in *Encounters with the Archdruid*.

John Burroughs (1837–1921), America's most popular nature writer in the late 1800s and early 1900s. The Burroughs Medal is now presented to contemporary nature writers.

Marjory Stoneman Douglas (1890–), protector of Florida Everglades.

Jane Goodall (1934–), **Dian Fossey** (1932–1985), and **Birute Galdikas**, naturalists, all recruited by paleontologist Louis Leakey to study primates in the wild: Goodall studies chimpanzees in East Africa (wrote *The Chimpanzees of Gombe*), Fossey studied mountain gorillas in Rwanda (wrote *Gorillas in the Mist*), and Galdikas has studied orangutans in Borneo (wrote *Orangutan Odyssey*); all spent years developing close relationships with their subjects, were filmed by the National Geographic Society, and worked for primate preservation. The mystery surrounding Dian Fossey's murder at her mountain station is described by Farley Mowat in *Woman in the Mists*.

George Bird Grinnell (1849–1938), editor of *Forest and Stream* magazine; called for hunting restrictions; helped establish the National Park Service, Glacier National Park, and the New York Zoological Society; started the first Audubon Society.

Benton MacKaye (1879–1975), creator of the Appalachian Trail, cofounder of the Wilderness Society.

Olaus (1889–1963) and **Margaret Murie** (1902–), wildlife naturalists in the Arctic and Wyoming, strong advocates of species and habitat preservation; helped establish Arctic National Wildlife Range and cofounders of the Wilderness Society, helped pass the Wilderness Act, authors of numerous wildlife books including *Two in the Far North* (Margaret Murie, 1962).

Katharine Ordway (1899–1979), preserver of tallgrass prairies.

President **Theodore Roosevelt** (1858–1919, president 1901–1909), outdoor lover, big game hunter, and creator of U.S. Forest Service and six national parks.

The reports on modern environmentalists end our historical study. We have seen America move from its own age of "innocence" when myths seemed to be reality and actions had no consequences, to an age of growing self-awareness and attempts to control our actions. We are ready to turn our attention to specific case studies and contemporary environmental issues. There are many directions to take and far too many issues to choose from. The perspectives we identified throughout the historical study will help us to understand modern conflicts over wolf reintroduction, cutting old growth forest, energy sources, endangered species protection, or clean air emission standards.

Works Cited

Works Cited for Students

Albom, M. 1997. *Tuesdays With Morrie*. New York: Doubleday. Chapters on family, money, and time complement Thoreau well.

Adams, Ansel. 1981. *Yosemite and the Range of Light*. Boston: New York Graphic Society.

Carson, R. (1907–1964). 1951. *The Sea Around Us*. New York: Oxford University Press.

———. 1964. *Silent Spring*. New York: Fawcett Crest.

———. 1965. *A Sense of Wonder* (1956). New York: Harper and Row.

Emerson, R. W. (1803–1902). 1979. "Nature" in *Centenary Edition, the Complete Works of Ralph Waldo Emerson*. New York: AMS Press. Defines Transcendentalism.

Faulkner, W. 1970. "The Bear" (1942). New York: Random House, Inc. A coming of age story about fulfilling dreams.

Giono, J. (1895–1970). 1989. *The Man Who Planted Trees*. Jean Roberts, trans. Toronto, Ontario: CBC Enterprises. (Also on audiotape, narrated by Robert J. Lurtsema, music by Paul Winter Consort. 1990. Earth Music Productions. P.O. Box 68, Litchfield, CT 06759). A fictional shepherd in Provence spends twenty-five years planting thousands of trees. For young readers, but good for anyone.

Henley, D., and D. Marsh, eds. 1991. *Heaven Is Under Our Feet, A Book for Walden Woods*. Stamford, CT: Longmeadow Press. Essays by sixty-six celebrities on Thoreau and the environment.

Hyde, P. 1992. *The Range of Light, with Selections from the Writings of John Muir*. Salt Lake City: Peregrine Smith Books.

Jewett, S. O. (1849–1909). 1925. "The White Heron" in *The Best Short Stories of Sarah Orne Jewett*. Boston: Houghton Mifflin.

Keene, A. T. 1994. *Earthkeepers: Observers and Protectors of Nature*. New York: Oxford University Press. Profiles significant environmental scientists, philosophers, and activists, from Linnaeus to Wendell Berry; attractive graphics and format.

Leopold, A. (1886–1948). 1987. *A Sand County Almanac* (1949). New York: Oxford University Press.

Lopez, B. 1992. *The Rediscovery of North America*. New York: Vintage. Also appeared in NRDC's *Amicus Journal*. A plea to replace dominance of land with intimate knowledge.

McPhee, J. 1971. *Encounters with the Archdruid*. New York: Farrar, Straus and Giroux. About the life and work of David Brower, founder, Friends of the Earth.

Mowat, F. 1987. *Woman in the Mists: The Story of Dian Fossey and the Mountain Gorillas of Africa*. New York: Warner Books.

Muir, J. (1828–1914). 1998. *My First Summer in the Sierra*. Galen Rowell, intro. Boston: Houghton Mifflin. (Also see *National Geographic*, 4/73, 433 ff. on Muir.)

Thoreau, H. D. 1965. *Walden*. New York: Airmont Publishing Co.

Thorpe, T. B. (1815–1878). 1989. "The Big Bear of Arkansas" in *A New Collection of Thomas Bangs Thorpe's Sketches of the Old Southwest*. Baton Rouge: Louisiana State University Press. A mythical bear is caught.

Additional Student Resources

Bonta, M. M. 1991. *Women in the Field: America's Pioneering Women Naturalists*. College Station, TX: Texas A & M University Press.

Fossey, D. 1988. *Gorillas in the Mist*, Boston: Houghton Mifflin.

Galdikas, B. and N. Briggs. 1999. *Orangutan Odyssey*. Introduction by Jane Goodall. New York: Harry Abrams.

Goodall, Jane. 1986. *The Chimpanzees of Gombe: Patterns of Behavior*. Cambridge, MA: Belknap Press of Harvard University Press.

Montgomery, S. 1992. *Walking with the Great Apes: Jane Goodall, Dian Fossey, Birute Galdikas*. Boston: Houghton Mifflin.

Pinchot, G. (1865–1946). 1998. *Breaking New Ground*. Washington, DC: Island Press.

Rich, L. D. 1970. *We Took to the Woods* (1942). Camden, ME: Downeast Books.

Strong, D. 1988. *Dreamers and Defenders: American Conservationists*. Lincoln, Nebraska: University of Nebraska Press. Profiles of Thoreau, Powell, Leopold, Carson, Olmstead, Commoner, and more.

Wallace, A. 1993. *Eco-Heroes: Twelve Tales of Environmental Victory*. San Francisco: Mercury House.

———. 1994. *Green Means*. San Francisco: KQED Books. Profiles each activist featured in the public television series of shorts: "Green Means."

Journals of Exploration and Settlement

Audubon, J. J. (1785–1851). 1987. "The Passenger Pigeon" in 1826 *Journal of John James Audubon*. Transcribed with notes by Alice Ford. New York: Abbeville Press.

Bartram, W. (1739–1823). 1996. *Travels and Other Writings*. New York: Library of America. Travels in North and South Carolina, Georgia, Florida, and territories of the Cherokee, Creek, and Choctaw.

Belknap, J. 1876. *Journal of a Tour to the White Mountains* (1784). Charles Deane, ed. Boston: Massachusetts Historical Society.

Beverly, R. 1705. *The History and Present State of Virginia*. As quoted in Leo Marx, *The Machine in the Garden*. 1964. New York: Oxford University Press, 75–88.

Byrd, W. 1987. *A History of the Dividing Line* (1728). New York: Dover.

Freneau, P. (1752–1832). 1787. *Journey from Philadelphia to New York*. Philadelphia: Francis Bailey. Freneau was a poet and essayist.

Knight, S. K. (1666–1727). 1972. *The Journal of Madam Knight*. Boston: D. R. Godine.

Percy, G. (1580–1632). 1967. "A Discourse of the Plantation of the Southern Colony in Virginia" (1606). Charlottesville: University Press of Virginia.

Sewall, S. (1652–1730). 1998. "The New Heaven Upon the New Earth" (1697), in *The Diary and Life of Samuel Sewall*. Mel Yazawa, ed. Boston: Bedford Books. Sewall associates an idyllic life in nature with heavenly grace.

Smith, J. (1580–1631). 1616. *A Description of New England*. Boston: W. Veazie. Smith describes the good life in America to entice new settlers.

Twain, M. (1835–1910). 1993. *Roughing It* (1871). Hurley, New York: Jerry's Books. The "Lake Tahoe" episode conveys both beauty and destruction.

Additional Resources

Andrews, B. et. al. 1990. *Journeys in New Worlds: Early American Women's Narratives*. Madison: University of Wisconsin.

Cronon, W. 1983. *Changes in the Land: Indians, Colonists, and the Ecology of New England*. New York: Hill and Wang.

The West

Bird, I. (1831–1904). 1999. *Lady's Life in the Rocky Mountains*. Norman: University of Oklahoma Press.

Cather, W. 1958. "Neighbor Rosicky," *Obscure Destinies*. New York: Alfred A. Knopf, Inc. Rosicky convinces his children that a farming life is better than the allure of cities.

———. 1988. *O Pioneers!* Boston: Houghton Mifflin. (See Chapter Six.)

———. 1991. *My Antonia*. New York: Chelsea House Publishers.

Cooper, J. F. (1789–1851). 1991. *The Pioneers*. James D. Wallace, ed. New York: Oxford University Press.

————.1993. *The Deerslayer*. H. Daniel Peck, ed. New York: Oxford University Press.

Evans, E. (1787–1866). 1819. *A Pedestrian Tour of Four Thousand Miles, Through the Western States and Territories, During the Winter and Spring of 1818*. Concord, NH: Joseph C. Spear.

Gerzon, M. 1992. *A Choice of Heroes: The Changing Faces of American Manhood*. Boston: Houghton Mifflin.

Guthrie, A. B. 1947. *The Big Sky*. New York: William Sloan Associates.

Lewis, M. and W. Clark (1770–1838). 1993. *Off the Map: the Journals of Lewis and Clark*. Peter and Connie Roop, eds. New York: Walker and Co.

Murphy, Virginia Reed or Patrick Breen, full text of their diaries of the Donner Party expedition are on the internet: "The Overland Trail Diaries," http:www.overland.com/diaries.html

Sanford, M. D. 1959. *Mollie: The Journal of Mollie Dorsey Sanford in Nebraska and Colorado Territories*. Lincoln: University of Nebraska Press.

Schlissel, L. 1987. *Women's Diaries of the Westward Journey*. New York: Schocken.

Shaw, A. H. 1915. *The Story of a Pioneer*. New York: Harper & Row. Shaw's family has a rude awakening when they arrive at their new Michigan "farm."

Stegner, W. 1991 *The Big Rock Candy Mountain* (1943). New York: Penguin Books.

Stewart, E. P. 1989. *Letters of a Woman Homesteader* (1847). Lincoln: University of Nebraska Press. (Also George, Susanne K., ed. 1992. *The Adventures of a Woman Homesteader: The Life and Letters of Elinore Pruitt Stewart*. Lincoln: University of Nebraska Press; and video, *Heartland*, based on Stewart's life.)

Whitman, R. 1977. *Tamsen Donner: A Woman's Journey*. Cambridge, MA: Alice James Books. A poetic simulation of the Donner party journey.

Whitman, W. (1819–1892). 1968. "Song of the Redwood Tree" in *Leaves of Grass*. Facs. of first ed. by Richard Bridgman. San Francisco: Chandler Publishing Co.

Wister, O. (1860–1938). 1999. *The Virginian: A Horseman of the Plains* (1902). New York: Grosset and Dunlap.

Additional Student Readings on The West

Austin, M. (1868–1934). 1932. *Earth Horizon*. Boston: Houghton Mifflin Co. Austin's autobiography.

————. 1987. *Stories from the Country of Lost Borders*. New Brunswick: Rutgers University Press.

Brown, D. 1991. *Bury My Heart at Wounded Knee*. New York: Henry Holt.

Catlin, G. (1796–1872). 1841. *Letters and Notes on the Manners, Customs, and Conditions of North American Indians*. London: C. Adlard, Bartholomew Close.

Clark, W. V. T. 1957. *The Ox-Bow Incident*. New York: Random House.

Cooper, J. F. (1789–1851). 1985. *The Leatherstocking Tales* (*The Prairie*, *The Last of the Mohicans*, etc.) New York: Viking Press.

Doig, I. 1984. *English Creek*. New York: Penguin. The first of a trilogy on the settlement of northern Montana by the fictional McCaskill family.

————. 1987. *Dancing at the Rascal Fair*. New York: Harper. The second book of the Mc-Caskill trilogy.

————. 1978. *This House of Sky, Landscapes of a Western Mind*. New York: Harcourt Brace Jovanovich. Doig's autobiographical account of growing up in Montana.

Ehrlich, G. 1985. *The Solace of Open Spaces*. New York: Penguin Books. A woman's sojourn on a modern Wyoming sheep farm.

Grey, Z. (1872–1939). 1980. *Five Complete Novels*. New York: Avenel Books. Classic western writer; dozens of books.

Guthrie, A. B. 1949. *The Way West*. New York: William Sloan Associates.

Kirkland, C. (1801–1864). 1969. *A New Home, Who'll Follow? or Glimpses of Western Life*. (1839). New York: Garrett Press. Pioneer life in remote Michigan wilderness.

L'Amour, L. 1986. *Last of the Breed*. New York: Bantam Books. One of many westerns by President Reagan's favorite writer.

Low, A. M. 1984. *Dust Bowl Diary*. Lincoln: University of Nebraska Press.

Luchetti, C. 1982. *Women of the West*. St. George, Utah: Antelope Island Press. Photographs, diaries, and oral histories.

McCarthy, C. 1999. *The Crossing (The Border Trilogy)*. New York: Everyman's Library. A young man returns a wolf to its Mexican homeland and begins a mystical quest.

McMurtry, L. 1985. *Lonesome Dove*. New York: Simon and Schuster. A cattle drive from the Rio Grande to Montana through the last of the old West.

Moynihan, R. et. al., eds. 1990. *So Much to Be Done: Women Settlers on the Mining and Ranching Frontier*. Lincoln: University of Nebraska Press.

Raban, J. 1996. *Bad Land: An American Romance*. New York: Random House. Traces the railroad's influence on settlement of arid lands and resulting economic and ecological disaster in eastern Montana and western North Dakota.

Rolvaag, O. E. 1955. *Giants in the Earth: A Saga of the Prairie* (1927). New York: Harper & Row. Norwegian homesteaders struggle to survive on the Dakota frontier (see Chapter Six).

Ross, N. W. 1985. *Westward the Women* (1944). Berkeley: North Point Press.

Silko, L. M. 1981. *Storyteller*. New York: Seaver Books.

Steinbeck, J. 1986. *The Red Pony (and The Pearl)*. New York: Penguin.

————. 1996. *The Grapes of Wrath*. Harold Bloom, ed. Broomall, PA: Chelsea House Publisher (see Chapter Six).

Stratton, J. 1981. *Pioneer Women, Voices from the Kansas Frontier*. New York: Simon & Schuster.

Trupin, S. 1984. *Dakota Diaspora, Memoirs of a Jewish Homesteader*. Berkeley: Alternative Press.

Waters, F. 1998. *Brave Are My People: Indian Heroes Are Not Forgotten*. Vine Deloria, Jr., foreword. Athens, OH: Ohio University Press.

Wilder, L. I. (1867–1957). 1981. *Little House on the Prairie* (1935). New York: Harper Collins Publishers. Children's novel about life on the frontier.

Works Cited for Teachers

Brox, J. 1995. *Here and Nowhere Else: Late Seasons of a Farm and Family*. Boston: Beacon Press.

Buber, M. 1970. *I and Thou*. New York: Scribners.

Jefferson, T. 1999. *Notes on the State of Virginia, 1784–1785*, Frank Shuffelton, ed. New York: Penguin Books. Jefferson argues for keeping America agrarian.

Marx, L. 1964. *The Machine in the Garden: Technology and the Pastoral Ideal in America*. New York: Oxford University Press. (Includes passages from Robert Beverly's *History and Present State of Virginia*, 1705, 75–88)

Nash, R. 1982. *Wilderness and the American Mind*, 3rd ed. New Haven, CT: Yale University Press. (Includes excerpts from Michael Wigglesworth's *God's Controversy with New England* and Cotton Mather's *Magnalia*.)

Stackpole, E. et. al. 1973. *History of the Town of Durham, New Hampshire*. NH Publishing Company.

Turner, F. J. 1962. *The Frontier in American History*. New York: Holt, Rinehart and Winston.

Additional Teacher Resources

Buell, L. 1995. *The Environmental Imagination: Thoreau, Nature Writing and the Formation of American Culture*. Cambridge, MA: Belknap Press of Harvard University Press.

Owens, C. 1984. *John James Audubon, The Birds of America*. The National Gallery of Art, Washington, DC. Exhibit brochure.

Smith, H. N. 1971. *Virgin Land: The American West as Symbol and Myth* (1950). Cambridge, MA: Harvard University Press.

Hudson River School Sources

"American Paradise: The World of the Hudson River School," (1987), The Metropolitan Museum of Art, NY. Distributed by Harry N. Abrams, Inc., 100 Fifth Ave., NY, NY 10011; an exhibit catalogue with 85 full-color and 172 black-and-white illustrations. Slides and accompanying text for "American Paradise" are available through the Uris Library and Resource Center of the Metropolitan Museum, NY, 212-570-3788.

Novak, B. 1995. *Nature and Culture: American Landscape and Painting*. New York: Oxford University Press. A study of Hudson River School artists and philosophy. (Reviewed by Robert Hughes in "The Unedited Manuscript of God," *Time*, August 11, 1980, 68.)

Hughes, R. 1994. "America's Prodigy," *Time*, July 11, 54. An essay on Thomas Cole.

McGuigan, C. 1987. "The Search for Paradise Lost, The Hudson River School Saw America as Eden," *Newsweek*. New York. October 12. Volume 110. Issue 15, 82.

Videos

Green Means, c. 1993. KQED, Inc., Environmental Media, P.O. Box 99, Beaufort, SC 29901. Two ninety-minute cassettes; thirty-two five-minute segments. "Less Is More" features Vicki Robbin and Joe Dominguez, writers of *Your Money or Your Life*.

Heartland. 1979. 95 minutes. Richard Pearce, director. Wilderness Women Productions, HBO video. Based on the life of Elinore Pruitt Stewart.

Land of the Eagle, "The Great Encounter." 60 min., PBS Video, 1320 Braddock Place, Alexandria VA 22314. Wildlife of Chesapeake Bay and settlers' journals from Roanoke Island. First of a series on history of American settlement and environmental issues.

Living the Good Life with Helen and Scott Nearing. 30 min., by John Hoskyns-Abrahall, Bullfrog Films, Oley, PA 19547, 215-779-8226.

"*The Wilderness Idea: John Muir, Gifford Pinchot, and The Great Battle for Wilderness*" (1989). 58 min. color, and "*Wild by Law: The Rise of Environmentalism and the Creation of the Wilderness Act*" (1991). 60 min., color. The story of Aldo Leopold, Bob Marshall, and Howard Zahniser and the passage of the Wilderness Act. Films by Lawrence Hott and Diane Garey. Florentine Films. (Direct Cinema Ltd. P. O. Box 1003, Santa Monica, CA 90410)

Slides

Slides of Yosemite National Park and Mono Lake with text of narration from John Muir's *My First Summer in the Sierra* available from E. Rous, Adams Point Road, Durham, NH 03824.

5

Issues and Actions

October 1976

Driving our old Econoline van, we descended today through geological time on narrow jeep roads into the silent depths of Canyonlands. Our campsite on the canyon floor is enclosed by overhanging redrock walls and strange, anthropomorphic shapes. Into one crevice, we have placed a jack-o-lantern, and the glowing pumpkin sends its orange light over the rock face to create a weird and eerie Halloween scene for our two-year-old daughter. Above all we feel the silence, each footfall, even a whisper, echoed back by our surroundings. Abbey country!

August 1993

It is the fourth day of a backpacking trip in Alaska's Brooks Range. We landed by seaplane on the Arctic divide and now hike along the Unakserak River to its confluence with the Alatna. Following animal trails that randomly emerge then melt away, we see no signs of humans, only tracks and scat of moose, wolf, and bear. We are trespassers in a wild country, a land that, until now, existed only in the dream world first envisioned when I read John McPhee's *Coming into the Country*.

The areas I study with students are areas I first learned to love through reading. Edward Abbey's passion for the American Southwest made me yearn to experience his world and despair at incursions that threaten it. And Alaska and its people are so vividly portrayed by John McPhee that I had roots in the state before I ever entered it. The literature of both regions features issues and interest groups that could be anywhere. By studying the environmental problems of a particular region, I hope to help students gain understanding of complex issues, practice critical thinking skills, and learn a collaborative approach to problem solving. Any area one loves and knows well can be studied in a similar way.

The Southwest

Using Edward Abbey's *Desert Solitaire* as the central text, we explore some key environmental issues in the southwest, including water supplies and rights, dam building, wilderness designation, and land use in national parks. To supplement *Desert Solitaire*, we also read excerpts from:

Encounters with the Archdruid by John McPhee, about David Brower, former head of the Sierra Club and founder of Friends of the Earth and Earth Island Institute
Cadillac Desert by Marc Reisner (with a public television documentary by the same name), a history of the settlement of the Southwest and the politicization of water resources
The Journals of Major John Wesley Powell on His Exploration of the Grand Canyon of the Colorado
The Place No One Knew, photographs by Eliot Porter of Glen Canyon
Materials about Glen Canyon Dam from the Bureau of Reclamation

Videos
Land of the Eagle, "Living at the Edge," on the Sonora desert
Interactions in Science and Society, #12: "Wilderness," ITV (instructional television video) series
Edward Abbey, A Voice in the Wilderness. Canyon Productions. Documentary film of Abbey's life and work

Links to Other Chapters
Animal Dreams by Barbara Kingsolver (Chapter Six)
"The Wilderness Idea: John Muir, Gifford Pinchot, and the Great Battle for Wilderness." 1989. Lawrence Hott and Diane Garey. Florentine Films. Highlights the controversy over the Hetch Hetchy Dam (Chapter Four)

Edward Abbey (1927–1989) came from a small Appalachian town in Pennsylvania and spent fifteen years as a part-time ranger in the West, a landscape he described and defended with passion, cynicism, and wit in twenty-one books. He writes with a directness, even an abrasiveness, that students find refreshing. His most famous book, *Desert Solitaire*, is a journal of two summers spent in Arches National Monument (now Park). Students get hooked on this book as soon as they read Abbey's introductory statement that he hopes people, particularly government officials, will find his views offensive!

The chapters of *Desert Solitaire* can be read independently of each other, and I do not assign the entire book. While this approach frustrates some students (and I encourage them to read the whole book), it is welcome to others and enables me to introduce a broader range of materials and writers. I first assign the introduction, the first three chapters ("The First Morning," "Solitaire," and "The Serpents of Paradise") and the rabbit-killing episode in the fourth chapter ("Cliffrose and

Bayonets"), and ask students to note (in reader response logs or with homework questions) Abbey's beliefs about nature, his writing style and personality, and his surroundings in Arches National Monument. "Rocks" and "Havasu," good adventure and mystery stories, are optional, extra-credit readings. The basic reading assignments in Abbey take five days. With additional reading in McPhee, Powell, and Reisner and time for films, research, and debates, the book can take two to three weeks.

In the opening chapters, park ranger Abbey makes it clear that he delights in the rugged isolation of his small trailer set back on the then-unpaved roads of Arches. He jokes about his rough workdays spent "watching cloud formations." He enjoys the terrain more than the passing tourists who seem to have only two things on their minds: how long it takes to see the park, and the location of the nearest bathroom. The early chapters provide an opportunity to show a video about the ecology of the desert (such as *Land of the Eagle*, "Living on the Edge") or to collaborate with an earth science teacher on the formation of canyons and rock arches.

I ask students to write about this question: Considering the juniper tree, the snakes, the generator and flashlight, and the rabbit in the first four chapters, what are Abbey's beliefs about how people should relate to nature? As Abbey searches to find his own role in the midst of his "desert solitaire," he experiments with killing a rabbit to experience the predator-prey cycle, rejects flashlights and his generator because they separate him from his environs, rejects the personification of nature, keeps away both rattlesnakes and mice with a pet gopher snake, and wonders what the snake and its mate wish to communicate as they slither toward him.

We next read "Polemic," Abbey's essay on the ravages of "industrial tourism," particularly its damaging effects on national parks. I ask students to explain the inherent conflicts in the National Park Service's stated mission to "provide for the enjoyment of same in such manner and by such means as will leave them unimpaired for the enjoyment of future generations." If "enjoyment" means providing concessions, accommodations, and easy road access to increasing numbers of people (136 million people in 1964, double that in 1994), then protection for future generations is threatened. Combining this chapter with current accounts of crowding in the parks (examples: *Time*, July 25, 1994; *Newsweek*, August 1, 1994), the class explores the national parks' problems. We list and discuss Abbey's proposed solutions: halting road construction, eliminating cars from the parks, and using existing roads for walkers, bikers, and buses serving elderly and handicapped visitors. Are these fair proposals? Should people be forced to walk or bike? Can the parks dictate how people view them? Some students argue that there should be places for those willing to make an effort, that the effort will increase the appreciation. Others counter that this position is elitist. Does insuring a wilderness experience for a few impose a hardship on the majority?

To bring these issues closer to home, I ask students how many of them have climbed Mt. Washington, the highest mountain in the northeast, and how many have driven the auto road to the top. There can be strong feelings about each mode of access. Some students cannot imagine hiking the mountain, yet were glad to be able to experience the summit. The hikers resent the crowds and concessions at the mountaintop. I sometimes divide the class into small groups to discuss recreational groups with conflicting interests regarding land use: cross-country skiers and snowmobilers, walkers and trailbikers, hikers and hunters, campers and preservationists. Each group presents the pros and cons of various land uses to the rest of the class and proposes ways to make the uses compatible. Dilemmas like these face every community; if students discuss complex local issues in which they take an interest, the challenges of solving regional and national issues may become more understandable.

As we go on to read "Down the River," we discuss the Grand Canyon exploration, modern controversies over dam building, and Abbey's beliefs about wilderness. When Abbey rafts the Colorado River through Glen Canyon, he journeys through a silent and beautiful world soon to be buried by Glen Canyon Dam under the waters of Lake Powell. His belief in the need for wilderness and his anger at the coming inundation are made passionately clear in the "Down the River" chapter.

We discuss Abbey's belief that "wilderness is not a luxury but a necessity of the human spirit, and as vital to our lives as water and good bread." Although Abbey describes his river trip as one of "effortless peace, deeper into Eden," he rejects a romanticized view of nature: "the love of wilderness is more than a hunger for what is always beyond reach; it is also an expression of loyalty to the earth . . . the true original sin is the blind destruction for the sake of greed of this natural paradise which lies all around us—if only we were worthy of it." And paradise, in Abbey's view, is every part of nature, "not a garden of bliss and changeless perfection" but a place of death and destruction as well as beauty and creation. "Paradise . . . is with us yet, the here and now, the actual, tangible, dogmatically real earth on which we stand." Not all of my students agree that their idea of paradise includes mosquitoes, rattle snakes, and poison ivy!

In conjunction with this reading, I ask students to brainstorm what they think of when they hear the word "wild." Here is one class's list:

uncontrolled	animals	peace
chaotic	jungle	escape
beautiful	no people	adventure
savage	uncivilized	frightening
untouched	deserted	mountains

The mixture of innocence and violence in this list reflects our conflicting views of wilderness as a place of peace and goodness to be preserved, or a fearful place to be tamed and conquered. In either case, Abbey's view that paradise is of this world and not apart from it supports the current emphasis on making all aspects of our life on the planet sustainable, not just preserving pockets of wilderness.

The ITV video on "Wilderness," #12 from the *Interactions in Science and Society* series, provides a good basis for discussion of the meaning and role of wilderness. The film defines wilderness as "anywhere people aren't." It presents another opportunity for students to consider the range of perspectives in American culture toward land, and they can take notes on the aesthetic, recreational, psychological, material, and scientific reasons for wilderness preservation.

As Abbey floats down the Colorado, he recalls with admiration the 1869 mapping expedition through Grand Canyon made by Major John Wesley Powell. We take a diversion along with Abbey and read excerpts from Powell's journal, a combination of eloquent description, scientific observation, and dramatic adventure. Powell traveled with ten men in three wooden dories on a journey that took three months and covered nine hundred miles. By the end, they were dangerously low of food. Along the way, Powell, who lost an arm in the Civil War, scrambled up steep rock faces carrying a transit and barometer to measure distances and depths in the canyon (a mile at the deepest). Although thousands of people now take float trips through the Grand Canyon, the fact that Powell was the first meant that he never knew what dangers lay ahead. Three of his men left the river a few days before the journey's end, only to be killed by Indians, while the rest of the party emerged safely from the mouth of the canyon. Modern river guidebooks mark the spot where this fateful split occurred.

Before leaving the "Down the River" chapter, students consider the pros and cons of damming rivers. In addition to Abbey's opinions, we refer to Marc Reisner's *Cadillac Desert*, John McPhee's *Encounters with the Archdruid*, and current news articles about dam relicensing. In 1963, Glen Canyon Dam was completed, filling in canyons explored by Powell and Abbey and backing up the Colorado River for two hundred miles to create Lake Powell. Information about the dam and lake are available from the Bureau of Reclamation and the Glen Canyon Recreation Area (see bibliography). The dam, part of a 150–year effort to irrigate the West, generates electricity which in turn helps the Bureau of Reclamation pay for irrigation projects. Inspired by the depression-era success of Hoover Dam downstream of Grand Canyon, the Bureau embarked on a massive dam building program, until by the 1990s there were 75,000 dams built on United States rivers. The Colorado River is now so "controlled" that its waters no longer reach its mouth. The convoluted politics and economics of the West's use of water and dam building are thoroughly documented in *Cadillac Desert* and the public television documentary by the same name. The public television *Planet Under Pressure* video on "Water" is also a valuable resource on problems with water pollution and diminishing groundwater, particularly in the Ogallala Aquifer in the western plains.

While power and irrigation were the main considerations when dams were first federally licensed, a 1986 amendment to the Federal Power Act says the Federal Energy Regulatory Commission (FERC) must also take into consideration fish and wildlife habitat, recreational use, and aesthetics when relicensing dams. One of the first dams to be torn down under these new regulations was the Edwards Dam in Augusta, Maine (summer 1999).

In *Encounters with the Archdruid*, writer John McPhee brings together two powerful and opposing forces of preservation and development, "archdruid" David Brower, and Floyd Dominy, head of the Bureau of Reclamation (both are also featured in the video, "Cadillac Desert"). McPhee, Brower, and Dominy travel on the newly created Lake Powell, then down the Colorado below Glen Canyon dam through Grand Canyon. As Brower and Dominy square off on the virtues and evils of dam building, McPhee leaves readers to make up their own minds. Brower vehemently opposes Glen Canyon Dam and compares it to flooding the Sistine Chapel. He expounds on the problems of siltation (9.5 million tons of silt settle behind the dam daily), the effects of scheduled water releases on riparian wildlife, the loss of water through evaporation, and the interruption of the river's natural scouring action on the formation of the canyon. Dominy calls his figures "unreliable" and his logic "nonsense." When he asks Brower to name the best source of electricity, the only answer Brower gives is "flashlight batteries." The writing is McPhee at his best, choosing details, finding irony and humor, describing characters, and repeating dialogue, but letting readers decide for themselves. Or does he? I ask students if they can detect any preference for either Dominy or Brower in McPhee's choice of detail. Whatever his attitude toward dams, McPhee's belief in the ultimate power of the river and nature comes through in his closing description of going through Lava Falls: "Water rose up in tons through the bottom of the raft. It came in from the left, the right, and above. It felt great. It covered us, pounded us, lifted us, and heaved us scudding to the base of the rapid."

There are interesting cross-references in these readings for students to discover. Abbey camps in the side canyon Powell called Music Temple. Further on, a campfire made by Abbey gets out of control, burning trees and shrubs, and the aftermath of this fire is documented by Eliot Porter in *The Place No One Knew*. When Brower wishes for the destruction of Glen Canyon Dam, Dominy suggests he read *Desert Solitaire* in which Abbey fantasizes that the button meant to open the dam would instead explode it, "reducing the great dam to a heap of rubble in the path of the river. The splendid new rapids thus created we will name Floyd E. Dominy Falls . . ."

Before leaving the Southwest, we return to *Desert Solitaire* to read the last two chapters and consider a final question: What are Abbey's beliefs about life and the fate of nature? In "The Deadman at Grandview Point," Abbey joins a search party for a missing man and contemplates the meaning of life, death, and his place in the universe; and in "Bedrock and Paradox," he states his conviction that nature will survive our most destructive attempts to change it. Abbey closes the book with questions about change: "When I return will it be the same? Will I be the same? Will anything ever be quite the same again? If I return."

Students often compare Abbey and Thoreau in personality, tone, and philosophy. Both chose solitude, at least temporarily, and both resented technological progress. My students find both men self-righteous, but one student astutely observed that while Thoreau seems to judge the reader, Abbey assumes the reader is on his side!

Writing and Projects The Southwest case study introduces students to the complexities of land use issues. How are the various, and often conflicting, interests of farmers, businesses, engineers, animals and fish, and outdoor enthusiasts to be met? Is the attempt to change nature on a large scale for human purposes a moral, aesthetic, or economic issue?

The reading in *Desert Solitaire* and supplemental reading and internet searches provide at least three interwoven threads for students to follow: adventure and recreation, water issues, and the controversy over dam building. I have explored these topics in a number of ways, always starting with student research. Students have written individual papers in which they set forth the pros and cons of an issue such as dam building and conclude with their own opinion, even if they cannot totally resolve the issues. Students have role-played stake holders in a controversy and staged a simulated hearing on a dam building proposal or an irrigation project. The class has also held debates in which various members argue for or against a specific proposal, such as whether or not to remove Glen Canyon Dam. While students enjoy the competitive format of debates, I have also experimented with formats that encourage negotiation such as those organized by the Environmental Issues Forums (see end of chapter).

The same skills are developed by combining literature and research to study America's last frontier, Alaska.

Alaska

Like the Southwest, Alaska offers students a look at adventure, nature studies, and an array of intense environmental and political-economic issues. Some of our best, modern nonfiction writers and environmentalists—John McPhee, Barry Lopez,

Joe McGinniss, Margaret and Olaus Murie, Robert Marshall, Jon Krakauer—have focused their attention on Alaska and the Arctic tundra. McPhee's *Coming into the Country* (1977) was my first introduction to Alaska and is still a favorite, but in recent years I have taught from Joe McGinniss' *Going to Extremes* (1980) because my students find it more accessible.

While a few of McGinniss' anecdotes might be a little risqué for some readers, they draw students into Alaska's issues in the late 1970s. By the last chapter on "The Brooks Range," McGinniss transcends the mild sensationalism of the early chapters with his appreciation of the beauty of Alaska's wilderness. One problem with reading McGinniss is that students can come away with negative stereotypes of both Native Alaskans and people from "outside." To counteract these stereotypes, I use Barry Lopez' accounts of native wisdom in *Arctic Dreams* or documentary films of traditional Inuit culture. John McPhee's *Coming into the Country* describes native Alaskan skills and traditions and includes material in which Eskimos and Indians speak for themselves about their plight in the modern world.

Before I give any assigned reading, I find out how much students know about Alaska, using a blank map of the state and a true-false oral quiz. I should do this more often because students enjoy it and get motivated to learn more. I take the information in the "quiz" from the opening chapters of *Going to Extremes*; we learn that there are four time zones in Alaska, the majority of Alaska is green half of the year, the only permanent snow is in the southern portion of the state (where precipitation is heaviest), Alaska was not covered by glaciers in the Ice Age, there are approximately one million people in the state (about the same as New Hampshire), and Alaska has fewer road miles than Vermont. Many students do not know that the largest city, Anchorage, is not the capital, or that Juneau, the capital, cannot be reached by road.

The final episode of the *Land of the Eagle* video series, "Last Frontier" gives a good overview of environmental history and current issues in Alaska. The film traces the devastating effects of Russian and American exploration and hunting, including the introduction of disease, starvation, slavery, and alcoholism to natives, and the decimation of fur seals, sea otters, walrus, and whales. In the closing portion of the film, we see the conflicting interests of oil and wildlife, and witness the effects of the 1989 Exxon Valdez oil spill in Prince William Sound. With the possibility of new sources of oil in the Arctic National Wildlife Refuge, the question of oil versus tundra preservation is still unresolved.

Like *Desert Solitaire*, *Going to Extremes* is written episodically, in a journal style, and it is possible to assign only selected chapters. Students are more likely to be engaged in the book's environmental and cultural questions if they are reading with a purpose. Therefore, I have individuals or groups of students choose issues to follow in the book, do further research, then present their information and opinions to the class. McPhee's *Coming into the Country* is also a source of information. Issues we have studied include:

- the Native Claims Settlement Act
- the Trans Alaska pipeline
- the Homesteading Act and open-to-entry land program
- the Arctic National Wildlife Refuge
- assimilation and preservation of native culture
- local control and states' rights versus federal law

In the first five chapters of *Going to Extremes*, McGinniss describes his journey by Alaska state ferry from Seattle to Haines with an eclectic group of Alaskans ("The Ferry"), the drive from Haines to Anchorage in a truck he calls "a hair dryer on wheels" ("The Road"), the oil boom's effects on Alaska's biggest city ("Anchorage"), and ice fog, cold, and the pipeline in Fairbanks ("The First Day North" and "Prudhoe Bay"). From these chapters, laced with amusing and ironic anecdotes about the extremes of Alaskan climate and lifestyles, students get a sense of who comes to Alaska, why they come, and what they find there.

"The Village" raises the poignant issue of how a young Inuit named Olive can find her place in the modern white world. Unhappy with her restricted life in a village of two hundred, she goes to work in Washington D.C., where she is even more alienated and out of place. The chapter shows how television disrupts native traditions like carving fish traps or celebrating the Slavic version of Christmas. As the following comments show, students find no easy answers to the dilemmas raised:

"The government probably shouldn't decide that the village needs television, but if people want TV, no one should tell them they can't have it either."
"But what is the point of people on the edge of the Bering Sea watching programs like "Starsky and Hutch" and "Charlie's Angels?"
"It will just make them dissatisfied with their lives."
"Yes, but it will also make them better informed about the world."
"You can't stop progress. If there is an easier way of life or a life with more luxuries, people are going to want it."
"There should be programs about their own traditions too."
"What about Olive?" What do you think will become of her?" I ask. But they are at a loss.

Olive joins the troubled characters in literature and real life who must bridge the gap between two cultures. Students often conclude that the best solution is to be respectful of all traditions and appreciate what each culture can teach us. The loss of cultural diversity is as tragic as the loss of ecological diversity, and the causes are similar: the failure to appreciate the inherent value in what exists and the belief that we have the right to change what exists to suit our own purposes. The simultaneous exploitation of native peoples and natural resources by Europeans in the East and by Russians in Alaska makes this causal link explicit. Students interested in lost indigenous cultures are fascinated and moved by *Ishi in Two Worlds* by Theodora Kroeber, the true story of the last surviving Yakima Indian in California.

The next chapter we read is "Crescent Lake" in which McGinniss tries a solitary, wilderness experience and hates it! The chapter begins with a sourdough's journal kept in 1917 for the seven months leading up to the writer's death in the wilderness. When McGinniss' three day experiment stretches into five days because of a blizzard, he begins to think he may meet the same end. Students compare his experience to Thoreau's sojourn at Walden Pond or to Chris McCandless in *Into the Wild*, and write about their own reactions to isolation and solitude.

In "Kahiltna Glacier," McGinniss joins Beth and Jack Hebert on the glacier before they ascend McKinley and hears about their three winters homesteading in the western Brooks Range. The chapter starts provocative discussion about why they went (it was beautiful and exciting), why they left (the valley got "crowded" with seven other cabins), and whether people should still have the right to build and live wherever they choose (1973 was the last year of Alaska's open-to-entry land program). At the end of the book, McGinniss' hiking partner, Ray Bane, objects to the Hebert's cabin and argues that "wilderness is to visit, not to live in." The chapter closes with yet another amusing profile, this one of a ragged but famed and skilled bush pilot, Cliff Hudson.

Having focused on personal experiences and anecdotes, McGinniss turns to political issues facing all of Alaska in the second "Anchorage" chapter. He describes the amount of federally controlled land in Alaska (more than half of the state), the amount turned over to natives in the Native Claims Settlement Act (44 million acres in 1971), and the proposal to set aside 114 million acres as wilderness, national monument, and national park. The remaining federal land in Alaska and 104 million acres of state land would be opened to development. McGinniss attends a hearing on the bill in Anchorage and quotes speakers on both sides of this proposal. I have students read this testimony aloud in class and role play advocates and opponents of the bill. They write and discuss their beliefs about Alaska's future and who should decide. By now, the pro-development and pro-preservation arguments presented are familiar to them.

Some of the land debated, and ultimately legally protected, is the setting of the last two chapters, "Bettles," and "The Brooks Range." McGinniss goes on a twelve day hike with National Park Service employees Ray Bane and John Kauffmann, to scout the proposed Gates of the Arctic National Park. (The same John Kaufmann appears in "The Encircled River" section of McPhee's *Coming into the Country*.)

Hiking with them is Boyd Norton, a nature photographer, who eventually published pictures of their trip in *Alaska: Wilderness Frontier*. The benefits of preserving a vast wilderness area continue to be discussed by the men as they travel. Many of their experiences—with bears, mosquitoes, tussocks, stream crossings, midnight twilight, and the sense of trespassing in the animals' kingdom—are so similar to my stories of being in the Brooks Range that students ask if we were all on the same trip.

The climax of the book comes when the men discover a hidden valley at the base of Cocked Hat Mountain that contains a mile-long meadow with "a tiny lake, like a liquid mirror, . . . nestled in the soft tundra, reflecting the towering grandeur" of the mountain walls on all sides. Ray Bane's journal continues: "My first reaction to the scene that confronted us . . . was awe. It was like entering a massive religious cathedral, empty of people. The air is heavy with silence and holiness." McGinniss describes the place as "Shangri-La. The meadow so pristine, so silent, so still. . . ."

> No one had anticipated that we would ever come upon such a place. No one had suspected its existence. This had begun as a wilderness trip; as a hike in a remote mountain range. But, as of now, it had transcended even that, and had carried each of us to a new and unexpected level of experience. We had been allowed to discover, and to enter, and to remain, for a few hours, in such a place, and it seemed we had been given a rare gift of immeasurable value. None of us was quite sure how to respond. The fact that, in all likelihood, we were the only human beings who had walked through this sacred meadow, who had sat high on this western barrier and looked back at this remnant of paradise, was more than I, at least, knew how to respond to. (1980, 281)

When students look closely at the language of these descriptions, they notice that both men use religious and mystical imagery. They "had been allowed to discover and to enter"; they "had been given a rare gift." What force is doing the "allowing" and "giving?" Being in the valley "transcends" adventure and is "a new and unexpected level of experience." Students will recognize this response by now as a deeply rooted human reaction to nature.

It is also significant that part of the power of being in this valley comes from the men's belief that they are the first to enter it. We discuss reasons for the appeal of being in untouched "virgin" land and also the dangers implicit in this desire. If the ultimate experience is being where no one has been before, what happens—to us and to the land—when everyone has been everywhere? (The relationship between sexual and environmental politics is explored in depth in Annette Kolodny's *The Lay of the Land*.) The discussion brings us again to Abbey's conclusion that "paradise" is here and now and that we must work to support a sustainable balance in our everyday world.

I ask students to contrast the tone and experiences at the end of the book with that of the earlier chapters, and to discuss the significance of the change. They note that the earlier portions of the book dealing with people are light and amusing, sometimes cynical, sometimes admiring, while the end of the book dealing with nature is serious and spiritual, full of awe at the power of bears and the beauty of the wilderness. One student said this suggests that while people may err and struggle to find their way, there is an enduring power in nature that can sustain us even as we flounder.

Writing and Projects The reading in McGinniss takes approximately seven days. Class time is divided between discussing the reading, watching slides or related videos, and doing further research on chosen environmental issues in Alaska. We might start class with a reading quiz or a quick write on an issue raised by the reading. Such in-class writings give students time to reflect on the reading, give everyone something to contribute to discussion, and, when collected, tell me how carefully students read. Reader response journals kept at home also serve these purposes well.

When the book is finished, the individuals or groups who gathered information about issues such as the pipeline or land preservation make presentations to the whole class. These presentations may take the form of poster displays around the room with students circulating from poster to poster, taking notes and evaluating the information. Students might prepare videos or computer-generated graphics. They might give a panel presentation in which each member represents a point of view about the group's issue, presents information, uses graphics to illustrate points, and engages the class in discussion of the issues. I give written guidelines for the sources students should use (internet, reference books, articles), the oral presentation (length, content, graphics, questions for the class), and the written follow-up (give arguments from all sides, state your own opinion and support it, cite sources). The clearer the guidelines, the better the presentations.

At the end of the book and after the presentations, I ask students to respond to a choice of questions, in journals if these were assigned, or as in-class essays. Students may generate their own writing questions. Some of the questions are:

- Who comes to Alaska and why? Give specific (at least three) examples from the book. Describe their interests and lifestyles. How do their interests conflict?
- Discuss McGinniss' writing style and consider how he creates his picture of Alaska. Consider: the overall structure of the book, sources of information,

ways of conveying information, use of humor, tone, objectivity versus subjectivity, and descriptive detail and imagery.

- Describe ways that traditional Eskimo life has been affected by white western culture. Discuss both the nature of the white influences and the Eskimo reactions. Consider pipeline work, the relationship between whites and natives in Barrow, the conflicts between old traditions and new white customs as shown in "The Village." Be specific. What suggestions can you make for improving the relations between white and Eskimo culture?
- Choose one of the environmental controversies discussed in the book (the pipeline, new drilling, creating a new national park, states rights versus federal regulation, the Native Claims Settlement Act, homesteading), discuss the various perspectives on this controversy as presented by the book and by classmates' presentations, and give your own opinion with explanation and support. Do not choose the topic you presented to class.

Presentations and final writing take several more days, so in all I spend about two weeks studying Alaska. The end-of chapter bibliography suggests individual choice readings to supplement this unit. I also watch newspapers and magazines like *Backpacker* or *Outside* for current news about Alaska. For example, Jon Krakauer's story about Chris McCandless (*Into the Wild*) first appeared in *Outside*.

Wolves

Whenever I give students a choice of case studies, wolves are their favorite option. A wolf study is a logical follow-up to studying Alaska, and McPhee's *Coming into the Country* presents some of the arguments for and against wolf control. Wolves offer an interdisciplinary topic that is interesting, timely, and has an array of good accompanying literature. We focus on two points of controversy: the reintroduction of wolves to Yellowstone National Park and a three-year wolf reduction program in the area around Fairbanks, Alaska started in 1993. I have written to Yellowstone and to Alaska's Department of Fish and Game for primary source materials, including research, news clippings, and hearing transcripts, on both of these issues. There is also a wealth of material in the media and on the Internet (see bibliography).

Before choosing sides for a debate on wolf hunts or wolf reintroduction, I try to discover students' natural leanings. I put a strip of masking tape on the floor and divide it equally into five sections. One end of the "value line" represents the point of view that wolves are dangerous predators who need to be controlled; the other end represents the view that wolves are beneficial to the ecosystem and should be protected. I role play each point of view, then ask students to stand anywhere along the line in a position that most closely represents their own view. I ask students to explain why they are standing where they are. In my own area, where people have no actual experience with wolves (though we have coyotes), students tend to support wolf protection.

I now divide the class into four teams: pro and con wolf re-introduction; pro and con Alaska wolf reduction. Some students may have to argue a point of view they do not support, but this is a good exercise in understanding the other side of a controversy. Students gather arguments for their side throughout the wolf unit and debate their questions when the reading is finished.

Along with research, we use three texts that can be a source of facts and arguments for the debaters:

Dayton O. Hyde's *Don Coyote* (1986)
Farley Mowat's *Never Cry Wolf* (1963)
Barry Lopez' *Of Wolves and Men* (1978)

There are both problems and strengths in the Hyde and Mowat texts. Hyde's book is about coyotes, which are not the same as wolves, a fact students sometimes forget. On the other hand, the history of the treatment of coyotes has much in common with the treatment of wolves. Hyde is a humorous writer with strong roots in the West. As a rancher, his argument that coyotes are part of a natural ecological balance and actually help rather than hurt a farm is all the more powerful. Hyde recounts his adventures (and misadventures) befriending the wild "Don Coyote," raising coyote pups, and building a dam to restore an ancient lake to his ranch. In the process, he learns to appreciate the benefits of fostering a natural system of checks and balances:

> What made me so different now from my neighbors was that they figured we humans had dominion over the land while I felt we had responsibility for it—for the soil; for every plant, bird, and animal that shared this planet with us; for the rivers, and for the air.

Farley Mowat's ability to poke fun at himself is equal to Hyde's. That and his passionate defense of wildlife have made him a popular nature writer who effectively raises readers' awareness of the plight of wolves, whales (*A Whale for the Killing*), woodland caribou (*People of the Deer*), and native peoples of the Arctic (*A Desperate People*). Once students get past the opening chapter satirizing Canadian bureaucracy, they really like *Never Cry Wolf*. The book teaches them much about wolf behavior and about negative stereotypes of wolves. Its drawback is that it errs on the side of idealizing and overly romanticizing wolves. For example, while wolves can exist on small rodents such as mice, they most often hunt large game. And while they usually hunt sick, wounded, or old animals, this is not always true.

113

The book that is most honest about putting wolf stereotypes, both negative and positive, into proper perspective is Barry Lopez' *Of Wolves and Men.* Lopez reminds us that we do not really know much about wolf behavior: They have not been systematically studied until recently and the percentage of observed wolf behavior is minuscule. Lopez divides his book into four sections: scientific observations, Native American beliefs, a history of wolf extermination, and the psychology of our view of wolves. Students use Lopez to gather information for their debate topics, or I divide them into four groups to report on each of Lopez' categories.

When we are ready to debate, opposing teams sit in designated pro and con seats. The issue is stated in the form of a resolution, for example, "Resolved that wolves should be reintroduced to Yellowstone National Park." Students have determined ahead of time who will give opening arguments, ask questions, make rebuttals, and give a summation. They have specified lengths of time for each phase of the debate. (Lynn Goodnight's *Getting Started in Debate* outlines procedures for organizing debates.) While formal debate inhibits the free-flowing discussion students are used to, it forces them to be well prepared and organized with facts and arguments. Other members of the class or invited observers determine who won the debate, based on a set of guidelines determined by the class ahead of time. Guidelines include extent, specificity and accuracy of data; organization and logic; effectiveness of counter arguments; and clarity and strength of presentation. Students need to be reminded that they are deciding who debated most effectively, not which side they agree with. Following the debate, the whole class can discuss the issue.

In addition to debates, we do the usual array of journals, reading quizzes, and opinion writings in connection with this reading. I try to arrange a field trip to a site with wolves such as Wolf Hollow in Ipswich, Massachusetts or a farm near us with wolf hybrids. We watch a documentary video, "The Wolf, Real or Imagined" (Weide and Hudak), and sometimes the film version of *Never Cry Wolf.* Some students will have seen Kevin Costner's *Dances with Wolves.* Part of the discussion of these films focuses on how our vision of wolves has changed since "Little Red Riding Hood" and why this might be. The closing lines of the *Never Cry Wolf* film provide a good basis for discussing how even the act of observing nature can change it: "In the end, there were no simple answers—no villains, no heroes, only silence. It all began when I first saw the wolves. By the act of watching them with the eyes of a man, I had pointed the way for those that followed—I turned away and didn't watch them go."

While studying wolves, we might return to Aldo Leopold and read "Thinking Like a Mountain" from *A Sand County Almanac,* in which he describes his participation in the shooting of a wolf and her pups. The video "Wild by Law" reenacts the episode and gives this text:

> We reached the old wolf in time to watch a fierce green fire dying in her eyes. I realized then, and have known ever since, that there was something new to me in those eyes—something known only to her and to the mountain. I was young then, and full of trigger-itch; I thought that because fewer wolves meant more deer, that no wolves would mean hunters' paradise. But after seeing the green fire die, I sensed that neither the wolf nor the mountain agreed with such a view. (138–139)

Seeing the defoliation of mountains and subsequent die-offs of deer that occurred when wolves were exterminated changed Leopold's views on wildlife management and taught him that all elements of a food chain are essential if the chain is to survive. This passage makes an impression on students and we draw on it for the debates. Leopold's insights are reinforced by using a Stella II computer modeling program that graphs changes in predator-prey populations. By experimenting with three variables—deer, vegetation, and wolf—students use the program to graph increases and decreases in populations over time and witness the results of eliminating predators from a system.

The discussion of the predator-prey relationship makes a logical opening for a discussion of hunting. While some of my students hunt, others oppose it. Fish and Game officers have come to class to discuss laws, game statistics, and game management philosophy and practice. Students share what they know about the animals they hunt and hunter safety. Those opposed to hunting present their views on animal rights and the need to bring natural predators back. The discussion between these two groups can be emotional, and I try to facilitate a dialogue that gives each group a new respect for the other's point of view.

Current Issues and Local Case Studies

At this point, students are ready to turn to current environmental questions and issues close to home. The skills of weighing evidence, understanding a variety of viewpoints, and trying to reach consensus are applied to environmental issues in our own time and place. In some cases, the students' research can also develop into action plans. There are many possibilities for local projects, and each classroom needs to get to know its community, its resources and problems, and the principal players. By contacting citizens and officials of local, state, and national groups personally, by mail, and by Internet, students have unlimited sources of information. I have used all of the following formats with students, but usually only one in a semester.

An Environmental Issues Scrapbook Students create a scrapbook of about forty articles about environmental news. These articles are collected over the course of a semester, arranged in an order students choose (e.g. from local to world issues or by type of issue), and presented with written commentary for each article or by section. We set aside several class days throughout the semester when each student shares one article. This provides a way to stay informed about current issues while we are in the midst of other units. At the end of the semester, each student gives a five-minute oral presentation on their scrapbook, telling how they organized the collection, what they learned in general from making the book, and describing one item in detail. We take time to pass the scrapbooks around the room and we display them in the school library.

Environmental Issues Forums The North American Association for Environmental Education has created guides to encourage dialogue within communities on four issues: solid waste, wetlands, clean water, and biodiversity. Each guide approaches its issue from three or four distinctly different and sometimes opposing perspectives. There are full-length (forty- to fifty-page) and shorter (sixteen-page) versions of each guide. The object of a single forum or a longer-term study group is to list the pros and cons of each perspective or "solution" and to work toward ways to resolve the issues. The information in the booklets is comprehensive and well balanced, and the format encourages respecting all opinions and working toward understanding and resolution.

I held two EIF forums on energy, a topic no longer part of the series. I divided the class into four groups, each representing one of the energy alternatives in the booklet (nuclear, fossil fuels, renewables, and conservation), and each group listed the pros and cons of their energy source on newsprint. To save time, we made the lists ahead and presented them at the forum. We invited parents, teachers, and two "experts" from the community—an electric utility executive and a researcher in acid rain. Because of the presence of adults, students took the issue quite seriously. We all particularly appreciated talking to parents and teachers in a new setting. The experts added a valuable level of knowledge, but students tended to focus the discussion too much around the visitors' opinions rather than their own. In the future, I will invite the specialists to class on a different day.

I-Search Projects An "I-Search" project, as developed by Ken Macrorie, is a form of research that asks students to begin their search with a question they care about, to tell the process of their search as well as their findings, and to give their conclusions about what they learn.

Every community has its own version of issues like endangered species, sewage treatment, solid waste, air and water quality, energy sources, wildlife and natural resource management, planning for development and open space, transportation, or wetlands. Every community has hot-button environmental issues that bring recreational, business, scientific, and aesthetic interests into play. To begin, each student brainstorms on paper questions they have about local environmental issues. Individual questions are shared in a group brainstorming session to trigger new ideas. I add what I know about our community to their pool of knowledge and suggest names of people and agencies to contact.

For the I-Search project, I require students to talk to someone in the community about their question, as well as use several print sources and Internet sites. The community contacts are documented by showing me a letter of inquiry, an addressed and stamped envelope, and notes from the interview. We talk about the importance of listening when interviewing and of asking follow-up questions based on what has been said, not just based on a prepared set of questions. Students are often very reluctant to make these community contacts and need encouragement. It helps some students if I make a preliminary call or if someone accompanies them for the interview. Hard though they find this, the skill of networking and using available resources is too important to ignore.

All students do an oral presentation and all turn in a final bibliography of sources, but a paper is only one of several forms the final project may take. Other options include a video, a bulletin board display, a multi-media computer presentation, or a documented action project (such as a roadside clean-up, starting a school recycling program, volunteering for an environmental monitoring program, etc.; see Appendix C). All final projects include a description and history of the issue, a discussion of causes and effects, pros and cons of possible solutions, and the researcher's recommendations.

Each student chooses a topic and develops a list of detailed questions. For example, Erin knew that a local river, the Lamprey, had recently been protected as a "wild and scenic river." She also knew that her friend's mother had been instrumental in bringing about this designation, so the I-Search question she chose was "Why should the Lamprey River be designated as "wild and scenic?" Her follow-up questions included:

How and why did this project start?
Who supported the designation and who opposed it? Why?
What does the designation mean about how the river can be used?

In conference, I suggested that she find out how long the process took and how consensus was finally reached; these ideas were added to her list. She also told me that she planned to do a hall display as her final project. The resources Erin turned to included her friend's mother, federal guidelines on wild and scenic rivers, testimony from hearings, plant and animal surveys conducted along the river, news articles, and river protection websites. Her final display included her own photographs of the river, lists of pros and cons for designating the river "wild and scenic," and a timeline of the approval process. She shared this display in her classroom oral report and later put it in a display case in the corridor.

Taking Action

> "It's hopeless. The problems are too big and things have gone too far. There's nothing we can do to save the environment."
> "I don't care. Even if things fall apart after I'm gone, I won't be here to see it."
> "Other people made this mess. Why does my generation have to deal with it?"

I've heard these views expressed by students far too often, and they are not the conclusions I am hoping for when I teach "Literature and the Land." Research shows that enjoyable childhood experiences in nature are the best way to insure adult stewardship of nature. Too much focus at a young age on vanishing whales and rainforests can lead to despair and resignation. Many students care deeply about the environment but feel overwhelmed. Some students are passive and un-aware, and a few apparently do not care. The latter need to be confronted with specific information about immediate problems—like the dramatic drop in sperm counts or the rise in skin cancer rates. To counteract feelings of hopelessness, I have students read about people who have worked for concrete, positive changes and encourage students to do projects in which they themselves can make a dif-ference. I hoped I was succeeding when I read this statement from Claire:

> With all of the environmental problems we face in this world, sometimes it feels like a hopeless cause, that whatever we fix will never equal the amount of damage done. But we need to learn that whatever is done, no matter how small, is a step in the right direction, and it is the combination of all of these small steps that will enable us to get to the goal . . of saving the earth's environment.
> —Claire H.

Readings about activists can be used to introduce community research and ac-tion projects or be interspersed while research is ongoing. This year, we reported on environmental activists while we read Barbara Kingsolver's *Animal Dreams*, a novel in which two sisters work to improve the environment, one as an agricul-tural worker in Nicaragua and one as a biology teacher in her hometown (see Chapter Six). Using materials such as those described below, students present in-dividual oral reports on the life and work of a range of activists—some famous, some relatively unknown.

One source of stories about ordinary individuals who have made a difference is the public television series of five-minute shorts called *Green Means*, narrated by Susan Stamberg. Examples of people and projects include Wyoming rancher Jack

Turnell who raises cattle while preserving native prairie grasses, New York volunteers who restore a Staten Island salt marsh, Wes Jackson who founded the Land Institute in Kansas to develop sustainable farming techniques, or students at Casa Grande High School in Petaluma, California, who cleaned up Adobe Creek and started a fish hatchery to restock it. In all, the video and the accompanying *Green Means* book present thirty-two international examples. The book, *Restoring the Earth* by John Berger is "about a few Americans who fervently believe a blighted environment is not acceptable and who are optimistic about restoring the Earth ecologically." In addition to conserving resources and preventing pollution, modern activists are working to restore damaged environments. One such activist is Marion Stoddart, a retired teacher, who helped clean up the Nashua River in Massachusetts, once one of the most polluted rivers in the United States.

My students read about Cathy Hinds ("Cathy Hinds," *Habitat*), a shy mother and high-school dropout from Gray, Maine, who in the late 1970s discovered contaminated water was causing illness, miscarriage, and death in her family and neighborhood. Hines faced enormous opposition but eventually a nearby hazardous waste dump was cleaned up and she became a regional coordinator for the National Toxics Campaign. In a similar but more famous case, homemaker Lois Gibbs fought indifference and hostility until the federal government was forced to evacuate Love Canal in New York state. Gibbs went on to run the Citizens' Clearinghouse for Hazardous Wastes. Both of these women were galvanized by threats to their families and both believe that the only way to bring about change is by working together at the local level. The book and film, *A Civil Action*, is the gripping story of Jan Shlichtman's legal fight to get damages from corporations that contaminated water and caused death and disease in Woburn, Massachusetts. Although his civil case failed, the EPA later used his work to fine the offending companies. Individual students read and present these stories and others about international figures such as Chico Mendes (Brazilian rubber worker), Ken Saro-Wiwa (Nigerian Nobel Prize poet and Ogoni tribal spokesman), and Rigoberta Menchu (Mayan community leader from Guatemala and Nobel Peace Prize winner). Mendes and Saro-Wiwa were killed for their environmental work; Menchu was exiled and lost her family. (See also the list of environmental activists at the end of Chapter Four.)

Following the oral reports on activists, students write papers defining an "environmentalist" and describing common traits. According to Rachel,

> All of these people . . have three important things in common: the desire to change the world around them for the better, the courage to take action for the cause, and the commitment to follow through until they accomplish what they set out to do.
> —*Rachel C.*

Students note that many activists are scientists who realize the importance of solving environmental problems and are committed to educating others. Others are writers who use their talent to communicate their love and concern for nature. Melissa underscores the importance of writing and education when she says:

> A common thread through most of them seems to be that they try to educate people about what they are doing, because they can't do it by themselves. Everyone has to know about the issues or they are never going to get fixed.
> —Melissa M.

Some activists are people with wealth or power who use their resources to defend nature. But many are ordinary people who are galvanized into action when their families or jobs have been threatened. Carrie and Jeremy both emphasize the critical role of ordinary people:

> The point I am trying to make is that any normal person is wrong if they think their opinion and their voice doesn't count or no one will care. Because everyone and anyone can make a difference in our world if they want to.
> —Jeremy F.

> I think it is amazing that such average people can make such a significant difference. It is easy to get overwhelmed by large problems like the pollution of the environment. However, these people had such drive and desire to accomplish their goal, that there was no stopping them until they did. These are the people that will save the world. I hope that I find a cause I feel this passionately about to fight for in my life.
> —Carrie P.

While students may not see themselves as activists on the scale of the examples in their reports, they can be inspired to look at their individual and collective lifestyles and consider what changes they could make to benefit their environment. Doing self-surveys and discussing personal lifestyle choices work well along with reading Thoreau's ideas about simplifying life (see Chapter Four).

As the great American coming-of-age symbol, cars are a good place to start. When I survey classes about the number of cars in their families, I find many families have a car for each driver. One student had seven cars in a family with four drivers. In our consumption-oriented society, only a few students see this as shocking. I ask students what priority they would give gas mileage when choosing a car to buy. I have them keep track of their gas mileage (in their own or their family car) for two weeks and make comparisons in class. We look at state and federal tax money that subsidizes highway construction. If we begin to also take into account the environmental and economic costs of getting, processing, and burning gasoline (a fifteen gallon fill-up results in 440 pounds of carbon dioxide; see Appendix E), we can begin to get a true measure of the costs and benefits of car ownership. We brainstorm ways to reduce automobile use: using public transportation (including the school buses!), carpooling, biking, and walking; but reducing car use is a hard sell to teenagers.

I ask students to monitor their use of other resources, such as electricity and water and to consider steps they can take to reduce their consumption. They can also monitor how consistently they recycle and what they do with toxic wastes. The reference book, *Students Shopping 4 * A Better World*, helps students make socially responsible choices as consumers. A video, "Your Money or Your Life," and two pamphlets, "How Earth Friendly Are You?" and "All Consuming Passion" (see end of chapter references), help students examine their habits as consumers. If they are not already convinced, the public television videos *Race to Save the Planet* ("Saving the Land") and *Interactions in Science and Society* ("Waste") effectively demonstrate the need for behavioral change. Students can consider their environmental impact both as individuals and as members of institutions—like school!

To assess their peers' beliefs about quality of life and material consumption, students construct questionnaires that ask about the relative importance of free time and conservation versus high salaries, expensive cars, homes, clothes, and vacations. Here is one questionnaire:

> If owning a large, luxurious home meant working an extra twenty hours a week, would you work the extra hours or choose a smaller home?
> Would you consider giving up your car and taking a bus if you could then afford to go on a special vacation every year?
> What matters more to you, free time or a high salary?
> How important are fancy clothes to you? (Do you make your own; shop in thrift shops, K Mart, or the Gap; buy designer clothes?)
> Would you buy an inexpensive, high mileage car or a fancy sports car, an ORV, a gas-guzzler?
> When you travel, would you choose low impact, inexpensive camping or luxurious resorts?
> Do you want a car for every member of your family? air conditioning? a heated swimming pool? an airplane? a yacht? a vacation home?

Many students may never have these choices but are still bombarded daily with messages that tell them they should want expensive material goods. If students are choosing luxury items, we discuss what would happen if everyone on earth had these things. Environmentalists have calculated that if everyone in the world consumed at the rate of North Americans, it would take two more planet Earths to support that consumption.

When Aldo Leopold defined land health as the ability of land to sustain itself, he did not offer a way to measure when an ecosystem had outstripped this ability. Using a method called "ecological footprinting" developed by William Rees from the University of British Columbia, some students learn how to calculate ecological impacts by taking into consideration such issues as distance a product travels, packaging, recyclability, energy efficiency, and natural resource depletion. Stella II computer software offers a modeling program that allows students to experiment with the variables of "stocks" and "flows" in an ecological system (see Appendix D). Rees' book, *Our Ecological Footprint* (1995) and its companion *Handbook for Calculating Appropriated Carrying Capacity* by Mathis Wackernagle, outline a philosophy of sustainability and give calculation procedures for determining individual and institutional impacts or "footprints." Using the Stella program and formulas in the handbook, students determine if and by how much an institution exceeds the "carrying capacity" of its site. Students report findings on their school or other institutions to the school board or to town governing bodies.

Students can also apply E. O. Wilson's theories about biodiversity and ecosystems using a sampling activity described in Appendix F.

All of these methods help students learn more about their impact on the world and begin to consider how they can keep this impact at a sustainable level.

Action Projects Students can resolve to change their personal habits in specific, environmentally conscious ways. They can also work on behalf of the larger community. Several years ago, students at our high school started SEAL, the Student Environmental Action League. It was these students, not adults, who started our paper, can, and bottle recycling program. The local university works with our chemistry classes to conduct "energy audits" of the high school. Our students have monitored tree health through Forest Watch; and every year students volunteer to monitor estuary water quality through Great Bay Watch. With classes, I have done campus and community clean-ups, planted trees and flowers, and built bluebird houses. My students have worked at fish ladders and carried buckets of salmon fry into remote streams for the Fish and Game Department. Each fall, students help on Coastal Cleanup Day. Our biology classes created an outdoor classroom using an old foundation in the woods and cleared a wheelchair-accessible trail to the site. A joint project with the middle school is proposed to extend the trail to a boardwalk and observation deck overlooking a small marsh between our two schools. Some projects carry on from one year to the next; some are done on an extra-curricular basis. For lists of resources, agencies, and websites for environmental monitoring and action projects, see Appendices C and G.

These projects take time and commitment on the part of teachers and students, and a class's desire to be more proactive on behalf of the environment can be frustrated by the limitations of a school schedule and class sizes. Since it helps to have other adults to work with and to have more than one class period, schools with block schedules and interdisciplinary teams have an advantage. But many schools have overcome these obstacles and engage students in exciting projects that give them first-hand experience and the satisfaction of achieving concrete results.

The gratification for a teacher comes when students are inspired to be activists on behalf of the earth, when they make personal commitments to live a sustainable lifestyle, or when they enter fields such as environmental science or outdoor education.

Works Cited

The Southwest

Abbey, E. 1968. *Desert Solitaire*. New York: Ballantine.

McPhee, J. 1970. *Encounters with the Archdruid*. New York: Farrar, Straus, Giroux. About David Brower, Friends of the Earth founder. Part III, "A River," chronicles his journey on the Colorado River with Floyd Dominy, head of the Bureau of Reclamation.

Porter, E. 1963. *The Place No One Knew*. San Francisco: The Sierra Club. Large format photographic collection of images of Glen Canyon on the Colorado River.

Powell, J. W. 1987. *The Exploration of the Colorado River and Its Canyons* (1895). NY: Penguin. The story of the first journey through Grand Canyon on the Colorado River.

Reisner, M. 1986. *Cadillac Desert, The American West and Its Disappearing Water*. NY: Penguin. A chronicle of western politics and water resources. A thorough and useful bibliography of books and articles with each chapter. (A PBS documentary series was based on this book.)

Videos

"Cadillac Desert" and "An American Nile." 1997. Public television video documentaries on water use and abuse in the American Southwest.

"Edward Abbey: A Voice in the Wilderness." Canyon Productions

Interactions in Science and Society, #12: " Wilderness" ITV (Instructional Television) Series. Broadcast on local public television stations with school year recording rights.

Land of the Eagle. Eight-part public television series on history of settlement and use of American geographic regions. "Living on the Edge" on the Sonora Desert; Sixty minutes. 1320 Braddock Place, Alexandria, VA 22314.

Planet Under Pressure, "Water, Water Everywhere." One of ten 20-minute ITV lessons on the chemical interrelationships of air, water, soil, and life.

Additional Resources

"Crunch Time at the Canyon," *Time*, July 3, 1995. Overcrowding and low budgets threaten Grand Canyon National Park.

Fradkin, P. L. 1981. *A River No More*, NY: Knopf. Standard resource on the Colorado River.

Informational pamphlets from the Glen Canyon National Recreation Area, PO Box 1507, Page, AZ 86040-1507.

Informational pamphlets about Glen Canyon Dam from the Bureau of Reclamation, US Department of the Interior: Upper Colorado Region, CRSP Power Operations Office, PO Box 1477, Page, AZ 86040; or Federal Building, PO Box 11568, Salt Lake City, UT 84147.

McPhee, J. 1989. *The Control of Nature*. New York: Farrar, Straus, Giroux.

Raban, J. 1996. *Bad Land: An American Romance*. NY: Pantheon Books. A study of the railroads' efforts to promote and settle the arid lands of eastern Montana.

Stegner, W. 1983. *Beyond the Hundredth Meridian*. Boston: Houghton Mifflin. A biography of John Wesley Powell by a great writer of the West.

"The Colorado, The West's lifeline is now America's most endangered river," *Time*, July 22, 1991. *Time*'s cover story.

Wallace, D. R. 1987. *Life in the Balance*. San Diego: Harcourt Brace Jovanovich. A companion to Audubon television specials.

Williams, T. T. 1995. *Desert Quartet*. New York: Pantheon Books.

Organizations

American Rivers. www.amrivers.org/hydro; 1025 Vermont Ave. NW, Suite 720, Washington, D.C. 20005

Trout Unlimited. www.tu.org/index.html. Formed to conserve, protect, and restore North America's trout and salmon fisheries and their watersheds.

Alaska

Kolodny, A. 1975. *The Lay of the Land: Metaphor as Experience and History in American Life and Letters*. Chapel Hill: University of North Carolina Press.

Kroeber, T. 1961. *Ishi in Two Worlds*. Berkeley, CA: University of California Press. "A biography of the last wild Indian in North America."

Lopez, B. 1986. *Arctic Dreams*. New York: Scribners.

McGinniss, J. 1980. *Going to Extremes*. New York: New American Library.

McPhee, J. 1977. *Coming into the Country*. New York: Bantam.

Norton, B. 1977. *Alaska: Wilderness Frontier*. New York: Reader's Digest Press. Photographs of the Brooks Range as seen by Norton and McGinniss, etc.

Videos

The Land of the Eagle, "The First and Last Frontier" on Alaska. Sixty minutes.

Scientists and the Alaska Oil Spill: The Wildlife, The Cleanup, The Outlook. 1992. Exxon Co. 22 minutes. The industry's view of the 1989 oil spill in Prince William Sound by the Exxon Valdez.

Environmental Organizations

Alaska Wilderness League, 320 4th St. NE, Washington, D.C. 20002, Phone: 202-544-5205; Alaska Coalition, 1-800-322-5205; Fax: 202-544-5197; www.alaskawild.org.

Additional Resources

Briggs, J., 1970. *Never in Anger, Portrait of an Eskimo Family.* Cambridge: Harvard University Press. An anthropologist's account of living for a year with an Inuit family.

Crisler, L. 1958. *Arctic Wild.* New York: Curtis Books.

Krakauer, J. 1997. *Into the Wild.* New York: Anchor Books.

————. 1997. *Eiger Dreams,* "Club Denali." New York: Anchor Books. Describes Krakauer's and others' attempts to climb North America's tallest peak (20,320 ft.).

Marshall, R. (1901–1939). 1970. *Alaska Wilderness, Exploring the Central Brooks Range,* 2nd ed. Berkeley: University of California Press. A travel account by an early preservationist who grew up peak-bagging in the Adirondacks and eventually founded the Wilderness Society.

Murie, M. 1997. *Two in the Far North,* 2nd ed., illustrated by Olaus Murie. Seattle, WA: Alaska Northwest Books.

Shields, M. 1984. *Sled Dog Trails,* Fairbanks, AK: Pyrola Publishing. Visitors to Fairbanks can meet the first woman to complete the Iditerod.

Wallis, V. 1993. *Two Old Women.* New York: HarperCollins. An Inuit legend of famine, perseverance, and reconciliation.

Articles

Alberstadt, M. 1987. "Ten Years of TAPS (the Trans-Alaska Pipeline System)," *The Lamp,* Fall, Exxon Corp, Florham Park, NJ.

Doherty, J. 1996. "The Arctic National Wildlife Refuge: The best of the last wild places." Traces the efforts to protect wild places in Alaska back to 1950 and Olaus Murie. *Smithsonian,* March. 32–40.

Ellis, W. Oct. 1971. "Will Oil and Tundra Mix?" *National Geographic.* One of many *National Geographic* articles on the pipeline.

Harmon, D. K. 1988. "Nature and Oil Lock Horns in Alaska." *Greenpeace,* April.

Rauber, P. 1992. "Last Refuge." *Sierra,* January/February.

Wysham, D. 1991. "Who Owns Alaska?" *Greenpeace,* July/August.

Wolves

Goodnight, L. 1988. *Getting Started in Debate*. Lincolnwood, IL: National Textbook Co.

Hyde, D. O. 1986. *Don Coyote*. New York: Ballantine.

Leopold, A. 1987. "Thinking Like A Mountain," *Sand County Almanac*. New York: Oxford University Press.

Lopez, B. 1978. *Of Wolves and Men*. New York: Scribner's

Mowat, F. 1963. *Never Cry Wolf*. Boston: Little, Brown.

Videos

Ballard, C., director. 1983. *Never Cry Wolf*. Walt Disney Home Video. $19.99. Contact local video distributor.

Costner, K., director. 1990. *Dances With Wolves*. Orion Home Video. $14.95. Facets Multimedia Inc., Image Entertainment, 9333 Oso Ave., Chatsworth, CA 91311, Tel. 800-473-3475.

Weide, B. and L. Hudak. 1992. *The Wolf, Real or Imagined*. Color; 28 min. Lone Wolf Productions and Montanans for Quality Television.

Additional Resources

Wolves and Humans, An Educational Resource for Teachers, The Science Museum of Minnesota, 30 East 10th St., St. Paul, MN 55101. Activities and information related to wolf biology, communication, territory, and pack structure.

http://www.iup.edu/~Wolf/ws.html, A site with many links to information, organizations, and publications (also search www.Yahoo.com). There may be more websites than wolves!

Organizations

Alaska Department of Fish and Game, 333 Raspberry Road, Anchorage, AK 99518 and 1300 College Road, Fairbanks, AK 99701. Source of information about Alaskan wolves and rationales for planned wolf hunts.

The Wolf Fund, Box 471, Moose, WY 83012.

U.S. Department of the Interior: Fish and Wildlife Service or National Park Service, Yellowstone National Park, WY 82190. The Park Service sent me an abundance of material on wolf recovery, including studies from Minnesota, environmental impact studies, hearing testimony, articles, and a long bibliography.

Issues and Actions

Berger, J. J. 1987. *Restoring the Earth: How Americans are Working to Renew Our Damaged Environment*. Garden City, NY: Anchor Press.

Dellabough, R., et al. 1992. *Students Shopping 4 *A Better World*. New York: The Council on Economic Priorities.

Harr, J. 1996. *A Civil Action*. New York: Vintage Books.

Macrorie, K. 1988. *The I-Search Paper*. Portsmouth, NH: Boynton/Cook Publishers, Heinemann.

Rees, W. E. 1996. *Our Ecological Footprint*. Philadelphia: New Society Publishers.

Wackernagel, M. 1997. *Handbook for Calculating Appropriated Carrying Capacity*. Philadelphia: New Society Publishers.

Articles and Pamphlets

Macdonald, A. 1991 (February). "Cathy Hinds: Portrait of a Grassroots Environmentalist." *Habitat: Journal of The Maine Audubon Society*. volume 8, no 1.

"How Earth Friendly Are You"" and "All Consuming Passion," The New Road Map Foundation, PO Box 15981, Seattle, WA 98115. A comprehensive self-survey of lifestyle values and practices, and a pamphlet of consumer statistics.

Environmental Issues Forums, "The Solid Waste Mess," 1994; "The Wetlands Issue," 1992; "Clean Water," 1995; "The Biodiversity Debate," 1997. Kendall Hunt Publishing Co., 4050 Westmark Dr., PO Box 1840, Dubuque, IA 52004–1840.

Videos

Interactions in Science and Society, "Waste Management." One of twelve 30–minute lessons. Can be pre-recorded from Instructional Television programming (see local public television ITV guide for broadcast times) and used for one school year. Teacher's Guide ($4.20) and computer program with simulations available from AIT, 800-457-4509.

Planet Under Pressure. Ten 20-minute lessons on the molecular and planetary chemistry of our earth's environmental problems: segments on global warming, ozone depletion, acid rain, and soil exhaustion. Pre-recording rights through ITV local programming.

Race to Save the Planet, "Saving the Land." Seven 15–minute lessons. Can also be pre-recorded; see ITV guide for times. Also available: *Race to Save the Planet Activity Guide*. 1990. WGBH Educational Foundation, Boston, MA.

Your Money or Your Life. About Vicki Robbin and Joe Dominguez who wrote a book by the same name. Available from The New Road Map Foundation, PO Box 15981, Seattle, WA 98115. www.newroadmap.org

Green Means. 1994. KQED San Francisco. Distributed by Environmental Media Corp., PO Box 1016, Chapel Hill, NC 27514. Two ninety-minute cassettes; thirty-two programs, each five minutes long, on current environmental activists.

Additional Resources

Berry, W. 1987. *Home Economics*. San Francisco: North Point Press.

Brown, L. R. Yearly since 1984. *State of the World: A Worldwatch Institute Report on Progress Toward a Sustainable Society*. New York: W. W. Norton.

Durning, A. T. 1992. *How Much Is Enough? The Consumer Society and the Future of the Earth*. Worldwatch Institute. New York: Norton.

Meadows, D., et al. 1972. *The Limits to Growth*. New York: Universe Books.

————. 1993. *Beyond the Limits: Confronting Global Collapse, Envisioning a Sustainable Future*. Post Mills, VT: Chelsea Green Publishing Co.

Schumacher, E. F. 1975. *Small Is Beautiful: Economics As If People Mattered*. New York: Harper & Row. Advocates a new, low-impact economics.

Wallace, A. 1994. *Green Means*. San Francisco: KQED Books. Profiles each activist featured in the public television shorts, "Green Means."

6

Fiction and Poetry

To people who think of themselves as God's houseguests, American enterprise must seem arrogant beyond belief. Or stupid. A nation of amnesiacs, proceeding as if there were no other day but today. Assuming the land could also forget what had been done to it.

Animal Dreams, *Barbara Kingsolver*

As Kingsolver makes clear, works of fiction can make very effective environmental statements. In assembling the *Norton Anthology of Nature Writing*, Robert Finch and John Elder included only nonfiction prose, which may be a defining characteristic of the "nature writing" genre. But given student interest and the centrality of environmental themes to many works of fiction and poetry, I work them into our predominantly nonfiction course as free choice or assigned reading. Fiction titles related to particular units such as colonial America, the West, or "Adventure and Survival" are discussed in Chapters Four and Seven. Poetry is considered with the Golden Age readings (Chapter Three), romanticism (Chapter Four), and journal writing (Chapter Two). This chapter addresses ways to incorporate separate units of fiction or poetry into a nature literature course.

Fiction

Am I alone? Sometimes it seems to me that adolescents have stopped reading books. When I ask even my college-bound students what they read during the summer, only a few have read a book or two. Some of my students announce, as though it were a badge of honor, "I haven't finished a book since sixth grade." This may happen because teenagers are so social and committed to extra-curricular activities. Maybe they have too much assigned reading. It may be a cultural problem rather than an adolescent issue: we live in a multi-media age. Whatever the reason, assigning reading in a widely heterogeneous group can be a challenge. Building in choices is one solution. Another is contract reading, which allows each student to work at an appropriate level of challenge.

Choice Reading

When we do a unit of choice reading, I give students a list of titles and show and describe books from a collection in the classroom; I may read a few passages aloud (see bibliography). I have students tell each other about books they like, and I encourage them to browse in bookstores and online. Students check their selections with me.

I generally offer students three assessment options when they do choice reading, options that work for individuals or small groups: essays, reader's response journals, and creative responses. Many students would choose creative response for every reading; therefore I do not always offer this option or I limit the number of times an individual may choose it.

The essay assignment is a traditional analytical paper:

Choose a theme, a focus, or a guiding question and write an analytical paper supporting that theme or exploring the question. The focus should have to do with people's relationship with nature. Use examples and quotations from the text to support your points.

Choice of focus due: First draft due: Final draft due:

Length:

While students have already written this kind of essay, I remind them that their purpose is not to summarize the book but to make a specific point about the book; events are cited in support of that point. We review guidelines for using quotations, and we discuss effective leads and conclusions. To create conference time for students to discuss their paper topics with me, I schedule reading and writing days.

A variation on the analytical essay is a format in which students choose a quotation from their reading that highlights a major theme of the book, then build their paper around the quotation. This format can be applied to writing about any reading and makes it easier for students to find something to write about. Since the choice of quotation is a key to the success of the paper, it is important to discuss the chosen passages before students start writing. An example of a central quotation in *Animal Dreams* might be:

"The very least you can do in your life is to figure out what you hope for. And the most . . . you can do is live inside that hope. What I want is so simple I almost can't say it: elementary kindness. Enough to eat, enough to go around. The possibility that kids might one day grow up to be neither the destroyers nor the destroyed." (326)

The paper begins with the quotation and a discussion of its meaning. Next, students discuss the passage in relation to the rest of the work, using other quotations and examples as support. Using the above quotation as a starting point, a student would show how the main character, Codi, and her sister Hallie tried to achieve a world with "elementary kindness" and without destruction. Finally, students draw conclusions about the theme addressed in the quotation. The virtue of this assignment is that it gives students flexibility to determine what they will write about while still providing a framework for the paper.

The response journal assessment option is:

Write a reader's response journal as you read the book. Write 500 words for each quarter of the book. You may also write more frequent, shorter entries that equal the same length. The entries should not summarize plot events but give your reactions to these events. What do you think of the characters? How are they like or unlike you? What do you learn from the book about people's relationship to nature? Use your entries to ask questions that arise as you read. The last entry should reflect on the book as a whole.

Due dates for handing in entries: 1. ＿＿ 2. ＿＿ 3. ＿＿ 4. ＿＿

Readers' response journals allow students to write about a variety of topics and incorporate more personal experiences and reactions. Students use their entries to ask questions about the reading, to react to events and characters, or to describe their own thoughts and feelings as they read. They do not summarize plot. They may also use the journal for creative entries, drawings, or collections related to the reading. The total amount of writing is longer than for an analytical paper because it has a looser structure. If books are being read individually, I use the journals to set up a dialogue between me and the student about the reading. Students may also exchange journals and respond to each other. If the same book is being read by a small group of students, sharing journal entries with other group members serves as a good catalyst for discussion. The reader response journal has been discussed at length by Nancie Atwell in *In the Middle* and Linda Rief in *Seeking Diversity*.

And finally, *the creative response* asks students to:

Choose a theme, event, character, or image from the book and do a creative project that expresses what you have chosen and its relation to the book as a whole. Choose a theme related to environmental issues. Possibilities for projects:

- Create a painting or drawing, or a series of visual pieces.
- Write a script and act it out; make a video or a radio show.
- Write and illustrate a children's book.
- Write and perform a piece of music.
- Write poetry or choose and illustrate a collection of poetry related to the reading; write an introduction to your collection.

- Make a sculpture or a mobile.
- Make a weaving or a quilt square.
- Make a well designed and carefully thought-out collage
- Take photographs and assemble them in a meaningful way; write an introduction and captions.
- Make a mural.
- Write a new ending for the book or write what happens after the book ends.
- Choose a character in the book other than the narrator, and write about an event in the book from that character's point of view.
- Your own idea.

Along with your creative project you must turn in a 500 word "rationale" or description and explanation of your work. The rationale should explain why you chose this medium and the process of creating the work; what you want the piece to show about the reading; what you learned about yourself, the art process, and the reading; and your feelings about the final product. Be prepared to discuss your project in class on the due date.

Artistic projects can be just as thought provoking as papers and more time consuming. They can also be a way for students to avoid the rigorous process of putting ideas into words. While we need to structure arts projects carefully, we do need to offer opportunities for creative expression to high school students as well as to middle school and elementary students. If we offer only one mode of response—verbal analysis—we cut students off from other aspects of themselves. An arts-based curriculum avoids this compartmentalization by integrating the arts with all subject areas. The best arts projects are those that combine several modes of expression. For example, students read a book, do an oral history interview related to the reading, write about the interview and the book, then create a visual or musical piece based on a theme in the interview and reading. All are shared in an oral presentation.

Kim made a children's book version of Richard Adams' novel, *Watership Down*, a story told by rabbits who are threatened by human encroachment and cruelty. Figures 6–1-6–8 are a sampling of her original text.

Artistic projects need clear guidelines and expectations. I tell students I expect them to spend ten to twelve hours (sometimes more) on a project and show them examples of work that clearly took that long. Students submit a plan for their project and may also write a progress report. The final, written rationale makes the difficult task of evaluating creative work easier. While I can't help being influenced by imagination and skill, I try to focus on effort and thought in grading these projects.

Contract Reading

With a contract, students choose how much reading they want to do and what grade they want to earn. As an example, I have twice used a contract for *Animal Dreams*, and parts of *Desert Solitaire* and *Going to Extremes*. The end of the term was approaching and we had not done all of the books I had hoped to read. I knew some of my students could manage the reading but not all of them. So I devised this plan. In the course of five weeks, students could read:

All three books for an A/A+
  Animal Dreams AND parts of *Desert Solitaire* or *Going to Extremes* = B/B+, *Animal Dreams* OR parts of *Desert Solitaire* and *Going to Extremes* = B-/C+,
  Parts of *Desert Solitaire* or parts of *Going to Extremes* for between C and D.

Figure 6–1. "Fiver felt something bad and very depressing coming." Fiver and Hazel see their land slated for a housing development and soaked in blood. They evacuate their warren.

Figure 6–2. They cross a river on driftwood . . .

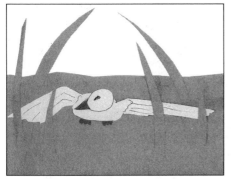

Figure 6–3. and help an injured bird.

Figure 6–4. After freeing rabbits from a farmer's hutch, ...

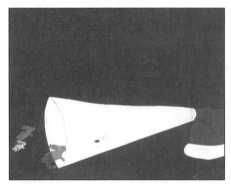

Figure 6–5. Hazel is caught in a headlight and shot at. . . .

Figure 6–6. then hides in a pipe, where Fiver finds him.

Figure 6–7. They battle an enemy warren . . .

Figure 6–8. and emerge victorious. "That is the story of *Watership Down*."

Reader response journal entries were due after a quarter of each book was read. A combination short-answer and essay test was given on each book—if students read all three books, they took three tests. I allowed time in class for reading and journal writing, and met periodically with small groups of students reading the same books. When I give this assignment, someone often complains, "I'd like to earn an A but I can't read that much." My feeling is that it is fair to give credit to the students who *can* read that much, and the reluctant reader is probably struggling to maintain a C anyway. If I could be sure of what each student is capable of doing, I could develop contracts that are fully individualized. By the end of the unit, students acknowledge that the system works out to be fair.

Analytical essays, reader response journals, and artistic responses are effective with class-assigned novels as well as with individualized reading. The following discussion of Barbara Kingsolver's novel, *Animal Dreams*, illustrates a student-centered approach to class study of an assigned novel.

Reading a Class Novel: Animal Dreams

In recent years, I have taught *Animal Dreams* because it is well written, students like the contemporary language and characters, and it raises important issues about pollution, environmental awareness, developing a sense of place, and the ability of a community to preserve its resources and heritage. *Animal Dreams* is the story of a thirty-two-year old single woman who returns to her hometown, Grace, Arizona, to teach high school biology, see her ailing father, and find her own sense of place and self. Like other Kingsolver novels, it follows many threads—love, death, teenage sexuality, parenting, environmental pollution, human rights, environmental activism, gender roles, cultural and geographic identity, stereotypes, and United States foreign policy in Nicaragua—all of which converge around the theme of connectedness—to people, to land, to the past and to the future.

Some cautions about teaching *Animal Dreams*: Students can be confused by the changes of point of view between Codi (Cosima) and her father (Homero). I point out that when a new point of view is used, the chapter is labeled with the narrator's name. As Homero's mind becomes more clouded, he confuses past and present, which also confuses some readers. Students often ask what is wrong with him, since Alzheimer's is mentioned only once. They also sometimes miss the fact that Codi had a miscarriage when she was fifteen. Chapter Twelve contains a discreet sex scene; teachers need to be their own judges of the appropriateness of this text for their classrooms. And finally, not all students share Kingsolver's vision that Grace is an ideal community. As one recently said, "If I came from a town with chickens scratching around in the dust, I'd want to get away too!"

Although I have chosen this book for the environmental issues it raises, I teach the book as a whole. Rather than give nightly assignments, I often divide a book into sections which are due every few days. This works well when intermingled with research projects or group presentations and gives students some flexibility about when they read. This year, I interspersed discussions of reading assignments in *Animal Dreams* with oral reports on environmental activists (see Chapters Four and Five). Students made the connection between the activists in their reports and the work of Hallie and Codi in the novel. We have also read *Animal Dreams* following *Desert Solitaire* and the supplemental readings on water problems in the Southwest (Chapter Five).

I often start by assigning students to take notes on one of the main characters. Students following the same characters can meet in small discussion groups first, then share their observations and examples with the rest of the class. After the first few chapters, one class noticed these similarities and differences in Hallie and Codi:

Both are tall, felt out of place as teenagers in Grace, and feel unloved by their father.

Hallie	lucky	*Codi*	unlucky
	committed to causes		doesn't get involved
	has principles		says she has no moral conscience
	has roots wherever she is		never feels connected

Codi's sense of being different, alienated, unloved and unappreciated is a feeling teenagers often identify with. Many also share her low self-esteem. For this reason, they find her slow but successful quest for self-acceptance and belonging particularly inspiring. As Mandy says, "We all have to go out and do what we truly want to do and find our place in life."

As they read, I also ask students to note images, scenes, or words that particularly impress them, along with their questions. If I open discussion by asking for these questions and impressions, I am allowing students to set the agenda for discussion. They generally bring up almost every idea I consider important, and what they miss, I can work in. If students are prepared with notes for discussion, the discussion proceeds well. I grade heavily for this preparation and participation, sometimes recording who contributed each day.

If students take notes while reading, they learn a method for paper-writing as well as preparing for discussion. When themes and images are noted with page numbers, students can review these passages, looking for links and patterns. There is no substitute for rereading a book, but few students make time for this luxury. Some images and themes students notice in *Animal Dreams* are:

- *Bones*: Mrs. Nash, the skeleton in Codi's classroom; the cow bones in World War II battlegrounds; the bones of war victims (including Hallie's) in Nicaragua; the over-irrigated, salted soil "gleaming like a boneyard"; infant bones buried in pueblo walls; coyotes burying bones in "God's backyard."
- *Death and graveyards*: the Day of the Dead; killing chickens; Loyd loses his twin at fifteen, Codi loses an unborn child at sixteen; Codi fails to rescue seven coyote pups; Loyd loses six mongrel coyote pups, all but his dog, Jack (Or was it seven pups? "Were they the *same* pups?" Beatrice asks. I wonder.); Codi loses her mother, sister, father, and child; Jack, Codi, Hallie, and Loyd are "orphans"; Codi lost her ancestors and her past; the river is dead and the water is killing the fruit trees.
- *Violence*: cock fighting, a bar fight, war, and the "violence" done to the river and valley by the Black Mountain Mining Company.

When students look for a pattern in these images, a theme of violence, death, and loss is clear. Poisons in the river water kill the orchard tree roots just as hate, misunderstanding, and prejudice have killed Codi's roots in her family and town. But there is also a pattern of reconciliation and rebirth: the town, river, and orchards are saved; Codi and her father are reconciled; Codi becomes loved and respected by the community; Codi accepts and returns Loyd's love; she also accepts her mother's death as a "finished life" and is pregnant herself with a new life. In Celina's words:

> When I put all these bone passages together, I think of life and death. You can see that the cows being buried showed death, but the bones helped new life grow. . . . Finally, because of bones in the ground [in the graveyard], Codi discovers her true family history and background. . . . She discovers her true self and I think she feels better knowing her place and not feeling like such an outsider like she did growing up. . . . She knows that her roots belonged to the place of her birth and feels one with herself.
> —*Celina D.*

Students can also look for patterns of opposites. We notice that, while Codi feels alienated from her family and home, Loyd feels connected. Codi feels inadequate and fears action, but Hallie finds self-worth in action, saying "it's what you do that makes you who you are." Codi feels like an "outsider"; Hallie feels at home wherever she goes. Homero hides his past; Viola embraces hers. Codi loses her own baby but saves Emelina's. Loyd is willing to die for "the land"; the Black Mountain Mining Company is willing to let the land die for money.

Students examine symbolism as well. The town of "Grace" is appropriately named, a town rich in Spanish heritage with an architecture that hugs its canyon walls and an "Eden of orchards" that supported its families before the mining company bought water rights and polluted the river. By "grace" and the efforts of the Stitch and Bitch club, the town gets listed in the National Register of Historic Places, and Black Mountain's plan to dam and divert the river is stopped. The townspeople's love and acceptance give Codi her sense of belonging—to Grace. Students note the colorful peacocks, symbolic of the town's Spanish history and hope for the future, a key to the fundraising efforts to save the town. Doc Homer's photographs are symbolic of his efforts to change reality and the past. Hallie is like the "semilla besada," the fruit tree that taps an invisible source of nourishment and outbears all of the neighboring trees, while Codi is rootless, always moving, until she finds a home in Grace. Codi looks for a female carob tree's male counterpart, and finds it near the train station, just as she returns to Loyd.

We also note the symbolism in the title of the book, *Animal Dreams*; animals dream about what they do all day. "If you want sweet dreams, you've got to live a sweet life," says Loyd. "It's what you do that makes your soul, not the other way around." Codi learns that she, like Loyd, is good at what she does. Her students test the river water and find it too acidic to support life; she teaches them about DDT, acid rain, ozone depletion, rain forest destruction, and the "real costs" of gasoline and stone-washed jeans. She prepares them to be "custodians of the earth."

Students see the importance of a sense of place in Loyd's love for the land and his ability to see small natural changes. The organic construction of pueblo architecture looks "like cells under a microscope . . . like something alive that just grew here . . . something nice that Mother Earth will want to hold in her arms." Loyd tells Codi, who has moved from place to place and person to person looking for the secret of life, "It's one thing to carry your life wherever you go. Another thing to always go looking for it somewhere else." Codi recognizes that her sense of herself is connected to being at home in a place when she says, "What you lose in blindness is the space around you, the place where you are, and without that you might not exist. You could be nowhere at all." Finding herself and home also means finding and reestablishing her family roots.

Building from details and patterns, students can see how everything in this book, and Codi's life, is connected. Codi's sense of self depends on her sense of place, of family, and of history. She carries the past—"Everything we'd been I was now," she says of her sister's death; and her pregnancy connects her to the future—"we contain our own future." Codi, short for Cosima, means "order in the universe," and by the end of this beautifully integrated book, we believe in this order with Codi.

As teachers, we can tell students the themes we see in a book and ask them to prove us right. Or, as I prefer, they can discover the themes themselves by being observant readers, by keeping track of what they notice, and by looking for patterns in these observations. If students practice this method of active reading, they will become more perceptive readers, and they will know how to approach literary analysis papers. This process can be the basis of analysis, response journals, or creative responses.

A few other novels well suited to a land and literature course include:

Growth of the Soil, Knut Hamsun. Written in Norwegian, this book won the Nobel Prize for Literature in 1920. The story chronicles the life of Isak, a simple farmer in Norway, and reveals his close relationship with nature and his indomitable spirit. This book is long and dated, but worthwhile.

Giants in the Earth, O. E. Rolvaag. Also first written in Norwegian, it is the story of Norwegian immigrants, Per Hansa and his wife Beret, settling the American prairie. The extreme weather, the isolation, and the physical and psychological suffering described make us appreciate the sacrifices made by those who first broke the plains. I have taught this book, but it is long—450 pages.

The Grapes of Wrath, John Steinbeck. As seen in *Of Mice and Men* when George and Lenny dream of living "off the fatta the lan,'" Steinbeck has a strong faith in the power of land to support the human spirit as well as human life. The use of farm land for economic gain before human sustenance, the separation of people from their land and their past, the consolidation of power and land in the hands of a few distant owners, all are viewed as sins against the land and the people in *The Grapes of Wrath*. Steinbeck's use of interchapters describing social and environmental conditions during the Depression gives this book a universal significance beyond the plight of one displaced family. "How can there be a whole chapter describing a turtle crossing a road?!" students will exclaim, but they enjoy decoding the symbolism of such events. Also long, the book is such an American symbol of injustice, exploitation, and human endurance, that it is well worth reading.

My Antonia and *O Pioneers!*, Willa Cather. Both are wonderful books. In *My Antonia*, Jim Burden travels from Kentucky to Nebraska, as did Cather, to live on the prairie with his aunt and uncle. His lifelong friendship with his neighbor, Antonia, is resumed when he returns from the city to visit Antonia's prosperous family and farm and regrets what he lost in leaving the land. The nostalgia for lost youth and a vanished wilderness are vividly expressed in images such as the wagon wheel silhouetted against the sunset or the old track disappearing in the prairie. But students expect a love story and may be too young to identify with nostalgia, so I prefer teaching *O Pioneers!*.

The bibliography lists other novels students can read as choice or class assignments.

Short Stories

A short story with strong thematic material about land is Borden Deal's "Antaeus" which, like Harriet Arnow's *The Dollmaker*, tells the story of a displaced southern farmer in a northern manufacturing city. T. J., a teenager, compensates for his loss by convincing his new urban friends to create a roof garden. Students read the story looking for differences in points of view between T. J., who sees the garden as useful and life-sustaining; his friends, who want it for recreation and status; and the building's owners, who are only interested in legal rights of ownership. The question of who has the right to decide how land is used is a provocative topic for class discussion. Some students will say it is solely a question of money and ownership; others will argue that the person who cares for the land should decide. Students also consider the meaning of the title, "Antaeus," the mythical wrestler whose strength comes from contact with the earth. This story is easy to read and I often use it as a first assignment, before starting the "Perception" unit, because it introduces two central themes in the course: the effects of different points of view and the importance of a strong sense of place. This reading serves as a good introduction to the Land Autobiography paper described in Chapter Two, which I also assign early in the course.

Other relevant short stories to study are London's "To Build a Fire" and Hemingway's "Big Two-Hearted River," one about the unfeeling, destructive power of nature, the other about the restorative powers of nature.

Poetry

How Poetry Comes To Me
It comes blundering over the
Boulders at night, it stays
Frightened outside the
Range of my campfire
I go to meet it at the
Edge of the light

Gary Snyder, from *No Nature*

Students read poetry in each thematic unit of this book, but they also enjoy a focused study of nature poetry. Along with reading, students write poems using exercises found in Chapter Two and the end of Chapter Seven. I create a class "anthology" of published poems (copyright laws allow a one-time use of one poem per author) along with brief biographical information. Students work alone or in pairs to gather more biographical data and other poems by their chosen poet. They generate questions about themes and images and lead class discussion of their poet. These guidelines help them prepare:

Check any vocabulary and allusions that are unfamiliar.
Paraphrase the meaning of the poem.
Consider the significance of the title.
Discuss the effectiveness of images and any use of symbolism.
Look at poetic devices like sound patterns, line length and breaks, word placement, and rhythm, and discuss what they add to the feeling and meaning of the poem.
Consider how the poem might resonate with personal experience.

Poets and poems I have chosen include:

Gary Snyder (1930–): "Water," "Riprap," "John Muir on Mt. Ritter," "Ripples on the Surface," "Mother Earth: Her Whales, " and any of the "Cold Mountain" poems (from *No Nature*)

Wendell Berry (1934–): "To sit and look at light-filled leaves," "The year relents and free," "Now though the season warms," "How long does it take to make the woods?" and "Slowly, slowly, they return" (from *Sabbaths*)

Mary Oliver (1935–): "When Death Comes," "Golden Rod," "Peonies," "This Morning Again It Was in the Dusty Pines," "Alligator Poem," "Hawk," "Goldfinches," "The Sun," "Winter," "Egrets," "First Snow," and "In Blackwater Woods" (from *New and Selected Poems*, 1992)

From *The Literature of Nature: The British and American Traditions*, Robert Begiebing and Owen Grumbling, eds. (includes biographies):

> Gerard Manley Hopkins (1844–1889): "God's Grandeur" and "Pied Beauty"
> Emily Dickinson (1830–1886): "I taste a liquor never brewed—," and "What mystery pervades a well!"
> Robert Frost (1874–1963): "A Dust of Snow," "A Brook in the City," "The Runaway," and "Directive"

From *Sisters of the Earth*, Lorraine Anderson, ed. (includes biographies):

> Joy Harjo (1951–): "Fire"
> Margaret Hasse (1950–): "Being Still"
> May Swenson (1919–1989): "I Will Lie Down"
> Elizabeth Coatsworth (1893–1986): "On the Hills"
> Nancy Wood (1936–): "My Help Is in the Mountain"
> Denise Levertov (1923–): "Come into Animal Presence"
> Edna St. Vincent Millay (1892–1950): "The Fawn"
> Barbara Mayne (1923–): "Changing"
> Marge Piercy (1936–): "Homesick"
> Adrienne Rich (1929–): "Contradictions: Tracking Poems, Part 18"

Joyce Carol Oates' poem, "Dreaming America," mourns the loss of American farmland and its replacement with highways and shopping malls, a loss she says teenagers seem unaware of. Her imagery makes a strong impression on students. She describes roadside signs as "eyeballs on stalks," and animals killed on roadways as ". . . transformed into rags/then into designs/then into stains/then nothing." For the power of its imagery to capture indifference in the face of destruction and for the questions it raises about responsibility, this poem is especially effective with students.

When the student-led discussions of these poets are finished, students choose an essay format. They can 1) write about several poems by one poet, 2) compare two poets, or 3) choose a common theme from several poets and use the theme as the focus of a paper. In addition, or as an alternative, they might create an anthology of poems, including a table of contents, an introduction, their own poems, a selection of published poems, biographies of the poets, illustrations, and a bibliography. The creative projects discussed under "Fiction" can also be assigned as an appropriate assessment project for a unit on nature poetry.

While I do not always have time to teach units of fiction or poetry, this reading provides an inspiring and enjoyable change from nonfiction nature writing, a change students and I both welcome.

Works Cited

Resources for Teachers

Atwell, N. 1987. *In the Middle: Writing, Reading, and Learning with Adolescents*. Upper Montclair, NJ: Boynton/Cook.

Rief, L. 1992. *Seeking Diversity: Language Arts with Adolescents*. Portsmouth, NH: Heinemann.

Additional Resource

Rosenblatt, L. M. 1983. *Literature as Exploration*, (1938). New York: The Modern Language Association of America. Emphasizes the response of the reader to literature over one "correct" critical interpretation and envisions a classroom in which teacher and students share responses honestly.

Fiction

Cather, W. 1994. *My Antonia*. New York: Signet Classic.

———. 1933. *O Pioneers!*. Boston: Houghton Mifflin.

Hamsun, K. 1921. *Growth of the Soil*. W.W. Worster, translator. New York: Knopf.

Kingsolver, B. 1991. *Animal Dreams*. Boston: G. K. Hall.

Rolvaag, O. E. 1928. *Giants in the Earth*. New York: Harper & Bros.

Steinbeck, J. 1996. *The Grapes of Wrath*. Harold Bloom, introduction. Bromall, PA: Chelsea House Publishers

Additional Novels

Abbey, E. *The Monkey Wrench Gang*.

Auel, J. *Clan of the Cave Bear*.

Atwood, M. *Surfacing*.

Arnow, H. *The Dollmaker*.

Borland, H. *When the Legends Die*.

Burroughs, E. R. *Tarzan*.

Callenbach, E. *Ecotopia*.

Craven, M. *I Heard the Owl Call My Name*.

Defoe, D. *Robinson Crusoe.*

Eckert, A. *Incident at Hawks Hill.*

Frazier, C. *Cold Mountain.*

Freedman, B. and N. Freedman. *Mrs. Mike.*

Gilman, C. P. *Herland.*

Hamsun, K. *Hunger.*

Hemingway, E. *The Old Man and the Sea.*

Herbert, F. *Dune.*

Hersey, J. *A Single Pebble.*

Hudson, W. H. *Green Mansions.*

Llewellyn, R. *How Green Was My Valley.*

London, J. *Call of the Wild.*

Matthiessen, P. *Killing Mr. Watson.*

————. *At Play in the Fields of the Lord.*

Melville, H. *Moby Dick.*

Michener, J. *Alaska.*

Mowat, F. *Lost in the Barrens.*

O'Brien, T. *Going After Cacciato.*

Quinn, D. *Ishmael.* A gorilla teaches a seeker of truth a new way of looking at our relationship with the world. (*The Ishmael Companion: Classroom Notes from Teachers.* 1995. The Hard Rain Press. PO Box 163686, Austin, TX 78716-3686.)

Rawlings, M. K. *The Yearling.*

Silko, L. M. *Ceremony.*

Stegner, W. *All the Little Live Things.*

Swarthout, Glendon. *Bless the Beasts and the Children.*

Swift, J. *Gulliver's Travels.*

Twain, M. *The Adventures of Huckleberry Finn.*

Unger, D. *Leaving the Land.*

Wyss, J. *Swiss Family Robinson.*

For Younger or Reluctant Readers

Eckert, A. W. *Incident at Hawk's Hill.*

George, J. C. *My Side of the Mountain.*

————. *Julie of the Wolves.*

O'Dell, S. *Island of the Blue Dolphins.*

Paulsen, G. *Hatchet.*

Richter, C. *Light in the Forest.*

Poetry

Anderson, L., ed. 1991. *Sisters of the Earth: Women's Prose and Poetry About Nature*. New York: Vintage Books.

Begiebing, R. and O. Grumbling, eds. 1990. *The Literature of Nature: The British and American Traditions*. Medford, NJ: Plexus Publications.

Berry, W. (1934–). 1987. *Sabbaths*. San Francisco: No. Point Press.

Oates, J. C. (1938–). 1975. *The Fabulous Beasts*. Baton Rouge: Louisiana State University Press.

Oliver, M. (1935–). 1992. *New and Selected Poems*. Boston: Beacon Press.

Snyder, G. (1930–). 1992. *No Nature, New and Selected Poems*. New York: Pantheon Books.

Other Poets

Blake, William	Coleridge, Samuel Taylor
Hall, Donald	Keats, John
Service, Robert	Shelley, Percy Bysshe
Tennyson, Alfred	Thomas, Dylan
Whitman, Walt	Williams, Terry Tempest
Wordsworth, William	Yeats, William Butler

7

Adventure

August, 1998

Our house is unrecognizable. In twenty-four hours, my husband, his brother Bernard, my son, daughter, her boyfriend, and I are leaving for a twelve day hike in Wyoming's Wind River Range. Gear is strewn everywhere, and people's individual piles are beginning to merge. Quick-drying, multi-colored t-shirts are piled on the couch; beside them, hats and mittens. Rain suits fill a chair. Wind pants fan out on the rug, along with borrowed and new sleeping pads, bags, and day packs. All have been laundered and sorted in anticipation of the arrival of the three young people who have only half a day to pack. In the den, five backpacks await our gear.

Small objects representing dozens of decisions litter every surface. Flashlights (are the batteries fresh?); film (prints or slides? how many? what speed? which camera?); maps and compass; writing and art supplies (pencils? paints?); fishing equipment (Bernard's department); a book (for the group? myself? how big?). Size and weight are always THE paramount issue. There are pots, stove, gas cans, cooking utensils, matches and lighters, along with cups, canteens, and spoons labeled for each person. A water pump (we repair the handle but forget to replace the filter) and iodine (not enough as it turns out). Extra garbage bags. Rope to hang the food out of bears' reach. Rain tarp and cord. Swiss Army knife. Emergency duct tape, string, and pack rings. The first aid kit has been checked and replenished. Soap, toothbrush, toilet paper. Chapstick. Pills. Sunscreen and bug repellent. Daily clothes must be selected: shorts, long pants, fleece, underwear, and multiple socks—always paring to a minimum.

Then the food. I discard all packaging and repack ingredients, all portions pre-measured with cooking directions enclosed. I am buried in ziplocks, masking tape, discarded boxes, and lumps of plastic filled with macaroni, rice, beans, spaghetti, tortellini, cous cous, tabouli, and felafel. There are instant soups and puddings, and the staples: coffee, tea, cocoa, sugar, salt, oil. Each lunch and dinner is bagged and weighs around four pounds. Multiplied by twenty-four meals plus oatmeal and pancake batter and two-pound individual gorp bags, each hiker's share of food is twenty or twenty-five pounds.

So many details. So much to remember. I lie awake at night worrying about what we may be forgetting. Is it worth it? In the last frantic hours before a departure, I usually say, "No!"

But once we are at the trailhead, boots laced up, packs cinched and everything we need on our backs, the chaos in the kitchen fades and I see only the trail unfolding ahead and the receding mountain ridges beckoning. I am independent, self-sufficient, and free. It's not that I'm entering a Garden of Eden. I'll get tired and short of breath; I will lose patience with searching for the perfect camp site; the bugs can be tormenting, the soup too slow to boil. I may not sleep well. Eventually, it is bound to rain and gear will get wet. But my responsibilities are only to myself and the group; our needs are simple—we respond to weather, tiredness, hunger . . . and the pure exhilaration of doing something hard and succeeding. And always, wherever and whenever I look, there is overpowering grandeur to lose myself in.

When I ask students why they sign up for "Literature and the Land," they often say, "I hear you take a lot of field trips." Inherently motivating, outdoor trips are a great way to make connections between reading and first-hand experience, and provide an ideal opportunity for building self-confidence and group cohesion. As Andrea, Chris, and Lisa make clear, outdoor adventures offer escape, the beauty of nature, challenge, a sense of achievement, and freedom:

Free

Here I came, to stone and sun
To billowing grass and clear blue sky
And in these hills I left my heart
Where dreams fly free and true
And the wild winds forever blow.

Now I've come, returned once more
To mountains tall and clouds so low
They hide the cares of the world below
And all I hear is the song of the wind
And the whispers of the stars . . .

Andrea K.

I wonder what it will be like to go back home? In the past week I have done more than I have ever done before. Everyday I have had a goal to accomplish and a task to complete. This is the life I prefer. I'm always busy, there is no time to worry or be bored. Out here I don't have to answer to anyone, just me and my friends. I wish it could last forever.

—*Chris R.*

I'm really proud of myself for coming on this trip. I never thought I could do it. But when we got to Mizpah Springs, the summit of a mountain, Lakes of the Clouds, and the Perch, I was really proud because I pushed myself and I stayed with it. I said to myself, "I did it. I really did it." I can do what I thought I couldn't.

—*Lisa H.*

146

Bastiaan offers perhaps the most important reason to take students on outdoor fieldtrips:

> Every time I go hiking or skiing, it reminds me that I need to do my part to help these places. For me, it is easier to understand it then, instead of people telling me I need to help.
> —*Bastiaan V.*

Some of my best experiences with students have been in the context of hiking and camping. I often learn more about them as individuals in a day of hiking (and they in turn learn about me) than I do in a whole semester in the classroom. On a mountain, their insecurities, generosity, humor, and grit all come to the fore. Students themselves recognize this. As Bianca wrote of our summer mountain trip in 1996, "I miss the people with whom I have spent the past week, getting to know them so much better than I ever would have in a week in school, getting to know sides of them I never would have seen." Less than stellar students often shine as leaders and helpers on hikes. Students' newly gained self-confidence and group trust carry back to the classroom and repay all of the effort that goes into a well-planned trip.

Trips also pose risks and danger. We have taken over forty trips without mishap, but people close to me have not always been so lucky. With the ever-increasing interest in outdoor adventure, students need to learn a proper respect for nature, safety, and leadership skills. While risk may be part of the excitement, it also means that groups need to prepare carefully for the responsibility of out-of-classroom experiences. Good reference books for leaders of outdoor trips include *The National Outdoor Leadership School Wilderness Guide* by Mark Harvey and *Outdoor Emergency Care* by Warren Bowman.

The "adventure" unit includes readings and films, group cooperation exercises, oral reports, and writing, culminating in one or more trips. I have spent as long as a month on this unit.

Group Problem-Solving and Trust-Building Initiatives

To prepare for a trip, we start with group exercises designed to build trust and encourage creative problem solving. *Silver Bullets*, developed by Project Adventure, is an excellent resource book describing these "games."

Some problem-solving initiatives are designed to demonstrate specific points. For example, in "Thumb War" students are instructed to grip hands with a partner and try to get as many "downs" as possible in a minute. Most students try to "win" this game alone, until they realize that by working with their partner and not competing, they can get dozens of "downs." Games like "The Longest Line," (two equal teams compete to form the longest possible line using their bodies and anything on their person) or "All Aboard" (a group of twelve to fifteen people tries to stand on a two foot square, low platform for five seconds with no feet on the ground) call for approaching problems in original ways and working well as a team. Many activities can be done on school grounds with equipment as minimal as ropes or balls.

For an intensive experience in trust and team building, there is nothing like a day at a ropes course. A typical ropes course has "low elements" such as rope spider webs or log teeter-totters for group problem-solving exercises, and "high elements" or high wires, which students climb and cross while tied with harnesses and climbing ropes to belaying partners. At each stage, facilitators help students reflect on their own and the group's process. Facilitators might ask students to try out different roles—if they are leaders, they should listen more; if they are quiet, speak up. If boys are dominating, they might be asked to be silent for an activity. The satisfaction we experience after accomplishing a group task and the exhilaration we feel at completing a high element is overwhelming and empowering. Without exception, students say a day at the ropes course is the best day they have ever spent in school.

> I am standing straight, eyes closed, surrounded by people with outstretched hands. As I roll around the circle I agree with myself to let go. I begin to breathe easily and let the hands carry me. Some of the people in my circle have been acquaintances, some close friends, some I have just met. What matters is that they all have two hands and with these they support me . . .
>
> In all the exercises, it was important to put aside preconceptions of other people, of yourself, and leave behind any arrogance and fear. It was necessary for the completion of each task to be unpretentious, to see yourself as one of a group of others with ideas different from but as valid as yours.
> —*Nahanni R.*

> I could believe in myself there and not only rely on me, but upon everybody's support too. For example, I would never jump from a spot forty feet high without everybody crying, "Come on, Ivan! Tell yourself that you can do it!" I told myself that, and did it. Support is a great thing, really.
> —*Ivan Z. (Russia)*

> I'm one person who has a hard time trusting people. Doing that circle, where I was in the middle, I thought was good for me. It started the day out with trusting my group. . . . The biggest highlight of my day was climbing up on the wire . . . Doug and Chris were my supporters. They were saying, "Rita, you can do it." I was so frightened, but I wanted to prove to myself that I could do it. I also wanted to prove to myself that I could trust Chris and Doug to help me if I fell. Another thing I liked was the group circle where you got to know everyone's feelings and let them know how

you felt. See, I'm not good with showing my feelings, but I felt very comfortable. All in all, this day boosted my confidence in myself and other people.
—*Rita L.*

The teamwork that we displayed on the spider web and rope swing/hoop obstacle was incredible. When someone touched the web, it wasn't, "It's so and so's fault." It was *we* touched the web. We all shared the responsibility. . . . I think that we all came a long way today! This was truly one of the best experiences of my life.
—*Laurie S.*

An intern, Stefanie Relles, devised two excellent activities to practice group skills and learn low-impact camping and map-reading in preparation for a group hike. Using "Cooking on Fires" in *The NOLS Cookery*, she has students bake cinnamon rolls on backpacking stoves or 'twiggy' fires (for which she obtained fire permits!). Cooking groups take into consideration nutrition and caloric intake, bear precautions, safety and sanitation, and removal of all signs of fire and food scraps. The mapping activity involves choosing a site on campus to map using contour lines, a scale, and a key. David Sobel's *Mapmaking with Children* has instructions for making contour maps of small plasticine or sand mountains in class, as well as for mapping outdoor topography (see Appendix B). Later, students will use topographic maps to work out the distance and elevation gain of our class hike. Students write an evaluation of their group's successes and problems and consider how they took leadership responsibility for themselves, the group, and the land.

Reading

While these group-building activities are being done in class, we also read fictional and nonfictional adventure literature. Jon Krakauer's two highly readable books, *Into the Wild* and *Into Thin Air*, raise provocative questions about risk taking and responsibility to self and others. Of Chris McCandless in *Into the Wild*, who died after 113 days alone in Alaskan backcountry, students either say he was crazy and irresponsible or admire him for following his dream. Carrie, not a risk-taker herself ("Taking risks seems so illogical. Why put yourself in danger?"), was convinced Chris was crazy: "Why else would he deliberately go out so unprepared?" Students put forth many reasons for Chris' actions: "He was disillusioned about his father." "He was tired of the grind of school and a conventional lifestyle." "He was idealistic and wanted to put his principles into practice." They made comparisons between Chris and Thoreau. By the end of the book, Carrie wrote:

I am tempted to call Chris' death senseless. I still believe that, with better judgement along with better supplies, he could have prevented his death. However, Chris died

doing what he loved. Following his heart, soul, and true convictions. Based on this fact alone, I think that his death was meaningful.
—*Carrie P.*

Into the Wild is highly readable and students make many connections between the book and other course readings such as Thoreau's *Walden*, Abbey's *Desert Solitaire*, and the "Golden Age" readings. Each time we confront the urge to turn our backs on society, we must stop and ask ourselves whether "going back to nature" is a realistic solution to our own or the earth's problems.

Krakauer's *Into Thin Air* is equally gripping. I once read parts of it aloud to a class and they loved it. One reluctant reader even got the book for Christmas. Students had dozens of questions about the world's highest mountains, the history of mountaineering, and the effects of high altitude. They debated why someone would choose to undertake such an expedition, the ethics of leading paying customers to the summit, whether people were properly prepared, and whether any of the expedition members were to blame for the tragic loss of life—eight climbers in all died on the day Krakauer's group summited. We saw the IMAX production, "Everest," by David Breashears, which documents this 1996 tragedy. The teacher's guide to the film gives good information and activities on history, high altitude adaptations and problems, wind chill, Tibetan culture, plate tectonics, the global positioning system, nutrition, and ethics. We used the guide's suggestion and made Tibetan prayer flags with environmental messages.

Students sometimes do independent reading during this unit. The readings are full-length works or magazine features about current or historical explorer-adventurer-survivors. I give students a list of possible books (see end of chapter) and a sampling of names such as Amelia Earhart, aviator; Reinhold Messner, climber; Catherine Destiville, climber; Steve Newman, around-the-world solo walker; Dan Buettner, around-the-world biker; Sir Edmund Hillary, climber; Tenzing Norgay, sherpa with Hillary ; Susan Butcher, four-time Iditerod winner; Colin Fletcher, backpacker; Teddy Roosevelt, hunter and adventurer; Piotr Chmielinski, Amazon paddler; Robert Scott and Roald Amundsen, South Pole explorers; Robert Peary, North Pole explorer; Jim Bridger, western explorer; Ernest Shackleton, British sailor and Antarctic explorer; Isabella Bird, Rocky Mountain adventurer; John Wesley Powell, Grand Canyon explorer; and Bruce Chatwin, travel writer.

Students do oral presentations in which they pretend to be their chosen adventurer. They might answer questions for another student who role plays a talk show host. They turn in research notes and a bibliography. Some questions they answer in their orals are:

What were the person's reasons for undertaking the adventure?
What makes the person exceptional? normal?

What personal qualities enabled her or him to reach the goal? What interfered?
Did doing this adventure accomplish anything for others? for the adventurer?
What impact might this adventure have on the environment?
What will happen to the person once they finish the adventure?

Writing Several creative writing assignments work well with the adventure reading. In one assignment, students plan a trip they would like to take. They can do
this individually or in groups. They draw a map and create an itinerary, a schedule, safety tips, and a supply list. They write imaginary log entries of what happens
on the trip, including a discussion of group leadership issues and precautions for reducing environmental impact. Students can also imagine being a member of one
of the historical excursions they have read about in this unit. For example, "Imagine that you are an oarsman on Powell's expedition through the Grand Canyon.
What do you see? What are your thoughts at different stages of the journey? Write
from the point of view of your character." A third assignment allows students
more flexibility and simply lets them write an imaginary adventure story using setting, character development, dialogue (or interior monologue), and plot. Will the
adventure be disastrous or successful? What will the characters learn? Students
have fun with this assignment.

Trips

We often do short nature walks as well as longer adventure trips. We have taken
walks in the woods and along shore meadows and marshes, taking advantage of nature reserves in our own and nearby communities. Local naturalists sometimes accompany us to share their expertise on soils, geology, birds, forests, animals, and
marine life. Students apply what they learn on these walks to looking at their land
journal sites.

I do at least one all-day trip with students in a semester, choosing places with
natural beauty, a literary or artistic history, and current or past environmental issues. Our trips range from rock climbing to hiking in the mountains, canoeing, or
exploring marine islands. We have combined forces with biology classes for
overnight camping in the mountains and on Cape Cod. And for five summers, I
have led overnight backpacking and writing "workshops" in the mountains and on
the lakes of northern New England.

Trip Reading

Since I choose destinations with a literary history, we read these texts before going
out. For example, if we go to Cape Cod, we read parts of Thoreau's *Cape Cod*,

Figure 7–1.

Henry Beston's *The Outermost House*, Robert Finch's *A Place Apart: A Cape Cod Reader* and *Common Ground*, John Hay's *Nature's Year*, and Mary Oliver's poetry.

For several years, I was lucky enough to accompany marine biologist Larry Harris on a research vessel to the Isles of Shoals. Dr. Harris's crew would ferry us onto Appledore Island to spend happy hours exploring while he and his students dove for specimens. The Shoals had seasonal fishing settlements even before people lived permanently in New England. By the 1800s there were two resort hotels on the islands, one owned by the father of Celia Thaxter who gathered a salon of writers and artists around her. On Appledore, my students located historical sites from a map and described the various adaptations of life in intertidal zones and from the shore to the center of the island. They wrote and drew. Once we brought microscopes and students drew something from three distances: far, medium range, and close-up. In the spring, we watched bird banders at work and avoided nesting seagulls. The activities on the island were designed to be interdisciplinary, as were the readings we did in preparation for the trip.

Before going to the Isles of Shoals, we read Lyman Rutledge's *Ten Miles Out* about Shoals history, Art Borrer's "Visitor's Guide to Appledore Island" on Shoals flora and fauna, *An Introduction to the Biology of Marine Life* by James Sumich, and

Figure 7–2. John's drawing from Appledore Island.

Celia Thaxter's poems and garden journal. We learned about writers who summered on the islands (Hawthorne, Emerson, Whittier, Twain, James and Annie Fields, James Russell Lowell, Lucy Larcom, Sarah Orne Jewett, Thomas Bailey Aldrich, Harriet Beecher Stowe, Elizabeth Stuart Phelps, Richard Henry Dana, William Dean Howells) and looked at slides of paintings by artists who also visited (Childe Hassam, Olaf Brauner, A. T. Bricher, Ross Turner, J. Appleton Brown, and William Morris Hunt). Were I to go now, I would add the recent book, *The Weight of Water* (1997) by Anita Shreve, about a double murder that occurred in 1873 on Smuttynose, one of the Shoals islands.

The trip I do most often is a day hike in the White Mountains. I have tried several mountains, but the one I return to again and again is classically shaped Mt. Chocorua, the closest mountain to school with a summit above tree-line. Chocorua offers a variety of routes to the steep, rocky summit including trails over glacial eskers and past glacial erratics, a ridge route over two lower summits, and a ledge trail through a grove of rare jack pines. The Champney Falls trail, named for painter Benjamin Champney, passes beautiful side-by-side water falls where students have "showered" on hot days. We have also hiked on cold, windy days in the fall when we could see snow farther north and every extra hat and glove in my pack got used.

In addition to journal writing along the trail, we do transects of plant communities at three elevations (deciduous, coniferous, and alpine) and develop

153

explanations for the different plant adaptations in each zone (soil depth, wind and sun exposure, extreme temperature changes, moisture), look for signs of human history (both use and abuse), draw, and photograph. Once again, the activities are interdisciplinary. If we have been to the Isles of Shoals, we compare our observations of marine (littoral) plant adaptations with mountain plant zones; the White Mountains and the Shoals share a similar pattern of social history (settlement, resource overuse, grand hotels and artists, tourism, conservation). While these details are specific to my location, the ideas are generalizable to any location.

Writing—Making Connections Students take notes on group presentations on mountain weather, geology, plants, animal life, and social history. After the hike, they write a "connections" paper in which they discuss and demonstrate how each element in the mountain's story, including their personal "story," is related to every other element. How does geology affect weather? How do both affect what lives and grows in the mountains? How do they affect your hiking experience? How have human uses of the mountain (exploration, farming, logging, tourism, conservation) affected it in the past and now? How do poems, stories, legends, and paintings affect our perception of the mountains? How would you describe your own experience of being in the mountains? What were the challenges of hiking and working together as a group? What is the significance of the idea of "dependence?"

When students see themselves as part of a larger natural history and system, their particular experience of a place is enriched. The same interconnections are there to be discovered on their land journal sites.

Writing on Extended Trips

Six summers ago, when a nature writing and drawing workshop I wanted to take was filled, I decided to organize my own. I proposed backpacking and camping in the White Mountains for five to six days, with time during the day for writing and drawing, and group sharing sessions each evening. My daughter and I co-led two trips the first summer and learned much from our initial experiences. For example, in order to have more time to write and draw, I plan an itinerary with two layover days and day-hikes. We reject the "bag as many peaks and miles as possible" philosophy in favor of having time for observation, reflection, and conversation. I also learned not to rely solely on a gear list—one of my first hikers showed up with a pack she hadn't used since she was ten. Being smaller, I ended up carrying it! From then on, I have held orientation meetings that include a gear check.

While week-long trips are not typically an option for classroom teachers, some schools use such experiences to foster growth in individuals and groups, and more schools should! Programs that do offer extended outdoor experiences such as environmental camps, alternative schools, and summer programs can be greatly enriched with a writing component.

I always start trips armed with structured activities for writing, knowing that I will use only a few of them. Since the trips are designed for writers and I ask students to submit a writing sample with their application, students are usually motivated to write and do not need writing prompts. But the prompts can help to get the pens started—not everyone is motivated all of the time! Students also make suggestions. Some of our ideas are:

1. Pretend you are something along the trail or on your person (ex. your boot), and write from that perspective.
2. Find something in nature to describe and use it as a metaphor.
3. Describe something at close, medium, and distant range.
4. Write a limerick about the trip or the group.
5. At a parent's suggestion, I read *The Artist's Way* and tried having students write stream-of-consciousness "morning pages" each day before hiking. This is a great warm-up, but made us late getting on the trail.
6. "My ten most important things." Each writer lists the ten things (or ideas) that mean the most to them. Lists are redistributed randomly, and each writer creates a story using someone else's list. This is a good getting-to-know each other activity and takes a day. When the final stories are read, the group has to guess who they are about and what words in the story come from the original list.
7. The "word list game." Each member of the group contributes a word and everyone writes their own story, using the list of words. Finding words rich in connotations is part of the fun. This activity has been repeated by popular demand every year since our first summer.

The last two ideas are particularly good for building comraderie in a group because they are cooperative.

Most students keep a log of the day's adventures and intersperse this writing with whatever inspires them. We write along the trail, after lunch, on summits or by waterfalls, and in the evening between setting up camp and dinner. One hiker, like John Muir, kept a small pad in her pocket, and stopped along the trail to write whenever something struck her. Sometimes we enforce a quiet time for writing and reflection.

After dinner, we share our day's work. The first night out, we talk about ways group members can help each other be comfortable sharing. They mention needing to trust the group to be supportive and to give specific feedback about what they like. "If you just say, 'It's good' or, 'I like it,' I feel like you didn't care enough

Figure 7–3. Natan and Anya write along the trail.

to really listen." Reluctant readers are encouraged but not forced, and, when they do decide to share, the group is supportive. As the week goes on, students become more and more motivated to have good material to read and show in the evening.

Their writings describe our surroundings, the group, the trip, personal and political issues, and fantasy adventures. This progression from outer description to inner reflection and imagination seems to be part of nature's method of inspiration. "Why do you think being in nature inspires writing?" Kaitlin asked me on a recent hike—a good question. First of all, and maybe most obviously, nature inspires us because it is beautiful, because there is so much to see, and it is always changing. It forces us to sit up and take notice. So we begin with description. The more grand the scene—a seascape, a mountain range—the more we are forced to see ourselves as a small piece of a larger whole. Nature transcends us and forces us to consider our role in the vastness of the universe. So we move from description to self-reflection, including thoughts that can influence our writing as well as our actions as stewards of the earth. When this writing occurs in the context of a supportive group engaged in a joint challenge like hiking, the results can be striking.

Figure 7–4. Kaitlin, Marci, and Andrea listen as Erin reads.

Her first year on the trip, Kaitlin wrote "Pathway to Heaven" about the Franconia Ridge trail:

If I ever saw a pathway to heaven
it would look like this.
Through sleeping eyes, I'd see
my spirit unfolding, like a pair of wings
shimmering ahead.
So, I'd follow,
running across a sighing path
until a clearing, where I'd see—
a great expanse of life and love
my earth.
Maybe I'd wave farewell.
Then I'd turn
to where a cliff side wound to the sky.
The sun would beckon,
drenching me in rainbow light
So I'd come.

Students have described sunsets,

> The sun is a brush, dipping into the cloud
> like a brush into paints
> together to paint a sunset.
> I am calm and alive.
> The sun silently hides behind the mountains,
> like a paint brush leaving the canvas.
> The colors leave a crisp, fresh smell,
> like a newly finished painting.
> Now only the finished canvas is left
> for us to watch.
> Natan D.

> **Dreaming**
> The sun sinks toward the horizon
>   As I climb into the sky
>   The stars begin to twinkle
>   Before I reach the cliff
> Where my journey will begin
>   Looking out and inward
>   I lean against the wind.
> And dive into a cobalt infinity.
>
> Andrea K.

the receding horizon,

—Chris Richards

Lighter and lighter, by and by, mountains touch the sky.

waterfalls,

> . . . up the flowing veil that frosts
>   granite in sun soaked silver,
>   combs of soft claws fall again and
>   again . . . .
> Chris J.

rivers,

The River
Water over rocks, rushing,
Hurrying to get somewhere.
Sunsparkles dance on curtains of foam.
Darkness spreads,
Fighting the current to cover the world
In night.
Laughing, shouting,
Thoughtful silences;
Layer upon layer of mountains
Stretching away in front of me
Forever.
I could hurry to their peaks,
Flowing ever onward like the river
Or I could wait, and look around me
At the life I'm passing by.
I could live for the journey,
Not the destination.
My gaze shifts back to the river—
Rushing hurrying, and I lie back on
My sunkissed rock
And close my eyes, smiling.
Marci K.

and a shooting star:

"Starlight, Starbright"
Huddled close
Friendship keeping out the cold
Searching for
Patterns in the sky and
Meaning in our lives
Suddenly

A miracle streaks by overhead
No one dares speak
Or even breathe
Its light reflects
In all our souls
Leaving wonder in its wake.

Marci K.

Not every piece extols the beauty of nature. Katherine's journal offers a different perspective:

One might think that an outdoor camping trip would be a relaxing experience. Free from the intricacies of living in a sheltered, monitored home, one would feel unburdened, and cleansed by the fresh environment. Reality states otherwise. Truth #1: I am sore in the shoulders from carrying a backpack that probably weighs a little less than that boulder over there. Truth #2: I must think things over more, things that would have passed without a thought at home. For example, I must think about

Hushed whispers, an occasional giggle—
Suddenly, in unison, an awed, "ahhh!"
Inside, the tent
I have to imagine it.
"That was the brightest, longest
shooting star I've ever seen!"

Figure 7–6. Emma R.

where to strategically put my gear so that it won't get wet, or so that I won't have to go searching through my bag for it.

—*Katherine T.*

Katherine, quiet her first year, wrote this poem.

> Somebody hold her
> I fear she shall fall
> Maybe no one cares
> Whether she falls at all
> Sometimes she wonders
> In her pool of tears
> If anyone will notice
> When one soul disappears.
> Katherine T.

By her third year, she had become one of the most outgoing and funny members of the group.

Figure 7–7. Katherine on Mt. Garfield.

Erin, practical, quick-witted fact-lover, is probably our strongest hiker. She once said, "I wish there was a place in the world where I could just walk forever." She used to exhibit little patience for soul-searching:

> Do you go to the mountains
> to discover yourself
> or to realize that
> life is not to be discovered
> and has better things to do?

or overly flowery verse: "I'm not good at being spiritual. I'm good at being superficial." Early on, she would sometimes say, "I don't know what to write." But by year three she found her voice and knew exactly what she wanted to say:

> **"My Revenge Poem:"**
> I was reading a poem
> Sometime near last week
> When I realized with horror
> This is much too bleak!
> "I am so sad," it said with dismay,
> "And my life is coming
> To take me away."
> This poem needs counseling,
> I thought to myself.
> And I put the anthology
> Back up on the shelf.
> Why are we always
> Thinking life is so bad?
> There's too much to do,
> Too much fun to be had!
> I'll write my own poem
> I decided, just me!
> So I wrote and I wrote
> And here's what came to be:
> The poem was bouncy,
> Its beat was incessant.
> It laughed and it smiled
> And it was rather pleasant.
> The poem rhymed too,
> It was as fun to read it
> As it was for the poet
> Who tried to conceive it.

This poem was pure,
Had no statements to make.
It would rather go frolic
Than be something fake.
I wrote it about
All I knew and could see:
The ocean, the universe,
My favorite oak tree.
And I like all to know
Though there's freedom of speech
While your poem's in jail,
Mine's at the beach!
Erin Q.

Group members write with affection about each other. In "The Trip," Marci wrote:

Between this year and last
We've changed, grown.
The trip is never the same, but the
Friendships born in the mountains will last
Forever.
Marci K.

At the end of every day, I give each hiker a bead. Sometimes the beads stand for an individual accomplishment that day—completing a difficult trail, extending a helping hand; sometimes they represent a group experience such as a brilliant, sunlit day. Students like this ritual, and if night is coming on at the end of a sharing session, they remind me to hand out beads before closing. At the onset of one trip, Marci presented us all with a necklace of thin ribbon and a handmade bead personalized with our initials. Each day, we add our beads to our necklaces. Marci's daily log entries describe her beads:

"Day one: two mountain-green beads to frame my shooting star," "Day two: . . . the purple flower bead, as beautiful as the flowers we saw that day," "Day three: . . . a new bead—red and bright for the beauty and intensity of the sunset we all caught in our own way," Day four: . . . "My newest bead hung nearby—blue for a rainless sky, green for the trees we descended into, large for our 7.2 mile marathon. . . ."

Kaitlin inspired others to acts of sharing when she illustrated my "Mt. Liberty" poem (see end of the chapter). Tricia followed with a poem and drawing for Kaitlin (Figure 7–8).

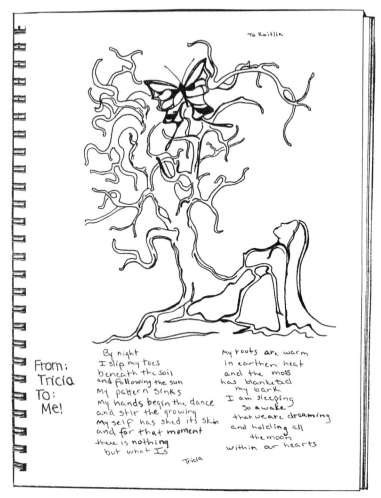

To Kaitlin

From:
Tricia
To:
Me!

By night
I slip my toes
beneath the soil
and following the sun
My pattern sinks
My hands begin the dance
and stir the growing
myself has shed its skin
and for that moment
there is nothing
but what Is

My roots are warm
in earthen heat
and the moss
has blanketed
my bark
I am sleeping
so awake
that we are dreaming
and holding all
the moon
within our hearts

Tricia

Figure 7–8. For Kaitlin by Tricia.

The students' creativity shows in ways other than writing: they make up stories as they hike; they sing, tell jokes, assume accents, and do impersonations. The second year, Andrea gathered a page of fellow hikers' quotations, and each year her list grew, until by the fifth year Andrea's quote collection was the glue holding our final book together. The quotations range from the sublime: "The hair flying in my face is like strobe lighting." (Andrea) and "I am a slave of my own self-consciousness." (Julie); to the ridiculous:

I invented compressed water: ten quarts in one bottle.—Erin
I don't want to get that beaver disease [giardia]. Actually, I've already drunk some of this, and nothing happened. Except I have this urge
to gnaw down a tree with my teeth.—Katherine
  So I was walking all alone and I started singing all of "Les Miserables,"
  and then I ran into these other hikers just as I got to "*Damn
  their warnings; Damn their lies!*"—Kaitlin
  Let's hear it for hypoglycemia and hiker dementia! –Katherine
  Someday I'm going to say something that isn't funny enough to go in that book.

  —Erin; That wasn't it.—Andrea

At a hiker's suggestion, we started a yearly tradition of writing farewell messages in each other's journals. Each message is done with thought, affection, and often a drawing. This can be a long process and is sometimes still being completed during the car ride home. The second year group decided to make a book of our writing and we each contributed a page. Later groups put together collections of writing, quotations, photographs, and drawings (Figure 7–9).

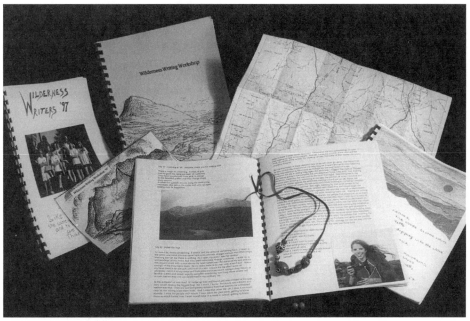

Figure 7–9. Wilderness Writing Workshop publications.

I don't think any of these ideas can be imposed. The most successful activities are those that arise spontaneously; all I do is provide the context and help build trust. The rest is up to the mountains and the group. As Kaitlin wrote, "You have given each of us a place we can always belong."

Teaching and learning happen in many forms and contexts. The trail can be a great humanizer, and on a mountain we are all learners and teachers. On these trips, as well as in the classroom, I realize how much I learn from my students and how much my life is enriched by their caring, their thoughts, and their creativity.

Mt. Liberty

Fog unfurls
whipping over the summit
     revealing
beautiful women
hair flying in the wind
beaming at the peak of their power—
    Liberty.

Figure 7–10. Mt. Liberty by E. Rous, drawing by Kaitlin S.

Works Cited

Leadership Sources

Bowman, W. 1993. *Outdoor Emergency Care: Comprehensive First Aid for Nonurban Settings.* 2nd ed. Lakewood, CO: National Ski Patrol System.

Harvey, M. 1999. *The National Outdoor Leadership School Wilderness Guide: The Classic Wilderness Guide.* New York: Simon and Schuster.

Rohnke, K. 1984. *Silver Bullets.* Iowa: Kendall/Hunt Publishing Co. A guide to initiative problems, adventure games, stunts, and trust activities.

Sobel, D. 1998. *Mapmaking with Children: Sense of Place Education for the Elementary Years.* Portsmouth, NH: Heinemann.

Additional Resources

Fletcher, C. 1971. *The Complete Walker: The Joys and Techniques of Hiking and Backpacking.* New York: Alfred A. Knopf.

Thomas, S. E., composer. 1985. *Adventure Education: A Bibliography.* Amherst, NY: Institute on Classroom Management and School Discipline. Department of Learning and Instruction, State University of New York at Buffalo.

Adventure Readings

Ambrose, S. 1996. *Undaunted Courage: Meriwether Lewis, Thomas Jefferson, and the Opening of the American West.* New York: Simon and Schuster.

Aspen, J. 1988. *Arctic Daughter: A Wilderness Journey.* Minneapolis, MN: Bergamot Books. A couple builds a cabin on the Chandalar River in the Brooks Range; a riveting survival story.

Brown, T., Jr. 1996. *The Tracker.* As told to William Jon Watkins. New York: Berkley. Brown apprentices to a Native American elder and learns the ways of survival and the wild.

Callahan, S. 1996. *Adrift.* New York: Ballantine. Callahan is lost at sea for seventy-six days.

de Voto, B., ed. 1997. *The Journals of Lewis and Clark.* Boston: Houghton Mifflin.

Irwin, B., with D. McCasland. 1992. *Blind Courage.* Waco, TX: WRS Publishers. A blind hiker completes the Appalachian Trail.

Jenkins, M. 1993. *Off the Map: Bicycling Across Siberia.* New York: Harper Perennial. Four Americans and four Russians bike 7,500 miles from Vladivostok to Leningrad.

Jenkins, P. 1979. *A Walk Across America.* New York: Fawcett Crest.

Johnston, T. 1992. *Shooting the Boh: A Woman's Voyage Down the Wildest River in Borneo.* New York: Vintage.

Krakauer, J. 1997. *Into the Wild.* New York: Anchor Books. The story of Chris McCandless' death in Alaska.

———. 1998. *Into Thin Air.* New York: Anchor Books. About the greatest climbing disaster on Mt. Everest.

Lansing, A. 1999. *Endurance, Shackleton's Incredible Voyage,* (1959). Wheaton, IL: Tyndale House Publishers.

Markham, B. 1983. *West with the Night* (1942). San Francisco: North Point Press. Stories of Africa and the first east-to-west Trans-Atlantic flight.

Matthiessen, P. 1996. *The Snow Leopard* (1978). New York: Penguin. A five week trek and spiritual journey in Nepal.

Melchett, S. 1992. *Passionate Quests: Five Modern Women Travelers.* London: Faber & Faber.

Morris, M., ed. 1993. *Maiden Voyages.* New York: Random House. Stories by over fifty women travelers.

Mowat, F. 1985. *Lost in the Barrens.* New York: Bantam. Two boys live alone in the wilderness after their canoe breaks apart in rapids.

Owens, M. and D. Owens.1992. *Cry of the Kalahari.* Boston: Houghton Mifflin. A seven-year study of wildlife in Africa. Also a National Geographic Special based on their work.

Read, P. P. 1992. *Alive.* New York: Avon. A Uruguayan soccer team crashes in the high Andes.

Slocum, J. 1978. *Sailing Alone Around the World.* New York: Dover.

Cape Cod Readings

Beston, H. (1888–1968). 1998. *The Outermost House: A Year of Life on the Great Beach of Cape Cod.* Thorndike, ME: G. K. Hall.

Finch, R., ed. 1993. *A Place Apart: A Cape Cod Reader.* New York: W. W. Norton.

———. 1981. *Common Ground: A Naturalist's Cape Cod.* Boston: D. R. Godine.

Hay, J. 1961. *Nature's Year: The Seasons of Cape Cod.* New York: Doubleday.

Oliver, M. 1983. *American Primitive.* Boston: Little, Brown and Co. Poems.

Thoreau, H. D. (1817–1862). 1997. *Cape Cod.* West Dennis, MA: Peninsula Press.

Isles of Shoals Resources

Faxon, S., ed. 1982. *A Stern and Lovely Scene: A Visual History of the Isles of Shoals,* (1978). University Art Galleries, University of New Hampshire, Durham, NH 03824. Slides and video accompanying Isles of Shoals exhibit available from UNH Gallery Outreach and UNH Media Services.

Rutledge, L. 1984. *Ten Miles Out, Guide Book to the Isles of Shoals.* Portsmouth, NH: Peter Randall.

———. 1965. *The Isles of Shoals in Lore and Legend.* Barre, MA: Barre Publishers.

Shreve, A. 1997. *The Weight of Water.* New York: Little Brown. A fictionalization of an 1873 murder of two women on Smuttynose Island.

White Mountain Resources

Campbell, C, et al. 1980. *The White Mountains, Place and Perceptions.* University Art Galleries, University of New Hampshire, Durham, NH 03824. Slides and video accompanying White Mountain exhibit available from UNH Gallery Outreach and UNH Media Services.

Dobbs, D., and R. Ober. 1995. *The Northern Forest*. White River Junction, VT: Chelsea Green.

Hawthorne, N. 1935. *The Great Stone Face, and other tales of the White Mountains*. Boston: Houghton Mifflin.

Heinrich, B. 1994. *A Year in the Maine Woods*. Reading, MA: Addison-Wesley. Notes and drawings about life in a north woods cabin.

———. 1997. *The Trees in My Forest*. New York: Cliff Street Books. About restoring 300 logged-over acres into a sustainable wood lot.

Olson, W. K. 1978. "Lightening." *At Home in the Wild*. Appalachian Mountain Club and Friends of the Earth. Washington, D.C.

Website

www.whitemountainart.com. A site with artists' profiles and pictures.

Epilogue
Opening the Doors

If the doors of perception were cleansed, everything
would appear as it is—infinite.

William Blake
from The Marriage of Heaven and Hell

In the end, we will conserve only what we love
and respect. We will love only what we understand.
We will understand only what we are taught or
allowed to experience.

Baba Dioum
African conservationist

It is the end of August and I am preparing for a new school year and a new group of students. I have seen the class list, and I know some of these students. Some like school, some do not, but all of them live in the world and make decisions that affect its future. Some will have children and they will do the same. How can I best prepare them to be responsible stewards of the earth?

Ultimately we teach students about the environment because we love our world and want to sustain it, and we hope they will share that love and commitment. Like Baba Dioum, I believe that the best way to bring about a change in perception and a commitment to sustainability is not to exhort or frighten but to share our knowledge and give students opportunities to appreciate the beauty and joys of nature. If students become aware of their own and others' perceptions and realize that perceptions have real consequences, they may begin to revision their relationship with the world. I have chosen to explore these perceptions and consequences through the study of language and literature.

It is hard to know what impact we have when we set out to teach young people. The following two very different final papers convince me that students do understand and care profoundly about the earth's future. The assignment was to find a central theme from the course and use five readings to discuss that theme. The

171

first essay by Tyler (printed as written) takes considerable liberties with the assignment but was an unusual and moving response.

True Story: Never Been, Never Will Be Proud

As I ran down the river dodging from rock to rock, hoping not to slip and fall. Three other's ran either beside or behind me. It was hot and the water felt great, it and the slow breeze cooled us down.

[As we waded downstream, we saw what we thought was a fish. It turned out to be an eel, which we had never seen before.] The color was the color of the rocks beneath it, light brown with long fins. . . . It was strange, not part of our world. At least we didn't think so! We just stood there, staring deep into this 'creature's' eyes, if that's what they are called for they looked nothing like eyes.

With that we decided to kill it, can you believe that? Kill it! So I grabbed a 2 × 4 that had floated down stream and slowly I brought it down in the middle of the eel—holding him there. As my friends took rocks and tried to kill it. It didn't work and the eel slowly then quickly swam away. We had no feeling at all for it. It shows how much life meant to us. . . . After this point I was just on for the ride—but I still stay on the ride.

[We noticed that the river was loaded with eels and made a decision.] Someone yelled out, 'Weapons.' Weapons? 'Why,' I asked myself for I dared not to ask out loud. [The others left and returned] with long sharp blades and hockey sticks with nails at the end of them. Approaching them I acted as if it was cool and we were going to have fun. Deep down I knew it was not going to be fun and I was lying to myself. I got a stick to hold the eels down while the rest of my friends did their things. Killing. . . . The first eel was sliced in half and then thrown on shore. (It was strange how I was being pulled two ways and wondered if my friends were also being pulled two ways.) I looked at "it," I'm using "it." The only way I could justify why we were doing this was that the eels were "bad," they would bite people . . . I swear I almost cried for that eel and the rest of the eels we destroyed.

We killed eight eels in total, although I did not kill a one, I believe I would if I was given the weapon to do so. That is what scares me. What if I do have a killer in me? With every slice of an eel, a smell filled the air . . . for me it has become the smell of death. . . . One of my friends had an eel hanging from a hockey stick and another slit it's belly open, yelling "Blood." Sick. [Later] I told a couple of people and they all said, 'No big deal.' But to me it was a big deal for I told myself I would never kill anything for no reason. Even though I didn't kill, I was part of it.

[Killing the eels was like killing wolves out of fear in *Never Cry Wolf*.] There are so many things I could do to help and change the way I affect the enviorment. Killing needlessly is definitely a NO! Why I ever thought of it I will never know. I just hope I remember it for the future. As in "The Tempest," in the fact that the characters must remember things from the past to move to the future.

I have nothing else to say except I will always remember the past so I can and will change the future. For some day the future will become the past.

—*Tyler L.*

The vividness of Tyler's descriptions and the depths of his remorse are convincing. Did his friends secretly experience the same regret? I wonder. The apparent callousness of their actions and of others' responses is, unfortunately, also believable. This experience had an impact on Tyler even before the course, but the course readings reinforced his impulse to be a sustainer rather than a destroyer of life.

The following essay by Abby applies the introductory theme of "perception" to the whole course. The essay, excerpted here, is carefully constructed with a quotation and a modern application for each reading discussed. While her approach is as philosophical as Tyler's is concrete, in the end they both arrive at a new vision of their role in the world.

Perception. You cannot escape it. It is the world through our eyes and ears, our fingers, our tongues and our noses. To everyone it is a different world. No two people, by definition, can see any one thing in the exact same way. One is taller or shorter than the other; . . . one is near-sighted while the other is far-sighted; one sees the glass half full and the other sees the glass half empty. These differences . . . may account for problems as serious as prejudice and violence, the state of the world, even the state of the earth.

Reality. What is it? Does it already exist or do we create it? Is it something we can change? Is it what exists or just what appears to exist?

Edward Abbey enters his trailer leaving the open Utah desert, the darkness of the night outside: 'I can't hear anything but the clatter of the generator. I am shut off from the natural world and sealed up, encapsulated, in a box of artificial light and tyrannical noise.' . . . He is confined by the reality of where he is. We are all confined by our perception.

. . . In *The Snow Leopard*, Peter Matthiessen tells us about Maya, a Buddhist theme: 'Maya is Time, the illusion of the ego, the stuff of individual existence, the dream that separates us from a true perception of the whole.' . . . Could this be the illusion one has that what one sees is the way it is and not just a perception? [Does a nuclear plant director "see" the effects of the waste created in his or her plant] on someone else's shore?

Another dimension of reality is time . . . 'I feel the summer/ in the spring' says the Chippewa song, and Momaday comments, 'Even as the singer sees into the immediate landscape, he/she perceives a now and future dimension . . . a state at once of being and becoming.' Perhaps reality is not only where you are as you perceive it, but when you are. Do automobile manufacturers consider whether or not their children will grow up with clean air, clean rain and a healthy ozone layer?

Once you create an understanding of reality, you can learn to manipulate it. [Annie Dillard describes using the 'artificial obvious' to help her find deer.] Creating a reality is similar to creating an illusion. When someone litters but knows it is not right, they create an artificial obvious that says it is OK.

Reality is a combination of what is there and what you perceive to be there. The way things are depends on you. Other things are affected by your existence in the same way that you are affected by their existence. [The observer affects the observed in quantum physics, just as people affect each other in their daily interactions.] . . . The observer is the participator . . . by living, by eating and sleeping, working and traveling, we impact all that is around us: our surroundings, other people, the earth which sustains us.

We look at the state of the environment today. Is the problem acid rain or ozone depletion, air pollution or toxic waste, wetland destruction or overpopulation? Fritjof Capra suggests in the movie "Mindwalk" that all of these problems are but the effects of a more fundamental crisis: a crisis of perception.

Our problem is the way we see the earth. We have created realities that give us the right to poison the water, run automobiles, fill in wetlands, destroy the rain-forests, dump toxic waste in the oceans, deplete the ozone layer. We seem to have created an artificial obvious that makes oceans look like we cannot harm them, forests seem so immense we cannot dent them, and air appear so vast that it can swallow whatever we feed it and never get sick.

We will never be able to correct the destruction only by recycling our paper and cans and taking our canvas bags to the supermarket. We have to learn to look at the world through different eyes, taste it with different tongues. We must work with our perceptions to change our perspective and create a reality in which we can respect the earth.

—*Abby C.*

As these two pieces show, young people love their world and want to make decisions that benefit rather than hurt it. Fostering and sharing their love, extending their knowledge, and strengthening their tools for responsible decision-making and action are what make teaching environmental literature worthwhile.

A tree frog hopped out of the deck chair I opened this morning; a beady-eyed blue jay is just now peering at me through the window; Tyler sees himself and his peers as the destructive "frontiersmen" in Gerzon's *A Choice of Heroes* and vows to change; Abby, inspired by Dillard and Momaday, envisions a new relationship with the earth based on respect. Each revelation momentarily swings open the doors of perception, offering a glimpse of a better world.

Appendix A
Schedule

Over the years, I have taught all of the material described in this book, but I can never teach all of it in one semester. I always do the perception unit, the Golden Age, the colonial journals, Thoreau, the Muir-Pinchot-Leopold readings, land journals, and readings associated with a field trip. Then I pick and choose depending on student interests, what seems timely, or the season. In the fall, I do the adventure unit early; in the spring, it might be last. While "Perception," the two history chapters, and "Case Studies and Action Projects" have a logical order, fiction and poetry, and the adventure unit can be done at any time. If I do presentations on modern conservationists, we might not do adventurers. If we spend time on research or action projects, we might not do fiction. I try to involve students in the decisions about what we will study.

The following are approximate (and minimum) time estimates for each unit.

Perception and introduction of land journals (Dillard, Momaday, Matthiessen, Lawrence): two weeks

History: Myths, the Golden Age, and "The Tempest:" two to three weeks

> Myths and the Golden Age (Native American tales, golden age myths and poems, writing): eight to eleven days

> "The Tempest:" two weeks

History: The New World: four to five weeks

> Settlement (Percy, Smith, Sewall, Beverly, Wigglesworth, Lopez, Audubon, Twain, Jewett): one week

> The romantic reaction (Emerson, Thoreau, Hudson River School): seven days.

> The Frontier: two to three days to do a few short stories and diary excerpts; two weeks to include a novel

> Early conservationists and preservationists (Muir, Pinchot, Leopold, videos): one week

> Modern environmentalists (Carson, oral reports): three to five days

Case Studies and Action Projects: four weeks and more

> The Southwest (Abbey, McPhee, Reisner, Powell): two to three weeks

Alaska (McGinniss, McPhee): two weeks

Wolves (Hyde, Mowat, Lopez): two weeks for reading and debate

Current issues and local case studies; "Issues and Actions": as much time as possible!

Fiction: Kingsolver's *Animal Dreams* or other novels. I often divide a book into thirds or quarters and spread the assignments over three to four weeks, with written responses due and discussion scheduled once a week. This works well along with poetry or research…

Poetry: With two students presenting two poets each day and everyone compiling individual poetry anthologies as an ongoing project: about two weeks.

Adventure: Krakauer, local history and literature readings, environmental impact and safety, field trips, orals: three to four weeks

Any of the material described here can be selected for short mini-units or longer units. For example, in a one-week unit with a focus on nature writing, students might do a few sensory exercises (Chapter Two), draft poems outdoors, share and rewrite, read poems by Mary Oliver or Terry Tempest Williams, read Borden's short story "Antaeus," and write the "Favorite Place" assignment (Chapter Two).

To focus on conflicting perspectives of land for about three weeks, a class can do the "Describe a Tree" exercise (Chapter One), read colonial journals, and view the Muir-Pinchot-Leopold videos (Chapter Four), comparing points of view of land in each case, then apply these views to a current, local environmental issue. The culminating activity would ask students to define and justify their own points of view toward land. During these three weeks, students might do individual choice reading of fiction, adventure literature, or nature writing, or have the option of doing research or a project on a current environmental issue (Chapter Five).

If you choose to emphasize personal lifestyles and sustainability issues, students could read Thoreau, Wordsworth's "The World Is Too Much with Us," and Barry Lopez' "Rediscovery of North America," view *Green Means* and *Living the Good Life*, write "Where I Want to Live and What I Want to Live For," (Chapter Four), and do the self-survey, interviewing, and ecological footprinting activities in Chapter Five.

Appendix B
Land Journal Data Collection and Research Entries

Research and collecting on students' land sites enrich the observations and personal responses written in weekly land journals. These activities extend student awareness beyond the personal and demonstrate how many fields of study are involved in understanding one piece of land. Students are more likely to do historic research or scientific sampling on their land sites if these activities have been modeled in the classroom first. These activities are ideal for language arts teachers working with social studies, math, and science teachers. Lacking a team, my interns and I lead some of the following activities, speakers visit class, and local foresters and wildlife specialists take us on short field trips. I have many occasions to be grateful to local historians and scientists who are happy to share their expertise with my students—and there is no reason to believe my area is unique.

The observation activities are divided into five categories covering geology, botany, zoology, social history, and the future. To consider the inter-relationships between these subject areas, we add a category on ecology. Students receive a checklist of questions (see below) in each category when they start writing weekly journal entries. As the semester progresses, we try to work some of the accompanying activities into our weekly class work. Of course, there is never enough time and we are lucky to do two or three of these ideas!

Geology

Describe geological features of your plot. You might use a transit and make a topographic map, or you can enlarge your portion of the USGS map. What kinds of rocks and soils are found on your site? How did the geological features on your land form?

Mapping part or all of the school grounds is a good team-building activity as well as a good introduction to mapping skills. David Sobel's *Mapmaking with Children* gives many excellent activities to teach map-making and map-reading. A professional surveyor can come to class and teach students to use a transit; this is a good opportunity to work with a geometry class. I ask students to invent their own unit of measure (e.g., a stick or person), sight along it to estimate changes in elevation, and use it to measure off distances on the ground. Their final maps include a scale, topographic lines, and a key. After making school maps, students map their land sites. We also practice reading contour maps, locate each student's land site on the local U.S. Geological Survey map, and use topographic trail maps to plan hikes. LandSat photos and global positioning systems can also be used.

To learn about soil types, we have dug test pits on school grounds and matched the soil samples with descriptions of soils in the U.S. Department of Agriculture's Soil Conservation Service soil survey for our county. This book also has soil maps on which students locate their sites.

Students use rock and mineral field guides to identify rocks found on their sites. An earth science teacher has taught my students about local glacial features such as eskers, rebounding, kettle holes, or erratics.

We link "geology" to other categories by considering what vegetation will grow in these soils, and what kinds of building development is possible on such ground.

Plant Life

Do a survey of the plants that grow on your site. What percentage of the land supports various types of vegetation (lawn, garden, pasture, trees)? Describe seasonal changes in vegetation—try to get beyond the obvious and notice new details. You might choose four to five representative plants to describe and research in detail. What clues can you find about how the vegetation has changed in the last one hundred years. Have some species been introduced from other areas, and how? You may include vegetation maps, photos, drawings, or pressed samples.

Our biology teacher, Bob Byrnes, taught us two methods for surveying plants. One is to mark off about a three-foot square or circle with a rope—in *Never Cry Wolf*, Farley Mowat used a hula hoop!—and count off every plant within the zone. Botanists used to do this by actually pulling out the plants, but this is no longer accepted practice. The other method is to do a transect by counting the varieties and measuring the sizes of plants along a ten foot line of rope. The count can be repeated randomly, or in a variety of plant zones. It can be done along with wild flower and tree field guides or an identification key, or students can simply develop their own categories and ways of differentiating the plants. I have done this activity on mountain hikes to illustrate changes in plant types and density in three elevation zones: deciduous, coniferous, and alpine. A local forester, Don Quigley, led a forest walk and taught my class about shade tolerant and intolerant species, plant succession from field to forest, and good forage for wildlife. Students then applied this information to describe forest conditions on their own sites.

The activity for deriving the "species area curve" in Appendix F can accompany plant surveying activities.

Students link the information about vegetation with the wildlife that lives on their sites.

Animal Life

What wildlife species live on your land? Include water life, insects, birds, and animals. How many do you observe? Where? When? What does your land provide for them to eat? to find shelter? What evidence do you observe of animal activity (e.g., scat, browse marks, burrows, food remains, tracks)? You might choose three or four animals and report on their seasonal and life cycles based on your own observations and research. How have animals affected your land? How have human uses affected the animals? Which animals succeed in areas highly affected by human use, and why? How have changes in the land affected wildlife? Has the wildlife changed over time? Have some forms been introduced from another area? How do the animals interact with each other? How does the presence of pets affect wildlife?

Students learn a lot just by exhaustively listing the birds and animals they see on their land. I keep a community wildlife list on the wall of our classroom where students list unusual animal and bird sightings. The list has included deer, moose, fox, coyote, otter, eagles, fisher, and the return of the great blue herons and swans in the spring. What warrants inclusion on the list sometimes sparks interesting debate: a Russian exchange student wanted to list squirrels but was outvoted by the class. What is unusual to one viewer is mundane to another.

At first snow, I give students a chart of animal tracks and scat types and send them out to be trackers on their land. They can learn to recognize other signs of animal activity as well—nests, dens, tunnels, webs, cocoons, bones, antlers, owl pellets, browse lines. The hunters among my students have a wealth of information to teach us about animal habits and tracking. If there is water on students' land sites, they can borrow a microscope and look for microscopic life with a field guide to pond water. One student wrote that she rarely sees animals but knows they are there by all of the signs they leave as they pass through. She liked knowing there is an unseen animal world paralleling, and occasionally intersecting, our own.

Social History

What natural and man-made changes have happened to your land over time? Describe present human uses and resulting environmental impacts of these uses on your land. What evidence reveals this land's history of past human use? What natural features have made these uses possible? Research your land's history and interview people who know your land.

As they describe present human uses of their land, students can consider the optimal balance between letting land develop naturally and "taming" it for human uses. Do they have lawns or gardens? How much of their land is paved over or built on? Are the forests managed? If the land is cultivated, is it for agriculture or aesthetics? What makes a plant a "weed?"

Students look for signs of past use in stone walls and barbed wire fences, cut stumps, new growth, gravestones, foundations, or garbage dumps. They look up their land on old maps and in local history books. We visit the local historical society and take walks with local historians. We go to the county registry of deeds to trace their deeds back to the "original" owners of their land sites (see Chapter Four). These deeds often reveal previous uses of the land, as well as former, natural and man-made landmarks. Students interview older neighbors who know their area well. They transcribe the interviews and make family trees, time lines, and maps. Because students have a personal interest in their sites, they find these historical research techniques relevant rather than dull and academic. Every piece of land has its own interesting story.

Future Use

What problems does your land face? How close is this site to being in a naturally sustainable cycle? What would it take to restore your site to this natural cycle? What are the pros and cons of doing such a restoration? What changes can you imagine occurring in the future? What do you think the site will look like in twenty years? fifty? What do you hope it will be like? What laws presently control how it is used? Should there be more or fewer rules? What would you recommend to insure the future you want for your land?

Students will often say they want their land site to stay the way it is. To learn more about the rules affecting land use, I have a copy of local zoning regulations in the room and ask students to look up the rules that apply to their sites. In addition to zoning, there are local, state, and federal environmental laws that may apply to their sites, such as shoreline setbacks, wetlands restrictions, tree cutting regulations, or hazardous waste rules. Town officials have come to class to discuss long range planning and the decision-making process for both growth and conservation. Students should be aware of various conservation tools such as easements, current use, and land trusts. We read about or visit sites that have been legally preserved in our area. If their sites are seriously degraded, they may want to research land restoration projects and consider what steps must be taken to restore their sites to a sustainable balance. Rather than be fatalistic, students consider what they want for their sites and what steps they can take to make their desires reality.

Ecology

After exploring as many of these categories as possible, what can you learn about inter-dependence in the natural environment? What happens when big changes occur in any one of the categories? (Give examples.) Is your site in a naturally sustainable balance?

Students understand the issue of "sustainable balance" once they have read Aldo Leopold's beliefs about only using a land's resources to the extent that the land can restore itself (Chapter Four). The resource allocation simulations in Appendix D can also be applied to these questions.

Any of the above questions can be considered in students' final evaluations and presentations of their land journals and sites.

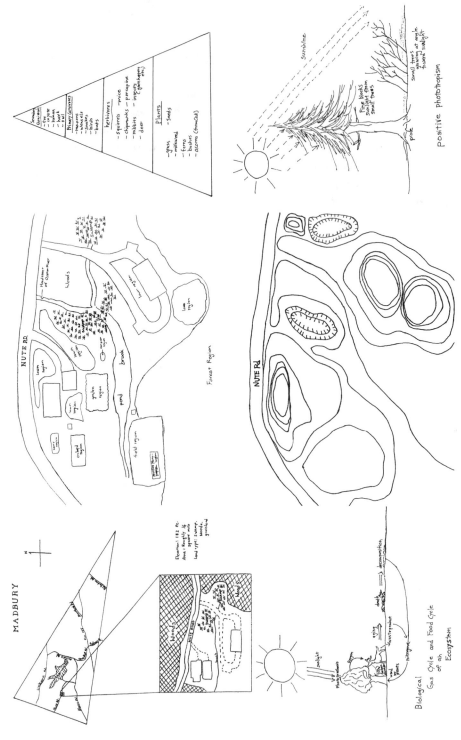

Figure B–1. Illustrations for a land journal presentation, with contour maps, bioregions, local food cycles, and an example of phototropism.

Appendix C

Monitoring, Restoration, and Other Volunteer Programs

ForestWatch
A program of the USDA Forest Service (www.fs.fed.us); See also www.forestwatch.org. Teacher materials and workshops. Students learn to do transects, count and measure tree species and varieties, identify invasive species, and monitor tree health through insect census and leaf damage. For example, students monitor white pines for the effects of low level ozone. Related programs include RiverWatch, PrairieWatch, and WetlandsWatch. Also Global Forest Watch (www.wri.org).

4–H Youth/Adult Science Clubs, Cooperative Extension (Adopt a Creek Programs)
Cooperative Extension programs exist at all land grant universities and offer many programs for urban kids. The Adopt a Creek program includes monitoring, tree planting, and weed removal. In San Luis Obispo, students measure creek flow, collect phytoplankton samples, and build large-scale watershed models. Information: Judy Neuhauser, 4–H Office, UC Cooperative Extension, 2156 Sierra Way, Suite C, San Luis Obispo, CA 93401; 805–781–5944. janeuhauser@ucdavis.edu

GLOBE
Global Learning and Observation to Benefit the Environment. (www.globe.gsfc.gov/cgi-bin/home.cgi) An international environmental education outreach program, directed by the White House, Washington DC. Links students K–12, teachers, and the scientific research community to learn more about our environment through student data collection and observation of the Earth's systems (atmosphere, hydrosphere, biosphere, and geosphere). Online teacher guide includes chapters on hydrology, soil, land cover and biology, global positioning satellites, and seasons. Also includes a

"toolkit" of measuring instruments and computer programs. Over 2,200 schools in 33 countries are involved in this program which started Earth Day, 1995.

GREEN (Global Rivers Environmental Education Network)

Offers *Watershed: A Successful Voyage into Integrative Learning*, published by the National Middle School Assoc., and a Low Cost Water Monitoring Kit. Available through Earth Force: vmeldrum@earthforce.org

National Volunteer Monitoring Conference

Six conferences have been held offering skill-building workshops, networking, presentations, field trips, and exhibits. Conference information is posted at www.epa.gov/owow/monitoring/vol.html

National Directory of Volunteer Environmental Monitoring Programs

Lists over 770 programs, including contact information, parameters monitored, and sources of funding. Online and in print: http://yosemite.epa.gov/water\volmon.nsf and (available at no charge) NSCEP 800–490–9198, fifth edition, publication number EPA 841–B–98–009.

Project WET (Water Education for Teachers)

WET Curriculum and Activity Guide, a national K–12 water education program including field sampling. Project coordinators in every state.

The Rivers Project   An interdisciplinary curriculum project in six subject areas (math, biology, chemistry, language arts, geography, earth science) offering materials and teacher training, and working with schools across the country. Curriculum ($23.95) and information about workshops available at www.siue.edu/OSME/river or contact founder-director, Bob Williams at rivers@siue.edu; 618–650–3788.

River Network   Offers monitoring, organizational development, and river restoration and protection programs. Publishes "The Volunteer Monitor," a free newsletter published twice a year for the exchange of ideas, monitoring methods, program descriptions, and advice. Address: 520 SW 6th Ave. Suite 1130; Portland, OR 997204; 800–423–6747. info@rivernetwork.org; www.rivernetwork.org

Save Our Streams   A program of the Izaak Walton League; has a K–12 curriculum using a biological stream monitoring method in which volunteers collect aquatic macroinvertebrates (insects and crustaceans), identify and classify them, and rate the stream's water quality based on the diversity of organisms found and their sensitivity to pollution. SOS sells monitoring equipment, an identification key, etc. SOS, Izaak Walton League of America, 707 Conservation Lane, Gaithersburg, MD 20878; 800 BUG-IWLA (284–4952). http://www.iwla.org

Student Conservation Association (SCA)

Since 1957, over 30,000 student volunteers have done conservation work in national parks, forests, and wildlife refuges. SCA, PO Box 550, Charlestown, NH 03603. www.sca-inc.org

Urban Environmental Education in Detroit

Case Technical High School, 2421 Second Ave., Detroit, MI 48201; Randall Raymond, 313–494–2605, x 315. A nationally recognized program helping urban youth make positive contributions to improve their urban environment.

WOW! The Wonders of Wetlands

An elementary and middle school curriculum, adaptable for higher grades. Instructions on setting up a field study (site selection, parameters to study, how to observe and collect information, presenting results). Published by Environmental Concern, Inc., 1995 and The Watercourse. Available from National Science Teachers Association, #OP517X, $15.95, 800–722–6782. www.nsta.org/scistore

Youth Conservation Corps

Combines community service with education and job training. Work may include environmental projects such as restoration or trail building. NASCC (National Association of Service and Conservation Corps) serves as a clearinghouse for information and assistance about Corps projects. NASCC, 666 11th St., NW, Suite 1000, Washington DC 20001; 202–737–6272. www. nascc.org

Appendix D
Environmental Simulation Games

FishBanks Ltd.

In this resource-allocation simulation, students work in up to six teams of three, each team in charge of a fishing company. A team "wins" by maximizing assets in the form of money or the value of the ships in their fleet. Play is fast paced and competitive. Teams that accumulate the largest fleets and seek rapid wealth deplete the stocks of fish below a recovery point, illustrating the dangers of overusing any natural resource; whereas teams that restrict growth can maintain a steady income. The game and debriefing take two to three hours. It can be led by one facilitator with one computer (Mac or PC) to run the program illustrating the effects of decisions on fish stocks. The game manual and computer program are available from:

Institute for Policy and Social Science Research (IPSSR)
Thompson Hall, Room G01
105 Main St.
Durham, NH 03824
Tel.: 603-862-2244
FAX: 603-862-4140

There is also an order form on the FishBanks website: http://www.unh.edu/ipssr/Lab/FishBank.html

Games on Sustainable Development

Also available from IPSSR is "Games on Sustainable Development" ($7.50) developed by Dennis Meadows and Barbara Van der Walls. The thirty-one page booklet describes six games led by one facilitator, requiring no computer, and taking from ten minutes to two hours. "The Tragedy of the Commons" and "Freeway Planning Game" involve decision-making about the allocation of natural resources. "Money in the Middle" and "The Trading Game" are about the distribution of wealth. The games are described at: http://www.unh.edu/ipssr/Games/gosd.html Another source of simulation games from IPSSR (see address above) is the *Systems Thinking Playbook*, also available on disk.

SimLife

A commercial computer game. Various windows allow players to create and modify terrain, climate, and life forms. In the scenario "Desert to Forest," players attempt to turn a desert, through the stages of plant succession, into a forest. "Battle of the Sexes" is about human evolution. The goal of "Feast and Famine" and "Carnivoria" is to design stable food webs and avert extinction. In "Terrible Lizards," players manipulate a dinosaur ecosystem. SimLife is available for both Macintosh and DOS.Windows.

Stella

A computer modeling program that engages students in systems thinking as they vary "stocks," "inflows," "capitals," and "outputs" to observe changes in a system such as a predator-prey-vegetation cycle (wolf-deer-shrubs) or a deforestation-flood-soil erosion-drought cycle. In the "Mahenjo Daro" scenario, students ponder the fall of an advanced civilization of 40,000 people with complex architecture and plumbing living in the Indus River Valley 4,500 years ago. Using *Stella* modeling, students graph the relationships between population increases and crashes, deforestation, and cyclical flooding to answer the riddle of why Mahenjo Daro eventually failed. The website for the Creative Learning Exchange (CLE) (http://sysdyn.mit.edu) has links to software developers of systems modeling programs including Stella. The website: www.hps-inc.com/edu/stella/stella.htm has ordering information and the opportunity to download a *Stella* demo.

Appendix E
Calculating Carbon Dioxide
Released by Burning Gasoline

Estimate the weight of a full tank of gasoline by using the following assumptions: water weighs the same as gasoline, gasoline is 100% carbon, and all of the gasoline is converted to carbon dioxide, CO_2. This is a rough calculation such as scientists often make to begin an investigation.

Use a scale to verify that one ounce of water weighs roughly one ounce; thus, one gallon (128 ounces) weighs roughly eight pounds. Students estimate the number of gallons per fill-up to find the number of pounds per tank:

(8 pounds per gallon) × (15 gallons per fill) = 105 pounds per tank

They also estimate the number of fill-ups per year and the number of automobiles in the United States.

To calculate the weight of carbon dioxide produced by burning gasoline, students can look up (on the periodic table or in a dictionary) the atomic weights of carbon (12) and oxygen (16) (CO_2 = 44: 12 + 16 + 16), then solve for X:

$$\frac{(8 \text{ pounds per gallon}) \times (15 \text{ gallons per fill})}{X} = \frac{\text{atomic of carbon (12)}}{\text{atomic of } CO_2 \text{ (44)}}$$

Solving for X, one gets 440 pounds of CO_2 per tank. In other words, the weight of the gasoline is significantly increased by the addition of oxygen atoms when carbon dioxide is produced. What is the annual national total if the typical car gets twenty-five miles per gallon, the typical car goes 10,000 miles per year, and there is one car for every two people in the United States?

To appreciate the significance of this calculation, students need to understand the relationship between CO_2 emissions, the greenhouse effect, and global warming. The PBS series *Planet Under Pressure* is a good resource for explaining the chemistry of the greenhouse effect.

This exercise was developed by Drew Christie for the 1994–1995 National Teacher Training Institute.

Appendix F

Calculating the Species-Area Curve

Backyard Biodiversity Survey: Deriving
E. O. Wilson's Biodiversity Curve

This activity helps non-specialists to develop a feel for biodiversity and its relation to land area. It explores how much land is needed to sustain species diversity and how much human activity affects local biological diversity (adapted from Henry S. Horn, "Biodiversity in the Backyard," *Scientific American*, January 1993, 150).

On a grassy playing field near the school, stake off sampling plots with string, using tape measures and large carpenters' squares, in the pattern shown on the Biodiversity Sampling Grid (Figure F–1). While one team marks off the plots, another team assembles a list of plant names found in the area (attach one live sample for each name). Students may find technical names using a key, or they may make up their own names, categorizing plants on the basis of size, shape, and color. The naming of "species" may be inexact and even creative—e.g. Sam's three-leaf. The focus of the exercise is on the distribution of different kinds of plants, not on scientific classification. Teams of students should then be assigned to each plot to count and list as accurately as possible the number of each listed species in their plot. One group of students can keep a tally sheet (Figure F–2) for the number of plants, by species, found in each plot.

Each group should graph cumulative total (y axis) versus cumulative area (x axis). Not surprisingly, the effort to find more species has diminishing returns. Ecologists have found that for many ecosystems S=c A(sq.) z, where S is the total number of species, A is the area, and c and z are constants fitted to the data. Note that the students' graphs look like parabolas turned on their sides (y=square root of x instead of y=x squared).

Students who are comfortable with logarithms can take the logarithm of both sides of the equation. log S = log c + log A. Use a calculator and plot log S (y axis) versus log A (x axis). Use a ruler to estimate the slope and the intercept. With your estimates of the slope and intercept, calculate c and z. If 90% of the land surveyed were converted to a parking lot, what percentage of species would remain on the undisturbed 10% of land?

191

Figure F–1. Biodiversity Sampling Grid

Thirteen sampling plots in a 256–square meter area. Plots one through four are one meter square; plots five through seven are two meters square; plots eight through ten are four meters square; and plots eleven through thirteen are eight meters square. Plots are numbered in a clockwise spiral pattern.

	1	2	3	4	5	6	7	8	9	10	11	12	13
poison ivy													
clover													
crab grass													
red flower													
long stem													
Sam's 3–leaf													
Stu's weed													
number of species													
cumulative species													
area													
cumulative area													

Figure F–2. Tally Sheet for Biodiversity Sampling

Appendix G
Useful Websites and Organizations

www.eelink.net

Amazing site—links to many important environmental education sites such as ERIC Clearinghouse for Science, Math, and Environmental Education; Center for Environmental Education; Eisenhower National Clearinghouse of K–12 math and science resources; Environmental Media Online Catalogue (teacher guides available for downloading). Lists organizations and projects, grants and jobs, classroom resources. Sponsored by North American Association for Environmental Education.

www.envirolink.org

An outstanding place to find links to hundreds of environmental organizations and websites. An environmental organization web directory (www.webdirectory.com) lists sites in thirty categories, including arts, news, and sustainable development. Lists journals, maps, and newsletters.

www.epa.gov

Environmental Protection Agency, resources for teachers and students, listings by region, grants, speakers, videos available through inter-library loan, student internships, links to other sites. For example, www.epa.gov/surf (EPA's Surf Your Watershed), and www.epa.gov/airnow/ozone.html (provides ozone maps for the area of your choice).

www.whitehouse.gov/PCSD

President's Council on Sustainable Development, 730 Jackson Pl. NW, Washington, D.C. 20503; 202–408–5296. Established in 1993 with diverse stakeholders to develop a "national sustainable development action strategy that will foster economic vitality while protecting our natural and cultural resources."

www.loe.org — National Public Radio's "Living on Earth." Gives transcripts and real audio of current and past programs back to 1992, text prior to '92, can search archives by topics.

www.econet.apc.org/econet/ — Econet: one of five networks operated through the Institute for Global Communications (IGC) network. Econet provides access to a variety of environmentally related home pages, conferences and resource centers, E-mail: anthony@econet.apc.org

www.enn.com:80 — Environmental News Network (ENN): a news and information service, with environmental news gathered from wire services, government agencies, industry, professionals, and special interest groups. Includes a calendar of upcoming events.

www.ciesin.org — Consortium for International Earth Science Information Network (CIESIN), 1747 Pennsylvania Ave., NW, Suite 200, Washington, D.C. 20006. Provides information to scientists, decision makers, and the public to better understand how human activity is driving global environmental change.

http://sysdyn.mit.edu — The Creative Learning Exchange, a resource for systems education. Provides models, lesson plans, videotapes, a newsletter, an idea exchange for teachers, and a self-teaching guide to the field of systems dynamics. A CD ROM containing these resources and a sample of the *Stella* modeling program are available from CLE, 1 Keefe Rd., Acton, MA 01720.

www. zigmacom.com/eco/html/ecological_footprinting.html — Links to resources on ecological footprinting, including Best Foot Forward. A source for the McDonough principles on sustainable living and

Green Design, published by the Sustainable Development Association, 4560 Mariette, Montreal, QC, Canada H4B 262.

www.cee-ane.org

Center for Environmental Education (CEE), Antioch New England Graduate School, 40 Avon St., Keene, NH 03431–3516; 603–357–3516; cee@antiochne.edu Lists K–12 environmental education and web resources collected by *Green Teacher Magazine*, the Green Brick Road, and CEE; resources sorted into categories such as programs, issues, clubs, periodicals, associations, government sites, and on-line networks.

http://library.thinkquest.org/ 26026

The Environment: A Global Challenge. Has over 400 articles in categories such as health, world outlook, current events, economics, organizations, and history. In "classroom connection," classes create accounts in a database and teachers exchange curriculum resources and lesson plans (elementary through university level).

www.plt.org

Project Learning Tree. Widely used and tested curriculum, pre-K–12, developed and sponsored by the American Forest Foundation and the Council for Environmental Education. Materials (free 402-page Activity Guide, K–8, and secondary materials) available with workshop attendance (workshops free or minimal charge). Not just about forests; curriculum covers all aspects of the natural and built environment, from the carbon cycle to packaging and resource allocation. State coordinators for every state listed on site. 1-888-889-4466.

www.ran.org

Rainforest Action Network. Lists actions and victories such as convincing Home Depot not to sell old growth tree products. Colorful and easy to follow. Has a "what you can do" feature.

http://whale.wheelock.edu

The WhaleNet educational website about the marine environment; includes monitoring, interactive books, a whale watch curriculum guide,

197

	slide shows, satellite tracking of tagged whales, a place to post questions to scientists, and links to information about marine mammals.
www.globalchange.org/gc.htm	Global Change. A review of climate change and ozone depletion. Hundreds of links to related sites.
www.nature.net	Discussion groups on birds, wildlife, nature photography, weather, camping, sustainability, etc.
www.ecobooks.com	Lists and reviews environmental books.
www.essential.org/monitor/monitor.html	Essential Information: founded in 1982 by Ralph Nader, provides a tool kit on fighting white-collar crime and gives a link to Geographical Information Systems (GIS), environmental maps constructed from computer and satellite data.

Yahoo! (http://www.yahoo.com/), the Environment and Nature category. Many, many subcategories and sites.

The GreenDisk Journal	A guide listing over 1,000 environmental Websites, listserves, databases, and bulletin boards. The Journal is available ($25, on IBM or Macintosh disks) from Greendisk, P.O. Box 32224, Washington, D.C. 20007.

Professional Associations:

www.asle.umn.edu	The Association for the Study of Literature and the Environment, an affiliate of the Modern Language Association. Site includes bibliographies of nature literature, news of conferences, and calls for papers.
www.naaee.org/index/htm	North American Association for Environmental Education (NAAEE), a network of professionals and students that promotes and supports the work of environmental educators in North America and more than twenty-five countries worldwide. Sponsors EETAP (Environmental Education and Training Partnership). NAAEE, 1255 23rd St. NW, Suite 400, Washington, D.C. 20037. Phone: 202-884-8912, Fax: 202-884-8701.

Bibliography
Additional Readings

Barbato, J., ed. 1996. *Heart of the Land: Essays on Last Great Places.* New York: Vintage.

Bast, J., et al. 1994. *Eco-Sanity: A Common-Sense Guide to Environmentalism.* Maryland: Madison Books. Questions some of the assertions and tactics of the environmental movement.

Bennett, G. F. and J. C. Bennett. *Environmental Literature: A Bibliography.* Park Ridge, NJ: Noyes Data Corp.

Bergon, Frank, ed. 1980. *The Wilderness Reader.* New York: Mentor, New American Library. Byrd, Bartram, Catlin, Roosevelt, Leopold, McPhee, etc.

Berry, W. 1990. *What Are People For?* San Francisco: North Point Press. Includes the essay, "Why I Am Not Going to Buy a Computer."

Bossel, H. 1999. *Indicators for Sustainable Development: Theory, Methods, Applications.* Winnepeg, Manitoba: International Institute for Sustainable Development. Presents indicators of sustainable development and quality of life, such as fulfillment, well being, and sustainability of resources for future generations, that go beyond economic indicators such as GNP. Prepared by the Balaton Group, international scholars and activists studying and implementing sustainable practices.

Brower, K. 1983. *The Starship and the Canoe.* New York: Harper & Row/Perennial Library. About astrophysicist Freeman Dyson, builder of "starships," and his son, George, who lives in a tree house in British Columbia and builds the traditional Aleut sea-going canoe, a baidarka.

Budiansky, S. 1993. "The Doomsday Myths." *U.S. News & World Report.* Dec. 13, pp. 81–91. Challenges warnings of environmental disaster.

Caldicott, H. 1992. "The Earth Is Dying. The Medical Implications of the Ecological Crisis." *Family Practice.* vol. 9, no. 4. Great Britain: Oxford University Press.

Capra, F. 1996. *The Web of Life—A New Scientific Understanding of Living Systems.* New York: Doubleday Anchor Books.

Dietrich, W. 1992. *The Final Forest: The Battle for the Last Great Trees of the Pacific Northwest.* New York: Penguin Books.

Durning, A. T. 1996. *This Place on Earth: Home and the Practice of Permanence.* Seattle: Sasquatch Books. The author goes home to the Pacific Northwest and examines the importance of a sense of place and an environmentally sustainable lifestyle and economy.

E: The Environmental Magazine. Bi-monthly editions. Articles on products, events, and issues. P.O. Box 699, Mt. Morris, IL 61054; http://www.emagazine.com

Ecodemia. National Wildlife Federation. 1–800–432–6564. ($14.95). The story of how American colleges and universities are adopting sustainable practices.

Gottliev, E., ed. 1996. *This Sacred Earth—Religion, Nature, Environment.* New York: Routledge. A collection of essays in categories such as "How Have Traditional Religions Viewed Nature?," and "Ecology, Religion, and Society."

Hardin, G. 1968. " The Tragedy of the Commons," *Science* 162. Dec., pp. 1243–1248. Explores the conflict between increasing populations and limited resources held "in common." Advocates mutually agreed upon coercion in the private management of these resources.

Hay, J., D. Ackerman, and A. Zwinger. 1998. *The Curious Naturalist.* Washington, DC: National Geographic Society. Tours of nine North American ecosystems with photographs, paintings, and instructions for field observation and collecting.

Hutchison, D., and T. Berry. 1998. *Growing Up Green: Education for Ecological Renewal.* New York: Teachers' College Press. Includes three philosophies of education: holistic, back to basics, and progressive.

Jackson, W. 1987. *Altars of Unhewn Stone: Science and the Earth.* San Francisco: North Point Press.

Lovelock, J. 1979. *Gaia: A New Look at Life on Earth.* New York: Oxford University Press.

Mander, J. 1991. *In the Absence of the Sacred: The Failure of Technology and the Survival of the Indian Nations.* San Francisco: Sierra Club Books.

McKibben, B. 1995. "An Explosion of Green." *The Atlantic Monthly.* April. Outlines positive environmental developments in the Northeast.

Meeker-Lowry, S. 1988. *Economics as If the Earth Really Mattered: A Catalyst Guide to Socially Conscious Investing.* Philadelphia: New Society Publishers.

Merchant, C. 1980. *The Death of Nature: Women, Ecology and the Scientific Revolution.* New York: Harper & Row.

Milbrath, L., and D. Suzuki. 1996. *Learning to Think Environmentally: While There Is Still Time.* New York: State University of New York.

Nash, R. 1989. *The Rights of Nature—A History of Environmental Ethics.* Madison: University of Wisconsin Press.

Orr, D. 1992. *Ecological Literacy—Education and the Transition to a Postmodern World.* Albany, NY: State University of New York Press.

———.1994. *Earth in Mind—On Education, Environment, and the Human Prospect.* Covelo, CA: Island Press.

Pollan, M. 1991. *Second Nature: A Gardener's Education.* New York: Dell Publishing. Explores our relationship with nature through gardening; questions emphasis on wilderness. Pollan edits *Harper's Magazine.*

Ray, D. L. 1987. *Trashing the Planet: How Science Can Help Us Deal with Acid Rain, Depletion of the Ozone, and Nuclear Waste (among other things).* New York: Harper Perennial. The former governor of Washington and chairperson of the Atomic Energy Commission advocates rigorous scientific inquiry and reasoned debate about environmental issues.

Rockefeller, S. C., and J. C. Elder. 1992. *Spirit and Nature: Why the Environment Is a Religious Issue. An Interfaith Dialogue*. Boston: Beacon Press. An anthology of religious teachings on the environment from world religious leaders. Based on the public television series, "Spirit and Nature," with Bill Moyers. United Nations World Charter for Nature in Appendix.

Roszak, T., M. Gomes and A. Kanner, eds. 1995. *Ecopsychology—Restoring the Earth, Healing the Mind*. San Francisco: Sierra Club Books.

Sauer, C. O. 1969. *Land and Life, A Selection from the Writings of Carl Ortwin Sauer*. John Leighly, ed. Berkley: University of California Press.

Schell, J. 1982. *The Fate of the Earth*. New York: Avon Books.

Spreknak, C. 1992. *States of Grace: The Recovery of Meaning in the Postmodern Age*. San Francisco: Harper.

Swartz, J., and D. Toomsen. *Environmental Literature for Young Readers*. Write to: Environmental Education Coordinator, Iowa Department of Public Instruction, Grimes State Office Building. Des Moines, IA 50319.

Waage, F. O. 1985. *Teaching Environmental Literature: Materials, Methods, Resources*. New York: Modern Language Assoc. of America.

Wallace, D. R. 1986. *The Untamed Garden and Other Essays*. Columbus: Ohio State University Press. Essays on nature writing, predators, etc.

Weisman, A. 1998. *Gaviotas: A Village to Reinvent the World*. White River Junction, VT: Chelsea Green Publishers. A group of scientists create a cooperative and sustainable community in the Colombian outback.

Williams, T. T. 1994. *An Unspoken Hunger*. New York: Pantheon Books. Essays on wilderness, feminism, and nature; Edward Abbey, Margaret Murie, etc.

Wilson, E. O. 1994. *The Diversity of Life*. Cambridge, MA: Harvard University Press/ Norton.

Index